THEY LEFT THEIR MARK

famous passages
through the
wine country

D1561174

Also by Joan Parry Dutton

California Houses of Gordon Drake (with Douglas Baylis)
Enjoying America's Gardens
The Good Fare and Cheer of Old England
The Flower World of Williamsburg
The Williamsburg Cookbook
Plants of Colonial Williamsburg

THEY LEFT THEIR MARK

famous passages through the wine country

by Joan Parry Dutton

Illuminations Press
St. Helena, California

Illustrations will be found following page 96

Picture Sources

1., 5. Joan Parry Dutton
2. Stevenson House, Monterey. Courtesy of California Department of Parks and Recreation.
3. *California Wineries.* Vol. 1. Vintage Image Publications, St. Helena, 1975. Courtesy of Jeffrey Caldeway.
4., 6. Courtesy of The Silverado Museum, St. Helena.
7. Courtesy of Kennedy Galleries, Inc. New York.
9. Courtesy of The Bancroft Library.
11. *Island in Time.* 1962. Courtesy of Philip Hyde.
12. Sierra Club Wildlife Calendar, 1979. Courtesy of Scott Ransom.
13. Courtesy of Geography and Map Division, Library of Congress.
16., 18., 19., 20.   Courtesy of Lowie Museum of Anthropology, Univ. California, Berkeley.
17. Collection of The Fine Arts Museums of San Francisco. Gift of Mrs. Samuel G. Fleishman. Photography by J. Medley.
21. *Forest Trees of the Pacific Coast.* George B. Sudworth. U.S. Department of Agriculture Forest Service. 1908.

Permission to quote has been given by: Mr. and Mrs. Frank H. Bartholomew to quote their poem inscribed on the display cask at the Buena Vista Winery Sonoma; Mr. Peter E. Palmquist for the content of *Carleton Watkins* in American West, Tucson, Arizona, July/August 1980; Dawson's Bookshop, Los Angeles, for passages (and content) from *The Life and Times of Cyrus Alexander,* 1967; Doubleday & Company, New York, for a passage from *A Writer's Notebook by W. Somerset Maugham,* 1949; Farrar, Straus & Giroux, Inc., New York, for passages from *The Life of Hilaire Belloc* by Robert Speaight, 1957; Mr. John Thomas Howell for the content of *A Collection of Russian Plants* in Leaflets of Western Botany, San Francisco, 1937; Hutchinson & Co., Ltd., London, for passages from *The Days I Knew,* by Lillie Langtry (Lady de Bathe), 1925; Napa County Historical Society, Napa, California, for passages from *The Oak Knoll Ranch* by Maggie Turner, 1948; Napa Valley Wine Library Association, St. Helena, California for passages from History of Napa Valley: *Interviews & Reminiscences of Long-Time Residents,* 1981; A.D. Peters & Co., Ltd., Writers' Agents, London, for passages from *The Contrast* by Hilaire Belloc, 1923; University of New Mexico Press for passages from *This Reckless Breed of Men* by Robert Glass Cleland, 1976; Yale University Library for passages from Robert Louis Stevenson's *The Amateur Emigrant* and two fragments of reminiscences about Jules Simoneau (Stevenson 6589 and 6846) in the Beinecke Rare Book and Manuscript Library. Permission has been sought from: Harper & Row, Publishers, Inc., New York, for the lines from *Life Was Worth Living* by William Graham Robertson, 1931; David McKay Company, Inc., New York, for passages from *This Life I've Loved* by Isobel Field, 1936; and W.W. Norton, New York, for passages from *Adventures of a Novelist* by Gertrude Atherton, 1932.

Library of Congress Catalog Number: 82-83659

ISBN 0-937088-05-6 (hardbound)
ISBN 0-937088-06-4 (softbound)

Manufactured in the United States of America

1   2   3   4   5   6   7   8   9   10

For Bill

William S. Dutton
October 25, 1893 — July 24, 1973

Patrons

Acknowledgements

This book came into being in various ways; first and foremost through the generosity of those who have backed it financially, and through the kindnesses of many people in many different ways. Adequate acknowledgment is beyond me. Those two small words "thank you" in no way express my appreciation.

As a first step, the Napa Valley Heritage Fund which supports the preservation of the cultural, historical and enviromental qualities of the Napa Valley region agreed to act as steward of the contributions, and the extraordinary thing is that all the contributions but one were made by old and new friends who live in the Wine Country. It was my luck that there was a publisher — Illuminations Press — here in St. Helena. Thus the book is, in a very real sense, the product of this community.

In addition to the financial aspect, I want to thank those who have made suggestions and corrections, and given much time and thought to reading the manuscript as a whole or in part:

Mrs. Yolande Beard, author of *The Wappo - A Report*; Dr. James D. Hart, Director of the Bancroft Library, University of California, Berkeley; Mr. Russ Kingman, of the Jack London Museum and Book Store, Glen Ellen; Mrs. Hildegarde Flanner Monhoff; Mrs. Virginia Snowden; Miss Ellen Shaffer, Curator of the Silverado Museum, St. Helena; Professor Stephen Watrous, Department of History, Sonoma State College, Rohnert Park.

I want to thank especially those who, for me, are very much a part of *They Left Their Mark*. Hildegarde Flanner Monhoff has given me valuable suggestions. Many a late afternoon, in summer and winter, over an iced drink, a cup of tea or a glass of wine, she would say, "Tell me now," and she would listen to the reiterated topic — 'the book'. Thus she has followed the course of the book from start to finish. Marie Rogers who over the years has sent me much information and helped my research in innumerable ways. We have covered many miles together. One of her photographs is on the back cover.

Maggie Wetzel for her encouragement, and for making me aware of "The Life and Times of Cyrus Alexander". She herself made two xerox copies of the entire manuscript, obtained professional advice on it, and spent considerable time in editing the major part. Jean van Löben Sels who gave me those two all important introductions — to David Marsten, President of the Napa Valley Heritage Fund, and to Gene Dekovic of Illuminations Press. And in our many luncheon conversations has helped me, as only a good friend can, to solve some of the conundrums that cropped up along the way.

     I also want to thank Mrs. Clayla Davis, Librarian of the George and Elsie Wood Library, St. Helena, and her staff, Mrs. Julie Fraser, Mrs. Millie De Jager, Miss Barbara Kaiser and Mrs. Barbara Stanton, for their painstaking and patient help in sifting through newspaper files, obtaining books on inter-library loan, and showing me items I might otherwise have missed.

     I also want to acknowledge in full my debt to all those past and present writers whose published and unpublished work is listed in the bibliography.

     Lastly, but by no means least, Mr. Gene Dekovic of Illuminations Press for his expertise and guidance that are an integral part of what I call putting a book together.

     As one of my literary friends in England writes in reply to my letters, "v.m.t." Very many thanks.

Contents

Foreword

Anything may happen in childhood dreams, but not once did I dream of ever living beside Spy-glass Hill of Robert Louis Stevenson's *Treasure Island,* one of the most famous hills in fiction, and searching for ghosts around it. This is the story of how both these unlikely events came about, and the extraordinary characters my husband and I encountered in our adventuring into the past.

First, to pinpoint Spy-glass Hill on the map. Others have identified it as one of the peaks of Mount St. Helena, a mountain within the Pacific Coast Ranges of Northern California, eighty miles north of San Francisco and forty miles inland from the Pacific Ocean.

Because of its position in the landscape, and because it rises so abruptly, the mountain looks a good deal higher than the measured altitude of 4,338 feet above sea level. Massive, forest-girt about its lower rocky slopes, it stands head and shoulders above all nearby hills and dominates the landscape far and wide. It closes off the northern end of Napa Valley, just beyond the town of Calistoga and straddles the boundaries where Napa, Sonoma and Lake counties meet.

The shape of the mountain is peculiar. From every point of the compass it presents a different appearance, so that, from one viewpoint to another, it is hard to believe you are looking at the same mountain. From the Napa Valley it appears as a single, almost flat-topped mass. Knight's Valley, immediately northwest of the Napa Valley, affords the only comprehensive close-up view of the mountain and its four peaks. The valley, some six miles long and half as wide at its widest, skirts the entire length of the mountain's western slopes. Unless you see the mountain from this viewpoint, you have not seen its full extent.

The spine of my story is Mount St. Helena and the countryside around it westwards to the coast, particularly Knight's Valley. The valley is still sparsely populated, still has a remote air about it, and few people are aware of its history.

Yet the story of both mountain and valley is the story in microcosm of the opening up of the west.

Two Russians from Fort Ross, the Russian settlement on the Sonoma coast, were the first to record their climb to the highest peak on the mountain. After the Gold Rush, prospectors swarmed across the mountain's slopes, searching for gold, silver and cinnabar. The Spanish and the Mexicans displaced the Indians, and the valley was named for an American settler, Thomas Knight.

With the opening up of the West the travelers came to California in droves. The trips they hoped most to make were to three natural wonders; the Geysers, in Sonoma County's northeast mountainous country, the Yosemite Valley, and the Big Trees, the sequoia. More people came to the Geysers, being nearest to San Francisco, than to either the Yosemite Valley or the Big Trees.

The most direct way to the Geysers was up the Napa Valley to Calistoga, and from there northward through Knight's Valley. Thus the valley road became one of the great roads of the Old West.

Travelers from the four quarters of the globe rode along it by stagecoach from Calistoga to the Geysers. The throng was so varied and fantastic that I wondered if there was any other byroad in Northern California where one could hear the phantom footfalls of so many different races and so many illustrious people. Certainly the cavalcade was as oddly assorted a company as Chaucer's pilgrims making their way to Canterbury, though the wonder they came to see appeared so appalling that it seemed more the work of the devil than that of God.

The region is also rich in literary associations. Robert Louis Stevenson, Hilaire Belloc, Jack London, and the Pennsylvanian traveler-reporter, Bayard Taylor, all came here. So did landscape painters, including Virgil Williams and Thomas Hill, as well as the photographer, Eadweard Muybridge, known as "the Father of the Motion Picture."

We were, of course, newcomers when we came to live in Knight's Valley in 1958. My husband, Bill, was a Pennsylvanian; I, English born and bred. We had not the slightest idea that our small ranch house was by crow flight but four miles from Spy-glass Hill.

1

Echoes of the Moving Footfall

A good deal of work had to be done on the small redwood ranch house we bought in Knight's Valley. Andy Tajha, a carpenter and builder, put the place in order and built on another room. Meanwhile, we stayed in what had been a foreman's cottage on a nearby ranch. Many an afternoon, when we did not go to see how Andy was getting on, we explored the countryside. Often, we followed the winding tracks the deer made between the manzanita bushes to the hilltop from where we could see Knight's Valley spread below. Aside from a patchwork of prune orchards and vineyards here and there, the valley appeared park-like, grazing land studded with big oak trees. We could see the rooftop of our house half-hidden in trees a mile away below our feet.

We moved in on April first. The following day, the heaviest rainfall of the rainy season dropped five inches in twenty-four hours. Next morning, as the rain ceased and the mist rose from the valley, the mountain peaks emerged capped with snow. A week later, it was a full, warm spring. The wild radish, white and pink, was waist high. There were flowers —poppies,lupins and wild mustard everywhere.

Neighbors who had a direct hand in the purchase and remodeling of the place gave us a welcome-to-the-valley dinner early one evening. This, by custom, was a complete surprise. They brought cocktails and appetizers, a roast turkey, salad, a high-tiered, homemade iced cake and after-dinner brandy. Everything was brought in, including paper plates, paper napkins and knives and forks.

It was dark by the time dinner was ready. We mustered the chairs in a circle under our rafters. For one fleeting moment, as we sat down to feast and celebrate, I couldn't help thinking that outside our house, which had been empty so long, there was no celebrating that night.

From amid the giant oaks and the tangle of shrubs, in the meadow about our acre, surely a thousand eyes beheld our lighted windows. A legion of small wild creatures no doubt listened apprehensively to the strange voices within. For them that night must have spelled calamity. Man had invaded their precinct, and without so much as the courtesy of by-your-leave.

Talk that evening was brisk, as might be expected. And among all the chatter — about racoons and deer, the falling-off in the lumber business, the summer feed for cattle assured by the torrential winter rains — one fact was uppermost. The mountain, Mount St. Helena, was the presiding genius of our neighborhood.

We were told that in time we would accept it as an intimate part of our lives, that it would influence all our days, as it did the lives of all people in the valley. We would come to know it as our guard and guide; a shield in summer against the sweltering heat of the interior valleys; a watershed that stored our winter rainfall and insured the continuity of our well. Returning from journeying, along any road, it would loom ahead to guide us home.

Talk of the mountain led to talk of Robert Louis Stevenson. We learned he spent his honeymoon in the early summer of 1880 at an abandoned silver mine on the slopes of Mount St. Helena, and recorded his stay in his book, *The Silverado Squatters.*

"He liked it here, you know. We hope you will like it too."

That welcome-to-the-valley dates our renewed interest in Stevenson and, through him, the beginning of our adventure into the past. Neither of us had read *The Silverado Squatters.* Before we could find a copy of our own, we borrowed a well-thumbed one from the public library in our nearest town six miles away, in easy-going, sun-bathed Calistoga.

Up to this time, though we were enraptured with the wild natural beauty about us and our view of the oak-studded parkland, the wooded foothills and the mountain silhouetted against the skyline, we felt there was something lacking in the countryside about us. It seemed bereft of any human past.

There were no field paths leading from footworn stile to stile along an ancient right-of-way to tell us that anyone had gone this way before. The trails of deer far outnumbered those of people. Most of the neighboring ranch houses were of wood and had an air of being built but yesterday. Up in the foothills a solitude I never felt before prevailed. The silence was unbroken by any sounds of human habitation; no sound of church bells came up from the valley on a Sunday morning. In short, I missed my Old World ghosts, those real or legendary characters who for may centuries have been an indelible part of British folklore and rural life.

The Silverado Squatters changed this viewpoint overnight. Stevenson had found, as we found, "the silence of nature reigns in a great measure unbroken." On one of his rides by hired rig he found "there was scarcely any trace of man but the road we followed." And that road, by today's meaning of the word, was but a rough trackway.

Then came the surprise. At various times, said R.L.S., the country about us had been overrun by men who "chasing Fortune; and Fortune found, still wander." Towns were founded overnight and as quickly abandoned if prosperity dwindled. People moved on, leaving what they had built as if it were a rusty tin can. "I suppose there are, in no country in the world, so many deserted towns as here . . . This stir of change and these perpetual echoes of the moving footfall, haunt the land."

Stevenson did not elaborate. He wrote about what he saw and the people he met. It was up to us to listen for those phantom footfalls and to explore the past.

Being neither professional ghost-hunters nor historians, we found our ghosts in a most haphazard way that took us ever backwards through time. The chapters in this book are not in chronological order because the people who were most remote in time and in places not marked on contemporary maps were the hardest to identify.

Clues were often hard to find and sometimes harder to follow. We did, of course, consult books about the region and the slim records. But unlike England, the Eastern states and the Old South, where so much of the past is known and documented, in Northern California much of the story and anecdote of the local scene is unrecorded except in barest outline.

There is a reason for this. California history has been so sudden and so violent, so short-lived in each successive phase, that the searcher may never get nearer to some of it than the echo of a passing footfall.

The pioneers who settled the land came west with little inclination to look back. They rarely thought of themselves as history-makers and certainly had little time or thought to record a present that often meant nothing but survival in a wilderness. Few jotted down travelers' tales told at those hospitable old ranch houses which kept open house for all those journeying north or south. Only a notation in a yellowed book, a signature in a hostelry register or a memory growing dim give a fleeting glimpse behind the scenes.

The face of the land about shows few traces of past occupation. A crumbling adobe wall may tell where a Spanish rancher had his home, a scar on the rocky earth where Cornishmen once prospected, a derelict mine shaft where Chinese mined precious ores, a glint of obsidian where an Indian sat in the sun and chipped an arrow head. But the telltale marks are mostly anonymous. Fire, too, has been a great destroyer, not only of scanty records and all manner of bygones and relics, but also of forests and timber-frame settlements.

All this made our adventuring the more intriguing. Discovering ghosts is far more thrilling than inheriting them willy-nilly like the family jewels.

2

Sam Brannan's Calistoga

Why, and in what circumstances did Stevenson come to Calistoga? How did the town come into being? This needs to be told before we meet Stevenson again, there and at Silverado.

Here is the opening sentence of Chapter I in *The Silverado Squatters:*

> It is difficult for a European to imagine Calistoga, the whole place is so new, and of such an occidental pattern, the very name, I hear, was invented at a supper-party by the man who found the springs.

The man's name was Samuel Brannan. But for him, Stevenson might never have come to Calistoga.

Sam Brannan did not, however, "found the springs." For centuries, the springs were known to the Indians as the Oven Place or Sweat House. The Californios called it *Agua Caliente,* which the first American settlers, who arrived about 1845, translated as "The Hot Springs." Those names stemmed from the hot sulfurous waters that bubbled and steamed from the soil of the townsite, and still do, affording baths for the sick, the aching and those seeking relaxation.

Sam Brannan appeared at The Hot Springs in 1859. As yet there was no town, only a straggling line of houses built with timbers cut from the big redwood trees and stretching along the trail at the western side of Napa Valley. A born promoter, Brannan instantly saw "The Hot Springs" as the place to build a spa which he envisioned as a future "Saratoga of the Pacific."

He was no idle dreamer but a doer of account, a Mormon elder who brought a shipload of emigrants, along with a printing press, around the Horn to San Francisco. His newspaper, San Francisco's first, *The California Star,* had reported the California Gold Rush to the world. Then as a banker and a supplier of stores to miners, opportunist Sam reaped a fortune.

At the age of 35, reputedly California's first millionaire, and seeking new schemes to promote, he bought one square mile adjacent to a small farm he already owned at The Hot Springs. Promptly he began to build his Saratoga and during a dinner speech, after a drink too many — so the story goes — instead of saying the Saratoga of California, his tongue slipped and he renamed The Hot Springs the Calistoga of Sarafornia. So it became known as Calistoga in fact, slip or no slip of the tongue.

A true son of the old San Francisco, Sam loved flamboyance: favoring tight buff trousers, flowered waistcoats (embroidered with rosebuds and forget-me-nots), red plush curtains, crystal chandeliers and champagne. He spared no expense on his dream resort to the end that the rich and great might luxuriate in the steaming sulfur baths. He planted vineyards and mulberry orchards with trees imported from China, hoping to launch a silkworm industry. He brought in blooded livestock and built carriage roads to nearby beauty spots. The resort boasted a dance pavilion, a skating rink, a mile-long track for horse racing, and several fine hotels, among them The Springs.

The Springs Hotel was the pinnacle of elegance in the sparkling new town. There were palm trees on both sides of the long driveway from the front gate to the entrance. Two-storied, crowned with several turrets of the most elaborate Victorian style, the Springs also included twenty-five private cottages, each with scalloped trim around the eaves.

On a summer day in 1862, the hotel and pleasure grounds were thrown open to the public. Sam chartered a ship to carry San Franciscans across the bay to Suscol, near Vallejo, where a train of stagecoaches and carriages awaited them. Sam, in person an imposing figure more than six feet in height, welcomed all guests in the portico of the hotel. After a banquet for specially invited guests, while the others were treated to a barbecue supper, everybody went to the race track to see Brannan's Arabian horses perform. At night, fireworks were set off from the top of Skating-Rink Hill.

There were a few years of thriving trade and traffic up and down Calistoga's broad main street, its boardwalks lined with fashionable shops, before discord jarred the harmony. The tea plantation didn't do well; the silkworm industry was a failure; the settlers who bought lots and built homes preferred a quiet village life to booming progress. Worse, Sam's good friend, Leland Stanford, decided that Calistoga was too far from San Francisco for the university he planned to build.

About dusk on a May evening in 1868, Sam attempted to repossess a sawmill and was shot. Partially paralyzed in his left hip, he had to walk with a cane for the rest of his life. But, by September, he was well enough to plan the celebrations for what was his crowning achievement — bringing the railroad from Napa to Calistoga. Its first passenger train in October brought hundreds of people to the opening of the depot.

Again he chartered a ship to carry the celebrants from San Francisco to Vallejo, where Sam greeted them as they disembarked. After a stop in Napa, they boarded the train and continued on to the new beflagged depot which Sam had built. Again Sam made a welcoming speech, this time from the balcony of the bathhouse in the Springs and again a vast barbecue was prepared and the same entertainments provided for all.

Sam, however, became disillusioned, and too good a patron of his own brandies and wines. As his drinking increased, so did his debts, and his friends deserted him. Because of his infidelities, his wife obtained a legal separation and was awarded half of Sam's property. Late in 1873, Sam leased what property remained to him, and two years later he was forced to sell all his remaining Calistoga property. He made yet another attempt to create a great resort in Mexico but this was unsuccessful. Sam finally settled on his ranch in Escondido, thirty miles north of San Diego, where he died, penniless but debt free, on May 14, 1889.

In a sense, Calistoga's memorial to Sam Brannan is in the Sharpsteen Museum at 1311 Washington Street, in the heart of town. This site was provided by the City of Calistoga, and Mr. and Mrs. Benjamin Sharpsteen munificently funded the building of the museum which they had so long envisioned to honor the region's pioneers.

Mr. Sharpsteen was for several years Walt Disney's Oscar-winning producer and production artist. Born in Tacoma, Washington, his father brought his family to live in Alameda, a small island with its southwesterly shores facing San Francisco Bay. Summers were spent at the property Mr. Sharpsteen Sr. had inherited from his mother in the northern end of Napa Valley. In the early 1930's, Ben, as he was called, purchased this property from his father. When Ben retired in 1959 he made the place of his boyhood summers his permanent home.

It was Mr. Sharpsteen's wish to portray in the museum a concept of Sam Brannan's Calistoga circa 1865, the peak years of the resort, in diorama and shadowbox form. To achieve this, he commissioned artists to create three-dimensional scale model villages and paint background scenes. Other permanent exhibits include one of William Spiers' stagecoaches, restored and placed in front of a life-size mural of a team of horses at the Magnolia Hotel, which was destroyed by fire several years ago. Bill Spiers, who came west from Missouri when he was nineteen years old, was one of Calistoga's great characters. Eventually, he monopolized the local passenger trade, served as a town councilman for thirty-six years, and was many times mayor.

While the museum was under construction, a group of interested persons financed the moving of one of Sam Brannan's cottages from the Spring Hotel grounds to its present site adjoining the museum. Named Sam Brannan's Cottage, it is identical to the one the Stevensons stayed in. Originally containing four rooms, it is now remodeled and restored with three rooms furnished according to the parlor and bedroom furnishing circa the late 1860's and early 1870's.

The continued development of the museum occupied Ben Sharpsteen daily until a day or so before his death on December 20, 1980. He was eighty-five years old.

By an odd coincidence, Sam Brannan's reign in Calistoga spanned the mining boom on Mount St. Helena, with the exception of the Great Western quicksilver mine that was worked profitably until the turn of the century. About the time Sam Brannan arrived in Calistoga, the drama of the California gold rush of '49 was played out. Prospectors, most of them empty of purse, were turning their backs upon the Gold Country to hunt for fortune wherever and in whatever ore it might be found. Among other places, they swarmed over Mount St. Helena, at the outset chiefly to mine silver, then quicksilver in what seemed a promise of a new El Dorado.

The mountain and foothills became a human ant-heap. For a radius of two or three miles, the ledges in sight of Knight's Valley were so pockmarked with miner's claims it was impossible to count all the excavations. At night the campfires made it appear that an army was encamped.

Chinese laborers, brought in by shiploads, worked the mines and built seemingly impossible roads with picks and shovels while American teamsters hauled away the loot in four- and six-horse freight wagons. From the Palisade Mine alone came the rare combination of gold, silver, copper and lead, returning its owners almost two-million dollars, worth infinitely more by today's dollar value.

No mine, however, showed more promise than the Calistoga, opened in 1872, four years after the first passenger train to Calistoga. In four months alone, it produced 2,300 tons of silver valued at $93,000. In 1874, with 1500 miners at work, plans were drawn for a town one and a half miles from the mine, and on October 11, amid the cheers of celebrators, it was named Silverado City. The mine superintendent promised in his dedicatory speech that Silverado City would surpass Virginia City, Nevada, in fame, wealth and size. He pointed out that inasmuch as it was nearer the top of a mountain than any town in California, its citizens would be "closer to Heaven than sinners usually get."

Streets were laid out, some of them running straight uphill: Fifth Avenue, Garnet, Pearl and Ruby, Gold and Silver, and of course, or the city would not be American, Main and Market Streets. With a great hurrah, they raised the "Stars and Strips" on the public square.

Silverado City did not live up to expectations. It died too quickly to gain a place on any official map. In 1875, one year after the miners' celebration, the mine and the town were no more. A fault in the rock stopped the flow of silver. Except for the hotel, the buildings were moved elsewhere. At the mine, a bunkhouse for miners and an assay office were left to fall into decay.

3

Virgil Williams
Knight's Valley Artist

Although the Stevensons may not have come to Calistoga but for Sam Brannan, it was the artist Virgil Williams and his wife Dora who persuaded them to do so. Their story needs to be told before we meet the Stevensons at Silverado.

Virgil Williams is thought to be a native of Taunton, Massachussetts. For ten years, thanks to his father's allowance, he studied art in Rome and during that time married a daughter of a well-known New York artist. But Williams was unable to keep his wife in her accustomed style and they soon agreed upon a divorce.

Returning home, Williams set up his studio in Boston. One day, B.B. Woodward, owner of Woodward's Gardens, an amusement park that was one of San Francisco's great show places, came to see him.

The Gardens contained a zoo, an aquarium, a lake with mechanical swans, a skating rink and a museum of freaks of nature. But it did not have the art gallery Woodward wanted. He looked at Virgil's work, liked it and offered to pay his passage and the cost of transporting his studio if he would create an art gallery in the Gardens and embellish it with copies of famous Italian masterpieces.

Virgil accepted. His innumerable copies of Italian masterpieces sold like hot cakes and at fantastic prices. His fortunes improved, he went back to Boston to marry art student Dora Norton. Together they returned to San Francisco and for a while Virgil continued to work at Woodward's Gardens. Subsequently, he became the founder and first director of the San Francisco School of Design (now the California School of Fine Arts), and remained director until his death. He was also one of the group of artists and authors who founded the Bohemian Club in 1872.

B.B. Woodward and Virgil Williams became close friends and Virgil and Dora often stayed at Oak Knoll, Woodward's vast Napa Valley ranch four miles north of Napa. There, Virgil loved to paint and to bask in the sunshine he had enjoyed in Italy. Fanny Osbourne, who was to become Stevenson's wife, and her first husband, Sam Osbourne, were other frequent guests. Sam also worked at Woodward's Gardens, and Fanny's friendship with the Williams began when she first studied art under Virgil at the School of Design.

To my mind, Sam Osbourne deserves a place in history all his own, and not to be remembered solely as Fanny's first husband.

Sam was a soldier when Fanny first met him. He was an adventurous soul, irresponsible perhaps as a family man — though his children adored him — but adaptable to all sorts of circumstances, and generous with what money he had. He improvised Negro ballads he had learned as a child on his grandmother's Virginia plantation. At the age of twelve, he picked cotton all day to earn enough to go to a circus that was forbidden him. He traveled widely in Europe, prospected in Nevada and, after working at Woodward's Gardens, became a shorthand court reporter.

Aside from their association with Oak Knoll, the Williams have their own part in the story of Knight's Valley and the road that runs through it. Virgil's painting of Mount St. Helena, from a spot about halfway in the valley, is now in the Oakland Museum. He knew the road well, for in time he and Dora bought their own small ranch in a remote canyon of the Sugar Loaf, a spur on the Knight's Valley side of Mount St. Helena. Their cottage was "among pine trees and hard by a running brook," and had a verandah that ran the full width across the front. Paintings hung in the living room were mostly their own. In a clearing among the pines was a garden surrounded by a picket fence.

There were two ways to their retreat. One was along the Knight's Valley road and up the narrow, precipitous Ida Clayton Road (named for pretty and popular Miss Clayton, teacher at the Knight's Valley School). After the turnoff leading to their cottage, the Ida Clayton Road continued up over the steep incline and down to the Great Western Mine on the northeast, Lake County side of the mountain some sixteen miles from Calistoga. The other way was by Lawley's Toll Road over the mountain from Calistoga to Lake County where the road from the Great Western joined it. These directions have little interest to travelers from afar, but they are still of interest to those who live here and the two routes also had a significance for the Great Western Mine.

Another intimate of Oak Knoll was Frank McDonald, orchardist to B.B. Woodward and to the ranch's former owner, J.W. Osborne (no relation to Sam Osbourne — the names are spelled differently). Eventually, McDonald bought his own ranch at the southern entrance to Knight's Valley, six miles outside of Calistoga. He set himself up as an orchardist-nurseryman, selling fruit trees up and down Napa Valley. Virgil Williams, who passed McDonald's house on the way to and from his cottage on Sugar Loaf, made sketches of various fruits McDonald grew to help him advertise his trade. We shall meet Louis and Fanny Stevenson at the McDonald ranch before we meet them at Silverado.

4

The Stevensons Arrive

Calistoga's boom days were over when the Stevensons arrived on the scene on May 22, 1880, six years after Sam Brannan had left, five after Silverado was abandoned. Teamsters still hauled rich loads of quicksilver from the Great Western Mine. The stagecoach was still worth a highwayman's holdup and people continued to come to Calistoga for the hot baths and the rides in the countryside but the spendthrift exhuberance was no more. Stevenson regarded it "as a pleasant place to dwell in . . . often visited by fresh airs, now from the mountain, now across Sonoma from the sea; very quiet, very idle, very silent but for the breezes and the cattle bells afield."

The place was, however, still fashionable enough to notice that the couple did not conform in any way to the kind of guests who usually registered at the Springs Hotel. Louis was a tall shabby young man with longish hair, stooping shoulders, sallow complexion, and gaunt as a wolf. Fanny was precisely the opposite, short and thickset. Louis was a Scot, Fanny a native of Indiana, and why they had come to Calistoga was anybody's guess. If their story had been known at the time all Calistoga would have been abuzz.

Only four years before, in 1876, they had met at the artists' colony at Grez-sur-Loing in France. Louis was then twenty six, the only son of a prosperous Edinburgh engineer. Acknowledged as a promising writer, he was bohemian in style and dress, and sometimes affected a smoking cap of Indian work, "its gold lace pitifully frayed and tarnished." He came to Grez after a canoe trip with his cousin.

Fanny was thirty-seven years old, living apart from her husband, Sam Osbourne of San Francisco. She was staying at Grez with her two children, Isobel and Lloyd, studying art. Her jaw was as determined as Napoleon's. She had beautiful white teeth and eyes that were "full of sex and mystery" and was known as "la belle Americaine." A vivid personality, she was also unconventional, wearing her wavy black hair short, rolling and smoking cigarettes.

Isobel, Fanny's teenage daughter, later described Louis' and Fanny's first meeting:

> One night we were at dinner; though the lamps were lit, it was not yet dark. We had finished our meal, and were talking idly and pleasantly over our coffee. Happening to glance at my mother, I saw that she was looking towards the window with an odd intent gaze. It was not exactly a window, but a half-door, and standing in the opening, the lights from the hanging lamps showing up his figure like a portrait painted against a black background stood a young man, slender, dark with a high color and yellow hair worn rather long. He was leaning forward staring, with a sort of surprised admiration, at Fanny Osbourne. Years afterwards, he told me he had fallen in love with her then and then.

On and off in the next two years, in the summers at Grez and the winters in Paris, Louis and Fanny saw a good deal of one another. But in 1878 Sam Osbourne stopped sending all support money, and Fanny promptly returned home to Oakland, across the bay from San Francisco, with divorce proceedings in mind.

A year later, hearing that Fanny was seriously ill, Louis against the advice of all his friends, and without telling his parents, set out to join her, traveling next to and comingling with the steerage to New York. He had very little money with him but ample clothing.

Arriving in New York, he received the news sent him at General Delivery that Fanny had recovered and was recuperating at Monterey, the seaport south of San Francisco. He spent a day of pouring rain going to banks, booksellers, publishers, moneychangers and railway offices. Then, leaving behind some of his rain-sodden clothes, carrying a small valise, a knapsack on his shoulders and in the bag of his railway rug the newly-acquired six fat volumes of Bancroft's *History of the United States,* he started straightway on his eleven-day journey across the country by emigrant train. He arrived at Monterey at the end of August, three weeks after leaving home and the Clyde.

Short on sleep and food, and worn out by the journey, Louis came down with pleurisy. Fanny nursed him through it and then she returned to Oakland. During Louis' stay in Monterey she was often on the move between the two places.

A few days after his bout of pleurisy, perhaps disappointed that Fanny had returned to Oakland so soon, or because of the sea fogs that encompass Monterey at that time of year, Stevenson rode up into the Santa Lucia Mountains. He slept out under a tree for two nights and was found in a stupor by some goat herders who took him to their ranch. When able, he returned to Monterey.

Every day Louis had one good meal at Jules Simoneau's little French restaurant. Between times the two men would play chess or talk over a glass of wine. Once, when Louis did not appear for two days, Simoneau went to his room, found him stricken with fever, and took care of him.

When Fanny finally decided to divorce Sam, Louis moved to San

Francisco, renting a room in Mrs. Mary Carson's lodging house at 608 Bush Street shortly before Christmas. It was a bleak interlude. "For four days I have spoken to no one but to my landlady or landlord or to restaurant waiters," he wrote in a letter to his friend, Colvin, on December 26. "This is not a gay way to pass Christmas, is it?"

His loneliness did not last long. Fanny came over from Oakland about twice a week and they would dine at a restaurant, at Mrs. Carson's, and with Dora and Virgil Williams. Virgil gave Louis a visitor's card to the Bohemian Club, which served as a passport to other friendships, in particular that of Charles Warren Stoddard, a thirty-seven-year old poet and romancer. Stoddard, a world traveler, had lived awhile in London and spent some time in the South Seas. His South Seas mementos and his book, *South Sea Idylls,* intrigued Stevenson and probably determined the eventual choice of Vailima as his home. Until the meeting with Stoddard, Stevenson had explored his own immediate neighborhood. Now with Stoddard he went for far longer walks, exploring the city far and wide.

It was a wet spring. Mrs. Carson's son Robbie developed pneumonia and Louis sat up for hours nursing the child. When Robbie recovered, Louis became ill again, falling into cold sweats and high fever with a hacking cough. He diagnosed his sickness as a galloping consumption. Fanny's sister, Mrs. Nellie Sanchez, and Dora Williams visited him almost daily. When Stoddard came to see him, he found him working on an essay, "submerged in billows of bedclothes" and looking like a half-drowned man. " Yet", Stoddard commented, "he was not cast down. His work, an endless task, was better than a straw to him. It was to become his life preserver to prolong his years. I feel convinced that without it he must have surrendered long before he did."

When Louis had sufficiently recovered, under Mrs. Carson's nursing, Fanny moved him to Oakland, first to a small hotel and then to the parlor of her house. Fanny had written to Louis' father about his son's penniless state and frailty and about the time the divorce was granted, came a cable, "Count on 250 pounds annually."

This was timely help, but it did not provide the means to stay at a mountain resort and the doctor had advised that Louis should be in bracing dry air away from summertime's coastal fogs. Dora and Virgil Williams, with a cottage on Mount St. Helena (which was too inaccessible for the Stevensons) knew that the mountain was dotted with abandoned miners' cabins. And Fanny, having lived with Sam Osbourne in Nevada boom towns while he was there, buying and selling mining rights, knew that boom towns often became ghost towns overnight and rents were free.

Everything pointed to going first to Calistoga at the foot of the mountain, and from there to look for a place in which to spend their honeymoon. Sam Osbourne wrote a note of introduction to young Mr. George W. Johnson, the new proprietor of The Springs Hotel.

For one reason or another, perhaps convention or superstition, Louis returned to San Francisco just before the marriage. On May 19, Fanny crossed the bay by ferry and was met at the wharf by Louis and Dora Williams. They proceeded to 521 Post Street, the home of the Reverend W.A. Scott, a prominent Scots Presbyterian minister, who married them in the drawing room. Dora Williams, Mrs. Scott, and "a cat that had followed Mrs. Scott into the room" were the only witnesses. For the record of the marriage Fanny described herself as a widow. Had the minister known she was a divorcee he probably would not have married them. After the brief service, the Stevensons took Dora to dine with them at a good restaurant, the Viennese Bakery, then went to the Palace Hotel to stay for two or three nights.

It may seem incongruous that a couple who were to seek a rent free place in a deserted mining town should stay at the Palace Hotel, which Appleton's General Guide to the U.S. and Canada (1879) listed as "the largest building of its kind in the world," with accommodation for about 1,200 guests. Conceivably this was the Williams' wedding gift. Maybe Louis and Fanny chose the Palace as a one-time celebration, a fling while the going was hardly good, but good enough. Neither of them had any illusion about Louis' precarious hold on life. He, himself, regarded the marriage ceremony "as a sort of marriage *in extremis* . . . I was a mere complication of cough and bones, much fitter to be an emblem of mortality than the bridegroom." The doctor had told Fanny that Louis had only a few months to live.

Whatever the reasons for going to the Palace, among so many guests, they were incognito. As Fanny recorded in a letter of a later date, they stayed there "seeing nobody we knew but Mrs. Williams." There was, however, another exception. Nellie Sanchez came over from Oakland with the twelve-year-old Lloyd and their dog Chuchu, "a setter crossed with spaniel." Lloyd, still usually called Sam, and so-called in *The Silverado Squatters,* was in school at Locust Grove, Sonoma, and was to join them in Calistoga.

On the afternoon of Saturday, May 22, Fanny, Louis and Chuchu set out for Calistoga, staying the night at a miserable, dilapidated hostelry in Vallejo. The next morning, at 9:10, they boarded the single day coach of the Napa Valley Railroad. Traveling at twenty-three miles per hour, with way stops at Napa, Yountville, Oakville, Rutherford, Bello, St. Helena, Barro, Bale and Walnut Grove.(Would Fanny have pointed out Oak Knoll shortly out of Napa?) The distance from Vallejo to Calistoga was forty-two miles, and Calistoga was the end of the line. Mount St. Helena loomed before them.

5

Sightseeing Around Calistoga

Almost three weeks went by before Fanny and Louis found a rent-free place. It was barely tenable but they could obtain fresh milk and collect their mail. In the interval, they made excursions in the countryside, sometimes by hired rig. Four days after their arrival at the Springs Hotel, the proprietor, twenty-eight-year-old George Johnson and his young wife, drove Fanny and Louis around in his buggy.

The first stop was to two Napa Valley vintners, neighbors to one another on a hillside, a short distance from Calistoga: Jacob Schram and Colin McEachran (mispelled M'Eckron by R.L.S.). The Schrams were not at home, but Collin McEachran, a Scot and a bachelor, showed them his Alta Vineyard stone cellar which was then but two years old. Next they stopped at the great grist mill built by an Englishman, Dr. Edward T. Bale in 1846, and Stevenson marveled at the "enormous overshot water wheel as tall as the trees that grow beside it." The tour was rounded out at the Beringer Brothers Winery. Their Los Hermanos vineyard, on the outskirts of St. Helena, was also a young vineyard, planted in 1876. Carpenters were still at work, adding a third story to the stone winery, abutting the carved-out hillside, which Jacob Beringer began to build in 1877. When it was completed, the *St. Helena Star* described it as "the most handsomely finished of any wine cellar in the Napa Valley."

Two days later, on May 28, Fanny and Louis went to see the Schrams, probably by previous arrangement. (Stevenson in *The Silverado Squatters* describes this visit and the earlier one to McEachran as being on the same day.)

Jacob Schram was sixteen when he came to New York from his native Rhineland, and for several years worked there as a barber. He came to San Francisco via Panama during the Gold Rush, and for a while continued his trade. Jacob had learned the art of the vintner in the Rhineland's Liebfrauenberg vineyard. One day he set out to scour the hillsides of the Napa Valley in search of land for grape growing. He found it two or three miles south of Calistoga. He was the first Napa Valley vintner to plant a hillside vineyard, and his winery built in 1862 was the first to have underground cellars dug in the rocky valley hillside.

His wife, Annie, a native of Germany, was buxom, friendly, as was Jacob, and a highly capable vintner's wife. Jacob hired Chinese workers to plant and care for his vineyard and in order to pay their wages, continued working as a barber at the White Sulphur Springs and in Calistoga. Annie managed affairs while he was away.

The house they built in 1875 testified to the Schram's prosperity. On the afternoon of the Stevenson's visit, Mrs. Schram entertained Fanny on the veranda with stories of her European travels while Louis in the company of Mr. Schram "tasted all." In his journal "all" amounted to some eighteen varieties of Schramberger — Burgundy, Hock and Golden Chassels. He also noted in his journal an item that he did not include in *The Silverado Squatters*. He had no wish to abuse hospitality or betray a confidence.

Mrs. Schram's "one trouble, worthy woman, is a question of clothing. Mr. Schram wishes her to wear corsets; God help us, in this hot weather; she has to wear them when she goes to pay a visit, hence pays no visits, hence as she says 'people hate her;' Fanny and she condoled over this for quite a while . . ."

It was probably during their stay in Calistoga that Fanny visited Frank McDonald's ranch in Knight's Valley. One Sunday, she and Louis had midday dinner there. Many years later, Mrs. Maggie Turner, Frank's shy little daughter, wrote briefly of these visits, saying that Lloyd was not along, and making no mention of Silverado. Frank McDonald was, of course, an old familiar of the Oak Knoll days. He and Fanny may have met in Calistoga and recognized one another or Virgil Williams may have told Frank the Stevensons' whereabouts. Here is part of Mrs. Maggie Turner's account:

> I was just a youngster, but I can see Mr. Stevenson now, sitting on our front porch talking with my father and mother. How he squinted his black eyes and looked me up and down! I was one of those long-legged skinny little girls that would get self-conscious at the least little thing. When I came out on the porch, here was this stranger who immediately turned to see the Scotchman's little daughter. His looking at me so hard gave me the creeps: I remember to this day how I felt. I refused to talk to him or eat dinner with him. Can you beat that? Chicken dinner, too, for company! . . .
>
> After dinner Mrs. Stevenson asked Mother if she might smoke, and I'll never forget how shocked we were; we'd never known a woman who smoked. She was strikingly unconventional in appearance — small and plump, with a dumpy figure and wearing her hair short in a day when women didn't. I remember once she wore a black and white Mother Hubbard from San Francisco. She was a great talker and she often talked with my father about her first husband, and in a very nice way.

Sitting on the veranda that Sunday, Stevenson would have seen the Knight's Valley view of the mountain, with its four peaks in a row from south to north. And he may have met the McDonald's neighbor just across the road, Clark Foss, whom he was to immortalize in *The Silverado Squatters*.

6

Stevenson at Silverado

It was Morris Friedberg, a bearded Russian Jew and owner of a general store in Calistoga, who offered to take the Stevensons to look at Silverado. The very name was appealing, and as Friedberg pointed out, it was close to the Toll House where the Lakeport stage stopped daily, delivered the mail and fresh milk, and being some two-thousand feet up on the mountainside, Silverado was above the fogline. (Friedberg, who Stevenson described as "the village usurer" appears in *The Silverado Squatters* as Kelmar, the only pseudonym he used.)

Friedberg and his family were going to Lakeport on May 30. He would take Louis and Fanny up to Silverado and look around there with them. They could stay the night at the Toll House, and he would pick them up early next morning on his way back to town.

On arriving at the Toll House that Sunday morning, Stevenson followed Friedberg into the bar, was introduced to the landlord and, after quite a handshaking all around, a little boy was detailed to lead the way. They came first to what had been The Silverado Hotel, where the Hansons lived as squatters. Rufus, wishing to avoid his creditor Friedberg, who was recognizable afar by the skull cap he customarily wore, had disappeared, but his wife led the way to a place she thought might do, a quarter of a mile farther up the mountain.

Clambering up an ore dump to the platform that partly covered it, they stood before a half-derelict brown wooden house that consisted of three rooms. The lower room, its rear wall flush against the hillside, was the onetime assay office: the door was smashed, one panel hung in splinters, not a windowsash remained. The upper floor, entered now by a board propped against the threshold, was twice as large as the lower: in it were eighteen bunks in a double tier, nine on either hand, in which, Stevenson reckoned, from eighteen to thirty-six miners had once snored together all night long. The third room, partitioned off, extended back upon the hill and was reached by a path leading upwards behind the rock to the door level with this higher ground. In it were uprights for more miners' bunks.

Close by, in a wooden shed built against a boulder and shaded by madrone trees, was a blacksmith's forge. And there was a tunnel cut horizontally into a ledge beside one of the mine shafts. Stevenson noted in his journal that "Mrs. Hanson said it would be a capital place to keep our milk and butter in. Wine, too, thought I."

Such was the Stevenson's first prospect of Silverado. "One way and another, now the die is cast. Silverado be it!" The triumphant Friedberg led the way back to the Toll House, and said he would call for them by six o'clock the next morning. When he had gone, Rufus Hanson came to make arrangements for the move to Silverado.

Towards evening, a wind sprang up among the trees on the other side of the valley. Sitting on the Toll House veranda, Fanny and Louis were "utterly stunned by the uproar":

> Sometimes, we would have it was like a sea, but it was not various enough for that; and again, we thought it like the roar of a cataract, but it was too changeful for the cataract; and then we would decide, speaking in sleepy voices, that it could be compared with nothing but itself. My mind was entirely preoccupied by the noise . . . For the most part, this great, streaming gale passed unweariedly by us into Napa Valley . . . So it blew all night long while I was writing up my journal, and after we were in bed, under a cloudless, starset heaven; and so it was blowing when we arose.

They were up and breakfasted by six o'clock next morning, but not until ten o'clock did Friedberg arrive. He delayed further by talking with the landlord, and he delayed again by stopping at the Guile Ranch a short distance down the mountainside. There was an age-long conversation with Mrs. Guile, more talk when Mr. Guile came in from his vineyard, but he did tell Louis he could supply him with Mission wine. It was past two in the afternoon (eight hours since breakfast) when they drove into Calistoga, "Fanny and I whitefaced and silent, but the Jews still smiling."

Ten days later, on June 9, one of those "beautiful still days, the sky one vast of blue," the self-styled King and Queen of Silverado and the Grand Duke Chuchu set out for their kingdom in a double buggy. Lloyd, the Crown Prince Sam, who had recently joined them at the Springs Hotel, rode ahead on a pony, leading the way like an outrider. They had with them some staples, fresh fruit and dried peaches, and bottles of white and red wine.

By mid-afternoon, the royal party reached the mine and the buggy went its way. While waiting for Rufus Hanson, who was to follow with the baggage, the packing cases full of books and a secondhand cookstove, they took stock of their abode. In the assay office, that would serve as the kitchen, was "a table, a barrel; a plate-rack on the wall; two home-made boot-jacks, signs of miners and their boots." The floor was deep in debris, but they had no broom to clean it up. The room immediately above, the bunk-lined bedroom, had even more hay on the floor, mixed with broken window glass.

Stevenson noted in his journal that he found the path to the Toll House, where he went to ask about hay for bedding, and then, having stowed the wine in the tunnel, there was nothing to do but smoke until Hanson came. In *The Silverado Squatters* he does, however, describe how, with the aid of a discarded miner's pick and shovel, he deepened the shallow pool that was fed by a spring on higher ground near the second bunk-lined room, so that there was water enough next morning. Bit by bit, Louis eventually made the pool into a small well, lining the rounded side with pebbles.

Toward nightfall, it was getting chilly, so they lit a fire in the blacksmith's forge. Between seven and eight, Hanson halted his wagon at the foot of the ladder that led up to the platform, bringing with him two of his wife's relatives to lend a hand. The men unloaded the baggage and the packing cases in short order, piling them higgledy-piggledy and upsidedown on the assay office floor. They had the cookstove but had forgotten the stovepipe and lost the lid. All three men adamantly refused to bring the hay from the Toll House until after they had their supper. "See how late they were! Never had there been such a job as coming up that grade! Nor often, I suspect, such a game of poker as that before they started," said Stevenson wryly.

While they were gone, too weary to rekindle the fire in the forge, the royal family dined "in the nightmare disorder of the assayer's office, perched among boxes. A single candle lighted us." At last, the hay was delivered, and one by one the family went up the plank bridge to their hay-filled bunks.

The next morning, with a good fire going in the forge, there was porridge, fried bacon and coffee for breakfast. For a while Louis rested at the door of the forge. "When I mustered my limbs together and got across to the house," he wrote in his journal, "I found there had been great doings in the Assayer's office. The broken door and the frameless window were all nailed up with white calico, which kept out the wind and let in the kindly daylight; and there was Fanny on her knees hammering up a door of the same material for the gaping eastern doorway. I was soon despatched to hunt leather for hinges, and in the dog's hutch beside the forge, I found a pair of old boots." The leather had, however, perished and a day or two later, the hinges parted, the door blew in on the stove and upset a frying pan of onions!

The idyll of those rainless summer days in the exhilarating mountain air had barely begun when Lloyd, in just under a week, developed diphtheria, and Fanny had hurt her thumb badly. Back they went, this time to a rented cottage in Calistoga. What Stevenson called a "melancholy interregnum" lasted ten days. On June 25 they returned to Silverado and the painter Joe Strong, husband of Fanny's daughter Isobel, went with them. Stevenson found him a "most good-natured comrade and a capital hand at an omelette. I do not know in which capacity he was most valued — as a cook or a companion; and he did excellently well with both." It was probably during this stay that Joe made a drawing of Fanny and Louis in the bunkhouse. This served as a frontspiece in the first edition of *The Silverado Squatters,* published in London. Joe made another very similar drawing — although not quite such a good one — for the first American edition. A third version of the same scene, copied obviously from Joe's drawings by some unknown hand, was used in some later editions and is far inferior to either of Joe's sketches.

Aside from his notes in the journal, Stevenson did no fresh literary work during the time at Silverado. But every morning he collected the day's supply of firewood for the cookstove and the evening fire in the forge. Later, he walked down the trail to the Toll House, to join and gossip with the little group awaiting the arrival of the two stages crammed with guests bound for the fashionable Lake County resorts — and bringing Stevenson's can of fresh milk and the mail.

> And then the first of the two stages swooped upon the Toll House with a roar and in a cloud of dust; and the shock had not yet time to subside, before the second was abreast of it. Huge concerns they were, well-horsed and loaded, the men in their shirt-sleeves, the women swathed in veils, the long whip cracking like a pistol; and as they charged upon the slumbering hostelry, each shepherding a dust storm, the dead place blossomed into life and talk and chatter. This the Toll House? — with its city throng, its jostling shoulders, its infinity of instant business in the bar? The mind would not receive it! The heartfelt bustle of that hour is hardly credible; the thrill of the great shower of letters from the post-bag, the childish hope and interest with which one gazed in all these strangers' eyes. They paused there but to pass: the blue-clad China-boy, the San Franciscan magnate, the mystery in the dust coat, the secret memoirs in tweed, the ogling, well-shod lady with her troop of girls; they did but flash and go; they were hull-down for us behind life's ocean, and we but hailed their topsails on the line. Yet, out of our great solitude of four and twenty mountain hours, we thrilled to their momemtary presence; gauged and divined them, loved and hated; and stood light-headed in that storm of human electricity. Yes, like Piccadilly Circus, this is also one of life's crossing places.

The solitude of those four and twenty mountain hours was not as great as Stevenson implied. Rufus Hanson, his companion, Breedlove, and Mrs. Hanson, came to be drawn by Fanny the day Joe Strong left. There is evidence that Andrew Rocca and his wife (who we shall meet later) came to visit at Silverado. On more than one occasion, Stevenson walked down the mountainside to Calistoga and hired Bill Spiers to drive him back. Bill Spiers was then twenty-seven, engaged in hauling bark to Napa tannery. In between times, he drove a rig for the owners of the Calistoga livery barn and eventually bought the stage line from Calistoga to the Lake County resorts and controlled all connecting lines. Thereafter, with the introduction and increase of the automobile, he supplemented his stagecoaches with motorbuses. Between 1912 and 1915, his entire transport was motorized. Reminiscing about Stevenson, he admitted years later to the late Anne Roller Issler (as she recorded in *Our Mountain Hermitage*) that he thought him "kind of a fool, livin' in that old shack writin' books" and would have taken more notice of him had he known "he'd be so famous".

It has been asserted that the Stevensons were visited by Dora and Virgil Williams, to whom Stevenson dedicated *The Silverado Squatters,* and that more often Fanny and Louis visited them in their cottage on the Sugar Loaf. There is no evidence of this and the walk across the mountainside from Silverado to the Sugar Loaf was quite long and rough-going. Moreover, Virgil was probably fully occupied with his teaching at the School of Design.

By mid-July, plans were being made to leave Silverado for Scotland. Louis, completely reconciled with his father and mother, was receiving affectionate letters begging Louis and Fanny to come home and bring Lloyd with them. Nellie Sanchez, Isobel and Joe came to stay. Isobel, in *This Life I've Loved,* found Louis amazingly better, he was like a different man. They had their meals out-of-doors and, as her mother was an excellent cook, they were good ones:

"She used the mouth of the old Silverado mine for an ice chest and storeroom; here hung sides of venison, pigeons, wild ducks and other game purchased from friendly neighbors" — chiefly, no doubt from Rufus Hanson who was a crack shot — and in the chill shadow were cans of fresh milk . . . About eleven o'clock in the morning and three in the afternoon we were all served with a rum punch, frothy with cream and delicately topped with a sprinkle of cinnamon." Dinner was eaten around the forge fire.

It was probably early in the week of July 19 when the squatters and their guests left Silverado for San Francisco. On July 29, Louis, Fanny and Lloyd boarded a Pullman bound for New York, arriving there on August 6. The next day they embarked, first class, aboard the *City of Chester* — one year to the day after Louis had sailed from the Clyde aboard the *Devonia.*

Traveling first class may seem as incongruous as the stay at the Palace Hotel immediately after their wedding. However, contrary to the general impression which Louis himself created, he was by no means destitute. His poverty was self-imposed, perhaps because he had an idealistic determination to prove he could make it on his own. He did succeed, thanks to Jules Simoneau, Mrs. Mary Carson and his other friends, but he did have funds available, and toward the end of his stay, drew the equivalent of two-thousand dollars, which was quite a sum in 1880. Fanny, in widowhood, became rich, and almost up to the time of her death in Santa Barbara in 1914, generously provided for Jules Simoneau in Monterey, and for Cummy, Stevenson's old nurse.

Stevenson, as is well known, returned to San Francisco briefly in 1888. The previous year his father died, and the doctors declared that Stevenson should no longer stay in Great Britain. The family — Louis, Fanny, Stevenson's mother, Lloyd and the Swiss maid, Valentine — set out for the health resort on Saranac Lake in Adirondacks in August 1887. The winter cold at Saranac Lake was harsh for them and a suggestion that Louis should charter a yacht and voyage in the Pacific was appealing. The following spring, Fanny set off for San Francisco to see her sister Nellie Sanchez and her daughter Belle Strong — and to make inquiries about yachts. In six weeks time, she cabled: "Can secure splendid seagoing yacht, *Casco* . . . ''

In May, Louis, his mother, Lloyd and Valentine started on the transcontinental railroad journey to San Francisco. Under doctor's orders, Louis was forced to rest at the Occidental Hotel. Fanny completed the arrangements for hiring the *Casco,* and, with the family, set about buying stores which included seventy pounds of plug chewing-tobacco, whisky, and Chinese custom-made dresses of lawn and muslin. On June 26 they set sail en route for the South Pacific. Belle Strong and Dora Williams waved from the wharf as the yacht was towed out toward and beyond the Golden Gate. Dora Williams somehow had managed to get a note on board for Fanny, it simply read "Ave atque Vale." Hail and farewell was a fitting tribute to her friends.

7

Remembering
Robert Louis Stevenson

Stevenson has had many biographers. Most of them have brushed off his stay at Silverado with a line. There have, however, been a number of books by California writers on his year in America. As far as I can learn, only two biographers, James Pope Hennessy and J.C. Furness, ever bothered to visit Silverado. Furness also traveled to all other places on the globe — except Davos, Switzerland — where R.L.S. made more casual visits.

In his *Voyage to Windward* (New York, 1951) Furness wrote: "Perhaps because of the special immediacy . . . of his writing about it, one feels more Stevenson in the air at Silverado than anywhere else except in Edinburgh and environs. This even excludes Vailima, the house in Samoa where he lived for years and died . . ." Hennessy, in *Robert Louis Stevenson* (London, 1974) wrote: "This is a silent and evocative place of intense natural beauty, and here it is easy to picture the Stevensons on their unconventional honeymoon. It is quiet and wild and solitary, and they seem to haunt it still."

The writing of "special immediacy" that Furness referred to was, of course, *The Silverado Squatters*. One reason why the Stevensons "haunt it still" is that *The Silverado Squatters* is a faithful piece of reporting on the local scene, and the scene itself has changed little.

Today, the mountain highway, for all the twists and steep grades, is easily and swiftly traveled compared with the Old Toll Road over which the six-horse wagons hauled the ore from mountain mines and the stagecoaches their passengers. At the summit of this highway is the entrance to the Robert Louis Stevenson State Park and the newly-made trail leads up through the forest to the mine. There is not a vestige of the old brown house but on its exact site, in a clearing among thickets of madrone and bay trees, is a marker; a block of Scotch granite shaped like an open book and supported by a stone plinth erected in 1911 by the women's clubs of Napa County. One page of the book records that Robert Louis Stevenson and bride stayed here while he wrote *The Silverado*

Squatters, and on the other page is a quotation from one of Stevenson's poems:

> Doomed to know not Winter, only Spring, a being
> Trod the flowery April blithely for a while
> Took his fill of music, joy of thought and seeing,
> Came and stayed and went, nor ever ceased to smile.

It is quibbling, perhaps, to point out that it was the journal and not *The Silverado Squatters* that Stevenson wrote while there but it does seem somewhat ungenerous not to have given Fanny a line, or at least inscribed her name. Her fortitude and ingenuity must have been taxed to the limit. To her goes the credit for Louis's regained strength in this lonely retreat. He lived, against the doctor's predictions, to voyage half around the world and back again and to write for fourteen more years before he died in Samoa at forty-four.

Stevenson's prophecy that trains would soon shake the mountain to its heart; that there would be many-windowed hotels lighting up the night like factories upon the mountainside, and that a prosperous city would occupy the site of Calistoga, has not been altogether fulfilled. The railroad has not advanced. In fact, Napa Valley has no passenger line, and the railroad now carries only freight and stops at Charles Krug Winery on the northerly outskirts of St. Helena. The freight consist mostly of pallets — fifty to sixty cases of bottled wine per pallet — from Krug, Beringer and other nearby wineries. There is but one modest hotel on the mountainside and the Robert Louis Stevenson Park now covers over 3,000 acres, including the Silverado mine and the site of the assayer's office. Calistoga remains a small town and a properous one, with motels as well as hotels to accommodate its visitors. Its white timber-framed houses, sheltered by vines and shrubs and wide-branching shade trees, still line its streets, but no longer can one hear the cattle bells afield.

Now, as then, life at the foot of the mountain "goes rustically forward. Bucks, and bears, and rattlesnakes and former mining operations, are the staple of men's talk." However, the talk today is more of coyotes, which have become a menace to sheep, rather than of bears, now rare visitors, and grape-growing, not mining, is a year-round topic.

In Stevenson's day, the wine-growing industry in California was still in the experimental stage. "The beginning of vine-planting is like the beginning of mining for the precious metals," wrote R.L.S., "the wine-grower also 'prospects.' One corner of land after another is tried with one kind of grape after another."

Today, the Silverado Country is Wine Country too. In Napa, Knight's and Alexander Valleys, prune and walnut orchards and pasture land have been almost entirely displaced by vineyards and portions of the hillsides in the Napa Valley are also possessed by the grapevine. The region has become famous for its fine wines.

Some of the wineries of hand-dressed native stone built mostly by the Italian Swiss still stand and wine still matures in the cellars tunneled in the hillsides. Stevenson would readily recognize the vineyards and wineries he visited, and would marvel at the seventeen-room Rhine House, which Frederick Beringer built later, and at the immaculately tended grounds surrounding it. These, planted with shrubs and trees, have long since matured and provide a superb setting. One tree, an enormous gingko, in fall foliage is mantled in sunlit yellow, and stands as one symbol of the valley's golden harvest.

Jacob and Annie Schram's elegant house is now occupied by Jack and Jamie Davies and their family. The grounds and winery are refurbished and Schramsberg's speciality today is sparkling wine under the label of Schramsberg Champagne. Benjamin and Rose Falk, the present owners, have replanted McEachran's Alta Vineyard in Chardonnay, and store their wine in the old stone cellar. In 1980, they commemorated the 100th anniversary of Stevenson's visit by releasing a special Napa Gamay with a portrait of Stevenson on the label.

Inevitably, so great an increase in vineyards has created a demand for new wineries, and some of these are as handsome and intriguing architecturally as are Beringer and Schramsberg.

There is another feature that Stevenson saw only in his imagination, and in another form. This is a modern spy-glass, a fire look-out tower that the Forestry Department maintains on the north peak of Mount St. Helena.

As for place names, "Silverado" has become a household word throughout the region. This, perhaps, is another reason why there is a feeling of Stevenson in the air roundabout. Those of his contemporaries who could say they knew or remembered Stevenson thereby added some lustre to their own names, a lustre their children also to some degree inherit. For them, and for the townspeople today, Stevenson ranks as Calistoga's all-time most distinguished visitor. But for Stevenson, Silverado City would be as forgotten as are scores of other ghost towns and cities. As it is, schools, streets, stores and lumberyards have made the name of Stevenson and Silverado synonymous.

Stevenson is also remembered in other places he stayed during his year in California. The house in which he lodged in Monterey is now known as The Stevenson House and is maintained by the State of California's Department of Parks and Recreations. It contains furnishings associated with R.L.S., early editions of his books, and among the drawings are some of Fanny's and Dora Williams's work, including Fanny's drawing of Louis wearing the pitifully frayed and tarnished smoking cap he wore at Grez.

San Francisco remembers R.L.S. by a memorial to him in Portsmouth Square: a bronze galleon in full sail atop a granite shaft, with these words from his Christmas sermon engraved on the shaft:

> To be honest, to be kind, to earn a little, to spend a little less — to make upon the whole a family happier for his presence — to renounce when that shall be necessary and not be embittered — to keep a few friends, but these without capitulation —above all, on the same grim condition, to keep friends with himself — here is a task for all that a man has of fortitude and delicacy.

There is also a plaque on the house that now stands on the site of

Mrs. Carson's lodging house at 608 Bush Street.

In St. Helena, eight miles south of Calistoga, The Silverado Museum displays one of the finest Stevenson collections in existence. The museum is the realization of the dream of Mr. Norman H. Strouse, a native of Olympia, Washington and former President and Chairman of the Board of J. Walter Thompson Company, the world's largest advertising agency.

In 1930, just fifty years after the Stevenson's stay at Silverado, Mr. Strouse, then 24 and beginning his career in advertising in San Francisco, purchased a beautiful edition of *The Silverado Squatters* printed by John Henry Nash in 1927. Impressed by his first reading of what he regards as Stevenson's great classic of the Napa wine country, Norman Strouse made the trip from San Francisco to the site of the mine assayer's office. He fell in love with the Napa Valley and Silverado cast its spell. He began to collect Stevenson memorabilia, paintings, manuscripts and letters. In 1968, he retired and returned to St. Helena where he and his wife fulfilled two dreams: they established the Vailima Foundation to support the Silverado Museum and they built their home, Skerryvore, on the Silverado Trail.

The Silverado Museum, established in 1969, is on Library Lane, and houses the Strouse's collections of Stevensoniana, a munificent gift. Since the museum was established, other important acquisitions have been made, largely by purchase, but occasionally by gift. There are original portraits of R.L.S., leaves of some original manuscripts, Stevenson's writing desk, hammock, inkwells and ten pieces of chinaware from Vailima, his plantation home in Samoa. There are also paintings by Thomas Hill, William Keith, Joseph Strong and Virgil Williams — and nine water colors by Dora Williams. Many who come to the museum are scholars bent on research but the museum also has a wide popular appeal. As of September 1982, more than one-hundred-thousand visitors have come from all over the United States and eighty-one foreign countries.

Robert Louis Stevenson is well remembered in California, and some may think that Calistoga has capitalized far too heavily on the association. He spent but three weeks there, and four weeks at Silverado, yet Frank Swinnerton, in his *Critical Study* of Stevenson (1924) considered that *The Silverado Squatters* marked "the emergence of a new Stevenson; chastened, experienced, matured: those of us who never take these voyages out into the unknown, who sit tight and think comfortably of such things as emigrant trains, cannot realize with what sudden effect the stubborn impact of realities can work upon those who actually venture forth."

Stevenson's year in California did, in fact, have a tremendous impact on his life and on his writings, and his Calistoga - Silverado stay was a turning point. He found a wife and family, and emerged a best-selling author. Three books stemmed from that year: *The Amateur Emigrant, The Silverado Squatters* and *Treasure Island.*

In addition, two essays, *"Monterey"* and *"San Francisco"* appeared under the title *The Old and New Pacific Capitals.* Two further essays have come to light: "San Carlos Day" appeared in the Monterey *California* of November 11, 1879 under the pseudonym "The Monterey Barbarian," and "Simoneau's at Monterey" a hitherto unpublished manuscript in the Beinecke Rare Book and Manuscript Library of Yale University; the title of this essay is a quotation taken from the text. Both essays are included in James Hart's *From Scotland to Silverado* (Cambridge, Massachussetts, 1926), the one appearing in a book for the first time, the other appearing for the first time in print. Also, more than one poem in *A Child's Garden of Verses* evokes memories of his California days.

The Wrecker also reveals something of what the region meant to R.L.S. *The Ebb Tide,* written the last year of his life and as George Stewart points out, "the presence and power of the city San Francisco hangs upon the edge of the story as Captain Flint hovers just outside the action of *Treasure Island.* "

To the end of his life, R.L.S. remembered America as "a great place for kindness." In his *Silverado Journal* he acknowledged that the country has "done me favours to confound my gratitude."

In terms of kindness, those he remembered with enduring affection were Jules Simoneau and Dora and Virgil Williams. Of all the inns and restaurants he had come across in his wanderings, not one he declared could be compared with Simoneau's at Monterey. "The talks we had upon all subjects . . . the long pleasant evenings by the stove . . . O mon bon Simoneau . . . your kindnesses are still remembered."

Six years after Stevenson left Silverado, on December 18, 1886, Virgil Williams was out on the mountain with his gun and his dogs — he loved to hunt as well as paint. He came home early, complaining of a pain near his heart. In the night he worsened. The cottage was too remote, the road too difficult for help to reach him in time. Only Dora was with him when he died about 2:00 a.m. The next day his body was taken to San Francisco, and the Bohemian Club and the Art Association gave him a noble funeral. Fellow artists Thomas Hill and William Keith were among the pallbearers. Dora wrote to R.L.S. to tell him the news. He replied: "Virgil's handsome face I see all over the San Francisco of my memory — San Francisco to me was only Virgil and yourself."

No doubt Stevenson would remember the kindliness of Fanny's ex-husband Sam Osbourne and there is a certain poignancy about Sam's end. He had remarried. Then came an evening when he did not come home as was his custom, during his second marriage. From that day on, no one heard a word about him: he had just disappeard. His wife kept the lights on every night thereafter, always hoping that he would reappear. His son Sam was so heartbroken that from then on he insisted on being called Lloyd by everyone.

To round out the Stevensoniana portion of this book, the argument or reasoning for the identification of Spy-glass Hill should be given.

8

Spy-glass Hill

In the various editions of Stevenson's works, only a portion of his journal is included. However, in 1954, the Book Club of California, in a superbly printed volume, *Silverado Journal*, published the complete journal from the original manuscript now in the Huntington Library. Except for one full entry to be mentioned later, the journal in its entirety is a very slim collection of notes of a few events and scenes. *The Silverado Squatters* was written largely from memory. Being such an accurate reporting of the local scene, it shows what an extraordinarily good memory Stevenson had.

The Silverado Squatters was first published in two installments in the *Century Magazine* of November and December 1883, with the additional subtitle, *Sketches from a California Mountain*. Simultaneously, it was published in London in November 1883, the same month and the same year as *Treasure Island*, and was followed by an American edition in late January 1884. *The Silverado Squatters* was fact; *Treasure Island* fiction, and the latter reveals that R.L.S. was a master at blending the real and the imaginary.

Our first reading of *The Silverado Squatters* had led us to other books on Stevenson's California days; one of these is included in the bibliography of George. R. Stewart's master's thesis, *Stevenson in California. A Critical Study (1921)*. In this thesis, Stewart identifies one of the peaks of Mount St. Helena as the Spy-glass Hill of *Treasure Island*. He is, I believe, the first to do so. It would be very hard indeed to discount this. Some credit a crag on Point Lobos, south of Monterey and Carmel, as Spy-glass, but I have seen no Spy-glass there. The point's rocky crags are often surrounded in sea fog, but certainly there is no peak on Point Lobos that a cloud could rest on and, except for the summer months, a cloud often rests on the north peak of Mount St. Helena.

The profile of Mount St. Helena, as already stated, presents a different appearance from one viewpoint to another. Stevenson's first view of the mountain was about midway in Napa Valley from the train, the day he and Fanny came to Calistoga, and, from midway in the valley, the mountain does appear to be a single, flat-topped mass. When he sat on the veranda the Sunday he had midday dinner at the MacDonald ranch, Stevenson would have seen the long silhouette of the mountain's western slopes, and the four peaks running south to north in a row. From this viewpoint, some see in this silhouette the figure of a woman reclining on her back; for Stevenson it suggested the outline of a sailing ship.

Here are Stevenson's descriptions of the mountain and of Spy-glass Hill as seen from the Napa Valley:

The tangles, woody, and almost trackless foot-hills that enclose the valley . . . were dwarfed into satellites by the bulk and bearing of Mount St. Helena. She over-towered them by two-thirds of her own stature. She excelled them by the boldness of her profile. Her great bald summit, clear of trees and pasture . . . rejected kinship with the dark and shaggy wilderness of lesser hill-tops.

The Silverado Squatters

By three or four hundred feet the tallest on the island, was likewise the strangest in configuration, running up sheer from almost every side, and then suddenly cut off at the top like a pedestal to put a statue on.

Treasure Island

And here is another aspect of the mountain and of Spy-glass Hill from a different viewpoint:

That hill to the nor'ard they calls the Fore-mast Hill; there are three hills in a row running south-ard - fore, main, and mizen, sir. But the main - that's the big 'un with the cloud on it - they usually calls the Spy-glass, by reason of a look-out they kept when they was in the anchorage cleaning; for it's there they cleaned their ships, sir, asking your pardon.

Treasure Island

Remembering that Stevenson was writing mostly from memory, this description of the mountain very nearly fits the Knight's Valley view, except that there are four, not three, hills in a row; and the north, not the middle peak, is the highest. A cloud often rests upon it when the other peaks are clear; and on some crystal-clear days, usually after a north wind, the Pacific Ocean may be seen from the north peak. All during his stay on the mountain, the sea was never very far from Stevenson's mind, as his chapter "The Sea Fogs" in *The Silverado Squatters* reveals.

The chapter is a partial rewrite of the one full entry that Stevenson made in his journal for Sunday, June 13; some passages being identical and others almost so. It is thus a firsthand account of a phenomenon of the Pacific Coast Ranges; of the velo clouds, or overcast that at times rolls in in opaque banks of fog, blanketing the Napa Valley. It is a spectacle that may be seen only on occasion, caused by a combination of certain variances in wind and weather. Stevenson saw it once and so have I. On just such a morning, a friend and I were up on the mountain just after sunrise, having been told by the Forestry Department that our chances to see the great sight were good. And we stood just

40

about where Stevenson stood, and saw what he saw:

> Gone were all the lower slopes and woody foothills of the range; and in their place, not a thousand feet below me, rolled a great level ocean . . . Far away were hilltops like little islands. Nearer, a smoky surf beat about the foot of precipices and poured into all the coves of these rough mountains. The color of that fog ocean was a thing never to be forgotten. For an instant, among the Hebrides and just about sundown, I have seen something like it on the sea itself. But the white was not so opaline; nor was there, what surprisingly increased the effect, that breathless, crystal stillness over all. Even in its gentlest moods the salt sea travails, moaning among the weeds or lisping on the sand; but that vast fog ocean lay in a trance of silence, nor did the sweet air of the morning tremble with a sound.

The spine of the story of both *Treasure Island* and *The Silverado Squatters* is Mount St. Helena and the immediate countryside around it. *Treasure Island* is a perfect illustration of Stevenson's ability to blend the real and the imaginary, to impose one scene upon another. Many of the imaginary scenes in *Treasure Island* are in reality those of Silverado. The "undulating, sandy country" on the Monterey peninsula is the land through which Jim Hawkins adventures on Treasure Island when he climbs upward to leave Monterey behind he strikes up into terrain akin to that of Silverado. The shrubs he delights in are those Stevenson saw around him on Mount St. Helena: "Thickets of green nutmeg trees were dotted here and there with the red columns and the broad shades of the pines, and the first mingled their spice with the aroma of the other." The wild nutmegs, sweet bays and chaparral, which still grow around Silverado, provided the verdant growth through which Long John Silver stumped with his peg leg on *Treasure Island.*

Writing about *Treasure Island* to his friend and editor, Sidney Colvin, Stevenson admitted that "The scenery is California in part, and in part chic." There was, in fact, a good deal more real then chic. *Chic,* as defined by *Larousse's Dictionary,* means having the ability to do something — to work or draw or paint from chic, that is without models and from memory.

R.L.S. himself, in the opening paragraph of his essay "Simoneau's at Monterey" has this to say about imagination; (and I am grateful to the Beinecke Library for permission to quote this passage):

> A place does not clearly exist for the imagination, til we have moved elsewhere. The tenor of our experience, one day melting into another, unifies into a single picture; out of many sunsets, many dawns, and many starry rambles, we compound a *tertium quid,* a glorified quintessence; the honey of honey, the cream of cream, a classical landscape, artificially and far more lively, winning and veracious than the scene it represents. For single glances may, indeed, be memorable; they are the traits of which we afterwards compose our fancy likeness, but the eye cannot embrace a panorama; the eye, like the etcher's needle, cannot elaborate from nature; and literature, which is the language of our thoughts, must be gently elaborated in the course of time. Hence, it is that a place grows upon our fancy after we have left it . . .

Doctor Hart, in *From Scotland to Silverado,* points out that R.L.S. sometimes chose words that had adventurous overtones or provided an alliteration, even though their precise meaning was slightly altered.

It is tempting to think that the title "Treasure Island" was inspired by a tiny island in San Francisco Bay, known and still marked on the map as Red Rock. Stevenson could have seen it from one of the city's hills, and may have heard that a Spanish hoard of gold and jewels, that no man has yet found, was said to be buried there. Woolworth, the owner, had built a cabin, put up a flagstaff and mounted a cannon. But the title was chosen by the publisher, and not by Stevenson.

How the book came to be written has been recorded, but is not often remembered. It was during the latter part of the summer of 1881 that the whole Stevenson family was staying in a cottage at Braemar, Scotland. To amuse Lloyd when the afternoons were cold and drizzly, Louis made colored drawings with pen and ink and the boy's shilling-box of water colors. On one occasion, he made a map of an island and "I ticketed my performance *Treasure Island.*" Poring over his map admiringly, "the future characters of the book began to appear there visibly among imaginary woods . . . The next thing I knew, I had some paper before me and was working out a list of chapters."

"On a chill September morning, by the cheek of a brisk fire, and the rain drumming on the window, I began *The Sea Cook,*" for that was the original title. Sitting by the fireside, Louis wrote a chapter every morning, and day after day, he read that morning's work aloud in the afternoon. Louis had counted on one boy in his audience, but found he had two; the elder Stevenson was just as entranced with the story as was Lloyd.

Louis' old friend, Mr. Henderson, the London publisher of *The Young Folks Paper,* had enlisted Dr. Alexander Japp to search for new writers for his periodical and to visit Stevenson. He arrived unannounced, and the first fifteen chapters of *The Sea Cook* were read aloud again. When Dr. Japp left, he carried the manuscript away in his portmanteau, confident that Mr. Henderson would serialize *The Sea Cook.* Stevenson set about his work again in a glow of promise. But in the sixteenth chapter, his inventiveness deserted him and his writing came to a dead stop. He was thoroughly embarrassed, for Mr. Henderson had promptly agreed to serialize *The Sea Cook* beginning on the first of October.

With the coming of winter, Louis, Fanny and Lloyd left Braemar, staying briefly at Weybridge, England, on their way to Davos, Switzerland, where they were to spend the winter again. Soon after their arrival on October 15, Louis looked over the unfinished tale, and "behold! it flowed from me like small talk; and in a second tide of delighted industry, and again at the rate of a chapter a day, I finished *Treasure Island!*" Stevenson was now using the title Henderson had chosen, the label Stevenson had given his map, and it appeared in *Young Folks* in seventeen weekly parts from October 1881 to January 1882, under the pseudonym, Captain George North.

Cassell and Company published *Treasure Island* in book form on November 14, 1883, and continued paying royalties until 1944. But, before the book came out, Stevenson had one other problem. The story had, as he put it, been written up to the map, and although he has sent it along with the manuscript, Cassell said they had not received it. Aghast, Stevenson had to make another map. As Stevenson said, it was one thing to draw a map and write a story to its measurements. It was something else "to have to examine a whole book, make an inventory of all the allusions contained in it, and with a pair of compasses painfully design a map to suit the data. I did it, and the map was drawn again in my father's office, with embellishments of blow whales and sailing ships . . . "

Incidentally, the site of the 1939 World's Fair was a flat manmade island created for that event in San Francisco Bay, and named Treasure Island. Erwin G. Gudde's *California Place Names,* according to one of the contributors W.L. Wright, the name "Treasure Island" was chosen "because it perfectly expressed a glamorous, beautiful, almost fabulous island that would present the treasures of the world during the World's Fair. It was no direct attempt to capitalize upon Robert Louis Stevenson, although the fact that he had made Treasure Island a household word was a factor in their choice."

Surely, the names of some of the characters in *Treasure Island* were taken from place names and the names of people Stevenson encountered at Silverado and elsewhere. Long John Silver's name may well have emerged from the name Silverado, a name that pleased him on their first prospect of the silver mining scene.

And what of the name Jim Hawkins? Andy Tajha had a carpenter friend to help him one day when working on our ranch house. His name was Chuck Hawkins, and he lived on the mountain not far from the Old Toll Road where Stevenson talked with neighbors while awaiting the morning stages.

I asked Chuck if his father might have been among them.

"Could've been," he said, pounding in another nail. "We Hawkins've been hereabouts for quite a spell."

"Then you could be Jim Hawkins' grandson?"

Chuck's hammer never missed a beat. "Could be," he granted.

9

The Great Western Mine

Of all the mines on Mount St. Helena, the Great Western was the longest steady producer. From it came quicksilver. Situated 1,850 feet up on the Lake County side of the mountain, it was most directly reached from Calistoga by the Lawley Toll Road up, over and down the mountain to a point known as the Western Gate, four miles south of Middletown. Mail and passengers were put off the stagecoach at the gate, to be picked up by some smaller conveyance from the mine and taken up the two-mile grade that joined part of the Ida Clayton Road to a branch road that led directly to the mine. All the information about Rocca and life at the Great Western, comes from *The Life and Death of a Quicksilver Mine* by one of Rocca's daughters, Helen Rocca Goss.

Andrew Rocca, the Great Western's superintendent and Trustee from 1876 to 1900, was an Italian from Genoa, and an old hand of the Gold Rush, who had learned to speak Chinese. This was no small asset at the Great Western "diggins" where the payroll listed some 200 Chinese and 25 whites, most of them also Gold Rush veterans.

The two chief buildings in the mining camp were the boarding house and the small school. Rocca and other white bachelors, engineers and assistant superintendents, lived in the boarding house and had their meals together in their own private dining room. The main camp was a Chinese world and, in reality, two camps. One was for Chinamen mostly from the Canton area, the other for those from other parts of China.

In the spring of 1879, Calistoga ran short of funds and closed its schools. One of the young teachers, Mary Thompson, was offered a teaching post for three months at the Great Western Mine and she accepted. She had a small sparsely-furnished room with a "thumb-latch" and had her meals along with the superintendents. At first she questioned how long she could make out in so remote a place but the three months went by, Mary stayed on, and it was not long before she wrote to her family in Sacramento County that she

44

was at the Great Western to stay. She and Andrew Rocca were married in April of 1880.

Construction began on a house for the superintendent and his bride while they occupied a set of rooms in the boarding house. Work on the new house was slow. It became evident that their first child would be born in the boarding house and the zinc bath the Roccas had ordered for their new home was set up in a room adjoining their boarding-house bedroom.

The zinc bathtub installed for Mrs. Rocca was an almost unheard of luxury in a mining camp at that time. On the day Dr. Parson came to attend Mrs. Rocca during the birth of her first child, Andrew proudly showed the doctor the bathtub and invited him to get in it. The doctor, who had never seen a bathtub, promptly did so, fully clothed even to his boots and a Prince Albert coat. It was a great Andrew Rocca story thereafter but at the time, Mr. Rocca was not amused that the doctor put the bathtub before the baby, even for a moment.

Another innovation was the telephone installed at the Great Western three years after the telephone was invented. A second telephone, installed later, served as the receiver of a new broadcasting service. Each morning shortly after the San Francisco papers reached Calistoga by train, the telephone operator rang one long ring, the signal for everybody on the line to listen in to the news. Then the operator read the headlines from the morning paper.

Daylight saving — fast time, the miners called it — was another modernity at the mine. Fast time was 45 minutes ahead of Standard and allowed the miners to be above ground in the daylight of early morning and late afternoon.

All this was in strong contrast to the Chinese world nearby: the camps a jumble of separate huts, each Chinese making his own small fire to cook his rice and heat water for tea. Later, one could catch glimpses of them through open doorways, wearing a kind of dungaree costume, squatting, eating their bowls of rice with chopsticks. Outdoors, they were identified by their "huge, wide-brimmed, conical-topped reed hats."

The Chinese New Year, which falls between late January and the third week in February was celebrated at the Great Western with firecrackers galore. It is recorded that in one year 110,000 firecrackers and numerous bombs were set off. The Roccas were overwhelmed with gifts, which began to arrive in proper, traditional order even before the New Year: narcissus of sacred Chinese lily bulbs, now commonly known as China lilies, litchi nuts, candied fruits and coconut, tangerines, chunks of sugar cane and jars of preserved ginger. And there were plain and brocaded squares of silk, umbrellas, Chinese slippers, fans, beautiful vases and bowls, china figures and hair ornaments. Rocca's Chinese miners thought well of "Bossy Man" and wanted him to know it.

In turn, Rocca respected their customs. The few Chinamen who died at the mine were buried temporarily in a clump of pines nearby. Later, the bones were disinterred and shipped to China, since it was the belief that no true

Chinaman could find eternal rest except in the soil of his native land.

Every month, Rocca went into Calistoga to get a sack of gold and silver coins to pay the wages of his Chinese miners, who put no faith in paper money. Highwaymen kept a lookout for him, sometimes lying in wait for a week. To fool them, Rocca made secret plans for each journey, varying the day, the hour and the route, but always riding between dark and dawn. Sometimes he used the Lawley Toll Road over the mountain, but more often he used the Ida Clayton Road.

This road provided a far longer and more difficult way to Calistoga by way of Knight's Valley: narrow, tortuous, almost perpendicular in places, it wound down past the turnoff to Dora and Virgil Williams' summer cottage on Sugar-loaf Hill to link up with the road through Knight's Valley. Rocca outsmarted the highwaymen and was never robbed.

Helen Rocca Goss, in *The Life and Death of a Quicksilver Mine*, says that her parents, Andrew and Mary Rocca, became acquainted with the Stevensons and saw them several times during their stay at Silverado. One of her elder sisters believed her parents saw them at Silverado and, at least on one occasion, at the Great Western Mine.

The Williams, at their cottage on Sugar-loaf Hill, were relatively close neighbors of the Roccas and perhaps friends, for the two men could reminisce about life in Italy. Dora and Virgil may have asked the newlywed Roccas — we remember they were married the month before Louis and Fanny — to call at Silverado. During their honeymoon, the Roccas rode around the countryside a good deal. It would not have been too difficult for the Stevensons to go by stagecoach from the Toll House to the Western Gate where they would be met and driven up to the mine. However this may be, the Roccas took to Louis instantly but found Fanny less appealing. Mary Rocca later said, they thought she was "rather dictatorial, too outspoken."

About a year and a half after R.L.S. was at Silverado, when he was at Hyères, in the south of France, he wrote a poem, "Windy Nights", that is found in *A Child's Garden of Verses*. Ill, temporarily blinded, his right arm strapped to his side, he lay in a darkened room, laboriously writing with his left hand on large sheets of paper pinned to a board. Was he not mindful of the wind that blew all night long on his first night on the mountain, of his own and the Chinamen's evening fires, and of the "Bossy Man's" long night rides?

> Whenever the moon and stars are set,
> Whenever the wind is high,
> All night long in the dark and wet,
> A man goes riding by.
> Late in the night when the fires are out,
> Why does he gallop and gallop about?
>
> Whenever the trees are crying aloud,
> And ships are tossed at sea,

By, on the highway, low and loud,
By at the gallop goes he.
By at the gallop he goes, and then
By he comes back at the gallop again.

I like to think of Andrew Rocca riding by our ranch house, his saddlebags heavy with gold and silver coins, and it is R.L.S.'s poem that keeps his image alive for me.

10

L.H.C. 5
Lillie Hitchcock Coit

Lillie Hitchcock Coit was one of the most remarkable characters San Francisco has ever known. The city loved her, perhaps more than any other person. Coit Tower on Telegraph Hill stands as a memorial to her. Her country homes were in the upper Napa Valley and there are people who remember the stories their grandparents told about Lillie.

Flamboyant, tomboyish, with a great capacity for mischief and pranks, Lillie Coit was not a frivolous person. Extremely independent, with a total lack of concern for what people thought of her, she was thoughtful of all others. She was a woman of courage and integrity and became fully aware of her responsibilities. Loyalty was her masthead. Men not only loved her but respected her. As Floride Green, who knew her well, reiterated: "she was never touched by a breath of scandal." She became a legend in her lifetime, the symbol of the volunteer firefighting men who, as George Barron pointed out in his speech at the dedication of Coit Tower, "met in the common purpose of preserving the city and remaining together as comrades and friends. In those stern pioneering days, a man was a man — and a fireman."

Lillie's parents came of Southern plantation-owning families. Charles was an Army surgeon; Martha, a proud socially ambitious, determined woman. Their only child was born at West Point in August 1843. Christened Eliza Wychie, she was always called Lillie.

In 1851, when Lillie was eight years old, Charles was promoted to Medical Director of the Pacific Coast Command and ordered to proceed to California. Sailing from Charleston on April 14, they reached San Francisco by way of the Isthmus of Panama on May 20.

In 1847, there were less than 400 people in the trading post on the San Francisco waterfront. At the time gold was discovered in 1849, there were 812. By the end of 1849, the population had swelled to 20,000 or more, nearly all men. In 1852, the year after the Hitchcocks arrived, the state census in

San Francisco was 34,776, and in 1860 the figure climbed to 56,802. San Francisco was thus an "instant city" and awash with tremendous wealth derived from the mines.

At the time of the gold rush, the early settlement at the waterfront spread rapidly across the hills: a city of a few adobe, but mostly wooden houses and tents. San Francisco's two great problems were fire and water.

In the seventeen months before the Hitchcocks arrived, the city had experienced five devasting fires, probably set by incendiaries to screen their plundering. The first volunteer fire fighting companies had been formed, and the city seal of 1850 depicted a phoenix, the bird fabled to be consumed in fire by its own act, and to rise in youthful freshness from its own ashes - thus it was an emblem of immortality. In the same year, the city erected a semaphore station on the summit of what became known as Telegraph Hill that was used to signal the approach of ships.

Shortly after the Hitchcocks arrived, more companies were formed and funds were allocated to build engine houses and to provide for the placement of water tanks and cisterns. The volunteer fire department now consisted of fourteen hand-drawn engines and three hook and ladder companies. And when it was dark, there was a band of boys who ran ahead of the engines carrying flaming torches to light the way.

The companies themselves raised the money for their engines and their uniforms. Among their members were bankers, butchers, doctors, clerks, lawyers, merchants, grocerymen and laborers — all regarded as distinguished citizens. They hosted formal dances and costume balls, and the companies became the main source of the city's social life. In their social activities and in their prowess in fighting fires, they were highly competitive.

Doris Muscatine, in her book *Old San Francisco,* records that the members of Company Number One, Two and Knickerbocker Engine Company Number Five came mostly from New York. Number Three's members were mostly Bostonians who considered themselves the elite. They had a gleaming twenty-thousand dollar silver-plated engine and at social affairs wore gold capes. Samuel Brannan, a member, presented the company foreman with a gold trumpet — the city's firechief carried a silver one. Pennsylvania Engine Company Number Twelve had its silver and gold-ornamented engine made in Philadelphia, and paraded in frock coats, patent-leather boots and stovepipe hats. Many of its members came from "First Families" and the company was dubbed accordingly "High-toned Twelve." Some companies, however, prided themselves on their simple dress and lack of showmanship. Almost thirty years later, Robert Louis Stevenson declared "that nowhere else in the world is the art of the fireman carried to so nice a point." Long before that, the name Lillie Coit had become synonymous with fire and men who fought it.

Before coming to San Francisco, the Hitchcocks had moved from one army post to another and Lillie, from babyhood, was the pet of each post and of the officers who took her riding with them. Lillie was an extremely intelligent and precocious child. Martha saw to her education; she was required to write a letter to her mother every day, whether or not she was with her. French lessons were also included, and continued into her teens. Along with an aptitude for learning very quickly, Lillie showed herself to be a tomboy and an almost irrepressible, high-spirited child. Her witicisms and her repartee astonished her elders. From the start, she preferred the company of boys to girls and men to women.

By December of 1851, the Hitchcocks were living in San Francisco's fourth and newly completed hotel, The Oriental, on Bush and Battery Streets. Nearby, Mr. Patrick Fitzmaurice was building another hotel to be called the Fitzmaurice House. Mrs. Fitzmaurice and Martha were friends, and on December 23, she sent Martha a note asking her to allow Lillie to come to a children's tea party at her fashionable boarding house. Her husband Pat, and her two youngest children, Joanna and Patrick, would come for Lillie and bring her home after the party. With that proviso, Martha let Lillie go.

Along the way, Pat Fitzmaurice stopped outside the half-finished Fitzmaurice House to confer with the contractor, and the children slipped into the building unobserved and climbed the stairs to the second story. Suddenly, a passerby excitedly pointed to the smoke billowing out of the half-open door. Where were the children? Pat surmised they were inside. Rushing to the doorway he called them; answering, they came running toward the part of the building that was on fire. Flames were already licking the stairway, so Pat shouted to them to go back to the stairway at the rear. Young Patrick, unheeding, seized the girls' hands, trying to get them down the front stairway. Lillie pulled back, urging them to follow her to the rear. But as she did so, a beam fell across the stairway, pinning Patrick and Joanna down into the flames and the two were lost. Pat tried to mount the stairway, but it gave way, and men who had followed dragged him outside.

By this time, Lillie was encircled by flames, though they were not yet near enough to burn her. John Boynton, a substitute of Knickerbocker Number Five, was on the roof. Hacking a hole in it, he let himself down on a rope. Telling Lillie to climb on his back and put her arms around his neck, he then inched his way up, and other firemen with ropes and ladders hauled them to safety. The next night, Christmas Eve, there was another fire. Boynton later recalled:

> As we dashed past the Oriental I saw the bright-eyed, piquant little girl I'd rescued. She was on the piazza of the hotel, holding fast to her mother's hand. As we swept by on the narrow street, she cried out to us, "Hurrah for my dear Number Five!" . . . That night when we returned our old-fashioned engine to its fire-hall we found a barrel of brandy, sent to us by Dr. Hitchcock with a thousand dollars towards a new engine . . . But it was Lillie Hitchcock's heart which throbbed with eternal love for the members of Number Five. From then on she belonged to us as much as we belonged to her.

From that time on, whenever the fire bell rang and she could escape her elders, Lillie ran beside Number Five Company hurrahing them on. One early incident did have a bearing on the future. Helen Holdredge, in her book, *Firebelle Lillie,* tells a story based on the diary of events kept by Mrs. Sarah Lee, whose daughter was a schoolmate of Lillie.

One January afternoon of 1852, Mrs. Lee saw Lillie, schoolbooks on her arm, running after Number Five's engine which was headed for Telegraph Hill. All the other children from The Oriental were following her. Number Five Company was having trouble pulling its engine up the hill. Lillie, throwing her schoolbooks on the ground, admonished the bystanders for not lending a hand. "Come on you men. Beat the other engines to the top!" There was no response, so Lillie grabbed the tow rope and began to pull with all her might. That was too much for the bystanders: men stepped out to lend their weight and Number Five beat its rivals and reached the hilltop first.

To curb Lillie's fire-chasing, the Hitchcocks periodically sent her to a boarding school. One day, at school, her desk-mate was holding a sharply pointed slate pencil in such a way that when Lillie turned her head the point struck her eye and cut the iris. For months, she had to stay in a darkened room in The Oriental, but her lessons continued, and young officers coached her in geometry and algebra. She made top grades in the examinations. When the sight of the damaged eye was restored, Lillie was out and about again. The Hitchcocks from then on made no attempt to stop her fire-chasing. Before long she became Company Number Five's mascot.

In 1861, the War between the States broke out. Although Lillie never wavered in her loyalty to the New York members of Number Five, she was as outspoken as her mother in support of the South. And when Lillie went so far as to help smuggle a Confederate on board a Navy ship, Dr. Hitchcock decided to pack her and her mother off to Paris for the duration. California had declared its support of the Union, and such family loyalty to the southern cause might, the doctor feared, hurt his reputation. He had long since retired from his Army post to go into private practice. It might also lead to the confiscation of their family properties should the South lose the day.

The Hitchcocks could well afford the visit. Just before her eighteenth birthday, Lillie's grandfather, Judge Hitchcock, had died in Maryland and left her $60,000 and other income-producing properties. Martha, who had sued one of her uncle's estates, was awarded a sum of about $100,000.

Lillie was almost as conspicuous in Paris as in San Francisco. Beautifully dressed, she and Martha soon became familiars at the court of Napoleon III and the Empress Eugenie. Lillie, who spoke French fluently, was asked to translate war communiques for the emperor, and with a series of letters became Paris correspondent for the San Francisco *Evening Bulletin.*

After a two-year stay, Dr. Hitchcock gave in to Lillie's pleadings to come back, on the condition that she would not discuss the war outside their home. San Francisco gave her a jubilant homecoming and, on October 3, 1863, Number Five Company gave her a certificate of full-fledged membership, making her, at the age of twenty, the only honorary woman member of a fire department in the United States.

It was said that Lillie had more proposals than any girl in San Francisco and that before and during the 1860s she was the talk of the town. Beaux, dinner parties and balls interested her far less than chasing fires. When the fire bell rang, whether she was on the dancing floor or at some social affair, she would leave and her waiting coachman dash her to the scene of the fire. The city as well as Number Five Company adored her.

In 1872 the City of San Francisco placed two photographs of Lillie and city documents in the cornerstone of the new city hall.

From the age of sixteen, Lillie was acclaimed as "the belle of San Francisco." However, Mrs. Crabtree, mother of Lotta Crabtree, the elfin entertainer of the gold country and the San Francisco stage, wrote in a family letter that when she saw Lillie for the first time, she found, surprisingly, that Lillie was not a great beauty as she had supposed. "She stood straight as an arrow, and her manner was ladylike." The secret, she concluded, of her peculiar fascination seemed to lie in her expression; there was a luminous quality about her mischievous face. Howard Coit, the man she was to marry, was also surprised when he first saw her, to find that she was "incandescent rather than beautiful."

When Lillie returned from Paris and received her certificate of membership in Number Five Company, the era of the volunteer firefighting companies was drawing to a close. The horse-drawn steam engine replaced the hand-pumper, the telegraphic alarm the manual bell, and other new equipment made many of the volunteers' tasks obsolete. By December 1866, the companies were disbanded and San Francisco had a paid fire department.

Lillie now became as addicted to poker as she had been to fire-chasing. On the way to Paris the ship's mate taught her to play and she soon played an excellent hand. Secluded in back rooms with the best men players in town she played, drank bourbon, and smoked a cigar or a cigarette. When she entered precincts barred to women, she dressed as a man.

Yet nothing diminshed her devotion to Company Number Five. As a veteran of the disbanded company, whenever she was in town, she attended the annual anniversary dinner on October 17, the Company's founding day. Dressed in the Company's colors, red and black, she wore a black silk skirt, a veteran's belt, a red fire shirt and a black tie. She usually carried her helmet. When she was out of town, she sent a telegram which was read aloud and toasting her became a company tradition. She continued to sign herself Lillie Hitchcock "5" and to wear a little gold "5" pin; and after her marriage everything she had, including her lingerie, was marked "L.H.C.5." The lace makers even worked "5" into the monogram on her fans.

Company Number Five's devotion to her also remained undiminished. In 1888, when she could not attend the thirty-eighth annual dinner, they sent her a perfect gold replica in miniature of a fireman's helmet. So much money had been subscribed that they put a diamond in the neck-protecting shield. With it came this note:

> The company being desirous of testifying their gratitude for the love and devotion manifested by you on all occasions from childhood days, beg leave to present to you the accompanying testimonial as a memento of the esteem and undying friendship the members esteem towards you as a lady and an honorable member of Knickerbocker Company Number 5 and beg your acceptance of the same.

Many things had happened in Lillie's life in twenty years, since the day when it was said that no one ever saw her enter a ballroom. But when a crowd of men came walking in, you knew she was in the center.

Lillie knew the first time she saw tall, handsome Howard Coit that this was the man she wanted to marry. Howard had been jilted on his wedding day in Arizona and he promised himself that he would never again be hurt by any woman. When he and Lillie met on various occasions, he seemed indifferent. But one night at a ball, he asked her if she loved him. After a whirlwind courtship she eloped with him and they were married in the Church of the Advent in November 1868.

Howard had money of his own, and was the "Caller" of the San Francisco Stock Exchange and later, President of the Board. The Coits thoroughly disapproved and the Hitchcocks were furious when they heard the news. Martha had hoped that Lillie would marry a man of social standing and from then on she did her best to undermine the marriage. For the first few years, all went well. The Howard Coits traveled a good deal and, in 1875, they were among the first guests to live in the new completed Palace Hotel.

Lillie's fascination with fire, when she so nearly lost her life in it, is an enigma. The break in her marriage was almost as surprising but there is some understanding of it. According to Helen Holdredge in her book *Firebelle Lillie,* in the late 1870s, Bill Emerson, a gifted tenor who made the song "I'm as Happy as a Big Sunflower" famous, came to live in a suite on the sixth floor of the Palace with his wife Mamie. The Coits lived on the first floor. Billy "gathered sunshine as he walked" and Mamie was a splendid raconteur and a beauty, elegantly dressed. In the Palace they were surrounded by admiring mining millionaires.

Night after night into the late hours, Lillie played poker with Billy, and Howard went up to the sixth floor to spend the time companionably with Mamie. When Mamie became seriously ill, Billy, continuing to play poker, neglected her. Howard waited on her instead. Martha Hitchcock, no doubt, passed the gossip on to Lillie and did her best to widen the rift. Lillie demanded that Howard stop waiting on Mamie. He refused to do so until the doctor pronounced her out of danger, and Lillie retorted that Billy Emerson, not Howard, was responsible for Mamie. In 1880, at Lillie's wish, they separated.

There was no question of divorce and there is evidence that both she and Howard were miserable without one another. As she later wrote: "No man ever had greater love than mine. My love was a delight. It was appointed and set aside for him alone."

Dr. Hitchcock, who had been ailing for several months, apparently spent his last days with Lillie at Larkmead. He was, however, confined to the house for only a few days before his death on April 3, 1885. Six weeks but a day later, on May 14, Howard Coit unexpectedly died in his sleep. He was forty-seven years old. Having set up trusts for his mother and sister, he left his estate valued at over $250,000 to Lillie. Utterly disconsolate, Lillie remained secluded in her Napa Valley home — "I've never loved any man in my whole life but Howard Coit," she once said. Slowly she picked up the threads of her old life and, by 1890, she left the Valley for good and again took a suite in the Palace Hotel.

11

Lillie at Lonely and Larkmead

In the early 1870s, Dr. Hitchcock bought 1000 acres which is now included in the Bothe-Napa Valley State Park, four miles north of St. Helena. In a wooded canyon, shaded by tall trees and close to Ritchie Creek, he built his country home. Martha Hitchcock named it Lonely. A few years later, Dr. Hitchcock built a house for Lillie, three miles from Lonely, on the east side of the valley. Lillie named it Larkmead.

As Lillie Hitchcock at Lonely and as Mrs. Howard Coit at Larkmead, Lillie was a familiar figure in the upper Napa Valley from the mid 1870s, until the late 1880s. She was the talk of the valley as she was of the city.

The Hitchcocks' near neighbors were the Lymans. Mr. W.W. Lyman Sr. bought his property, which included the Bale grist mill, about the same time. His son W.W. Lyman, Jr. who will be ninety-eight in January, 1983, in taped interviews and in his memoirs, tells about the people he has known in this area. When he was seven or eight years old, his mother and father took him to one of San Francisco's best-known restaurants. Lillie was also there, sitting with three men friends at a nearby table. He was introduced, and what he still vividly remembers, and what impressed him most at the time, was that Lillie's fingers were covered with rings, even her thumbs. In his teens he would go to see Lillie when she was at Lonely — "a big woman with a rather deep voice."

Probably some of Lillie's happiest and saddest days in Napa Valley were at Larkmead during her marriage and separation. The house, an Indian bungalow, with wide porches all around and two intersecting halls, twenty feet wide, was situated on the valley floor. Even with the doors of the intersecting halls wide open, to catch every breeze, it was not a cool retreat like Lonely.

At Larkmead, with her French maid and Chinese servants, Lillie lavishly entertained her San Francisco men friends. Poker was played into the early morning hours. Sometimes, dressed as a man, she went to a bar in St. Helena to play poker with men, drink bourbon with them, swear as they did, and smoke a cigar or cigarettes "but she behaved like a lady in other ways."

Aside from entertaining, Lillie went hunting with her hunter, Mace, a young country boy. Larkmead was filled with her trophies of the chase. Everyone in the valley knew that Lillie was "a dead shot." She wore hunting boots and a hunting suit made in London — a white shirt, a jacket and a skirt which was a brazen ten inches above ankle-length. She rode a horse like a cavalry officer and she drove her splendid four-in-hand with style. Some of the best stagedrivers came to instruct her, including, so it is said, the famous Clark Foss. "She could tool her four-in-hand over any mountain road."

Mrs. Marielouise Kornell who, with her husband Hanns, owns the Hanns Kornell Champagne Cellars (formerly Larkmead Winery) on Larkmead Lane, spent her happy girlhood summers at her grandparents' ranch with its vineyards to the south of Larkmead house. She loved to ride. Distressed, her grandparents hoped she would not ride like a man, as Lillie Coit had.

Grandfather Carlo Rossini was a great raconteur and told many stories about Lillie. Marielouise Kornell remembers that Lillie was oftentime used as an illustration about how "a well dressed woman does or does not behave." Grandfather thought Lillie should dress and behave in the valley as she did when she met with the San Francisco society; not to do so was "an offense to the local people." He also thought it bad taste for Lillie to wear a ring on every finger. Marielouise Kornell feels that Lillie's honesty won her some credence. In spite of disapproving of some of her ways, her grandfather had an affection, an admiration and even respect for Lillie, recognizing that she was one of the strong and vital characters of her day.

Mrs. Tateler (Bonnaffon) Mitchell also remembered the days she spent at the ranch house her grandfather, Dr. Cole of San Francisco, built on land he bought on the road just north of Calistoga which leads to Santa Rosa. The Coles knew the Hitchcocks well and used to visit them at Lonely. In a 1964 taped interview, Mrs. Mitchell recalled that:

> when Mrs. Coit lived and partied at Larkmead, there was a saying that "Larkmead was the hottest spot in the valley, and Lillie Coit was the flame." After the death of her husband, Mrs. Coit was always in the company of two or three men. These were not love affairs, nor was there any question of sex involved — Mrs. Coit just liked men.

Lillie's Larkmead ranch comprised four hundred acres, of which one hundred and thirty acres were in vines. For eight years. from 1893 to 1901, Lillie, living again in the Palace Hotel, rented the ranch to François Saviez, a native of the south of France, who became one of California's most successful viticulturists. Lillie occasionally came up to stay a day or two and look around, and sometimes Saviez went to the city to consult with her. In 1901, François Saviez purchased an old ranch house along with two hundred acres adjoining Lillie's land. His son, Cyril Saviez, who was born in the ranch house, and now lives in a modern ranch house built on the site of the earlier one, showed me the old road into Larkmead. It ran from the highway up Larkmead Lane and, just before the second small bridge which crosses Selby Creek, turned left to follow the creek a short way before turning left again and from there on ran straight on between an avenue of mulberry trees to the house. The portion of the road from the turn-off at the bridge is now vineyard land.

In her interview, Mrs. Tateler Mitchell recalled that the house stood empty and unattended for several years, and was looted. "It was possible to see pieces of Mrs. Coit's furniture in houses all up and down the Valley." Some pieces may still exist in one house or another but who could say whether any one of them came from Larkmead which eventually fell into disrepair. Three tall, spindly palm trees planted close to the house remain, and the name "Larkmead" has a place on the map as Larkmead Lane. This runs straight from the highway to the Silverado Trail.

In 1967, Sloan and John Upton established their vineyard on the land surrounding Lillie's old home and have aptly named it Three Palms Vineyard. It would have been far easier to have felled the palms, but in deference to local history landmarks and with pride in owning the land Lillie once owned, they worked around the palm trees and let them stand — pointers to where "Larkmead" stood.

The Larkmead winery was established in 1879, and was probably a wooden building. On its site, a stone building called the Larkmead Cellar was built. It is this cellar, on Larkmead Lane, which now bears the name, Hanns Kornell Champagne Cellars, and the family home is on the land that once belonged to Carlo Rossini. There is a continuity in the life and the land of the upper Napa Valley which is almost unique in California.

It has frequently been said that Lillie met Fanny and Robert Louis Stevenson during their stay at Silverado in 1880. This is not so. The records show that she and Martha were in Washington D.C., Europe and New York from January 11 to June 5, and did not return to California that year.

Lillie would, however, have known Jacob and Annie Schram. They were neighbors of the Hitchcocks at Lonely, and across-the-valley neighbors of Lillie at Larkmead. Jacob may well have advised Lillie on her vineyard, and she in turn would surely have visited Schramsberg. However that may be, the plaque presented to Schramsberg at the time it was listed as a historical landmark in 1957 (by reason of it being the first hillside winery in Napa Valley) recorded Robert Louis Stevenson's visit. The names of Ambrose Bierce and Lillie Hitchcock Coit were also inscribed as "other cherished friends."

One person Lillie did meet in Napa Valley was to become her dearest friend — Floride Green. The Greens, of an illustrious Southern ancestry, had lost all in the Civil War and came to California. Floride graduated from St. Helena High School and Lillie apparently had an instant liking for her when they met. Determined that the young girl should have as good a time as possible, Floride was admitted into the "Coit circle" — so much so that it seemed the Coits might adopt her. After Lillie left Larkmead, she kept in touch with Floride.

In 1899, after a brief illness, Martha Hitchcock died at the age of eighty-one. Remarkably able and highly successful in managing the family finances, she had looked after Lillie's affairs as well as her own. Lillie now turned to one of her father's old friends, Major Joseph McClung. Lillie's cousin by marriage, Alexander Garnett (also spelled Garnat), was a problem. A gambler and a drunkard, he had come to live in San Francisco sometime previously, intent on freeloading on the Hitchcocks. Lillie allowed him to handle a few minor affairs and paid him accordingly. Garnett continued to pester her.

I have read three versions, all of which differ in details, on the extraordinary event which impelled Lillie to leave San Francisco and make a home in Paris. I have chosen to quote Mrs. Tateler Mitchell again, for, although she was not a witness of what happened, she was indirectly and by some bizarre chance involved in the incident. One late afternoon in 1903, she was walking with her aunt and uncle, Major McClung, in the Palace Hotel, where she was to make her debut. Her aunt asked the Major to go upstairs to "tell Mrs. Coit that Tate is coming out tonight and ask her to come down."

> He did. He knocked on the door, and Mrs. Coit told him to come in. A man by the name of Garnat was standing there with a pistol on her like this (gesture) because she wouldn't give him any money. My uncle jumped at him and turned his hand down like that (gesture) and, in that moment, when he turned his hand down, Garnat pulled the trigger, and the shot went through my uncle. He only lived twenty-two hours after that . . . Mrs. Coit told my aunt what had happened.

Putting her affairs in the hands of a bank, Lillie left for Paris after testifying at Garnett's trial, and Floride Green went with her. Fearing that Garnett might again try to kill her when he got out of prison, she resolved not to come back to the city while he was alive.

For eighteen months Lillie and Floride traveled widely. On October 27, returning from a trip to Damascus, Lillie drew up her horse at the foot of the Lebanon Mountains and announced she must have a glass of champagne. A bottle was taken from her baggage.

"Whose birthday is it?" Floride asked.

"Number Five's," Lillie replied.

There was no ice. The party waited until the guides brought snow down from high up on the mountains. When the bottle was chilled, the party solemnly drank to Number Five.

After eighteen months of travel, Floride returned home to her mother and Lillie settled in Paris. There she was surrounded by the grandsons of her San Francisco beaus. Almost twenty years later, in 1923, when Lillie was eighty years old, she received the news that Alexander Garnett, after serving fifteen years in San Quentin, then committed to a mental institution in Virginia, had died. Straightway, Lillie packed up in the Hotel Wagram on the rue de Rivoli. She was surrounded by baggage when William Gwin III, grandson of one of her old San

Francisco friends, called by to see her.

"I'm going home," she said. Reminding her that the San Francisco she had known was — after the 1906 earthquake and fire — vastly changed, Gwin could not dissuade her. In an article he wrote for the *Argonaut* of February 1, 1957, entitled "Louise," Gwin recalled part of their conversation.

"Willie, there is something you must do for me. I had a maid once, the only French maid I ever had who really cared for me. Her name is Louise. I want her to take me to California."

Lillie had learned from the hotel night porter that Louise had become a prostitute and the places she frequented. Gwin found her at the Two Palm Trees bar. The barman, by a tilt of his chin, indicated where a "hard-eyed, thin-lipped, bosomy" French woman was sitting. Gwin moved over to her corner table. "Her jet-black hair was plastered down tight on her forehead. She had an aquiline nose, finely modeled. In detail she was a good-looking woman, but forbidding and aggressive."

"What do you want?" she rasped.

"Louise," I said, "do you remember Mrs. Coit . . . ?"

"L'Americaine." The hard eyes, the thin lips softened; "it was as though a veil had been drawn aside to let you look into another room the face of the woman underwent such a change." It was Louise Subas who accompanied Lillie home.

Floride Green came to see Lillie in her suite at the Fairmont Hotel. Standing at the window overlooking the bay, watching the white tracks of the ferry boats, Lillie said, "Floride, I don't know my own city."

One of the first things Lillie did was drive up Telegraph Hill to see about buying it for the city. She did not know that in 1876, a group of prominent men had already done so. She signed her last will and testament on the first of October, and a few days before Christmas, had a stroke and was moved to the Dante Sanitarium. She lost all power of speech but understood all that was said to her. Floride visited her daily, ministering, comforting and amusing, and spent many nights in the Sanitarium when she felt Lillie might need her presence. In January 1929, a cousin living in Texas petitioned the Superior Court for a guardian for Lillie and her considerable property, and the Wells Fargo Bank was appointed.

Lillie died, shortly before her eighty-sixth birthday, on July 22, 1929. Two days later a crowd gathered in Grace Cathedral as the coffin covered with lilies was borne through the streets. Some distance from the cathedral twenty-two blue-uniformed men representing the San Francisco fire department fell in ahead and led the procession. At the cathedral steps, three of the four living volunteer firemen stepped forward and preceded the pallbearers; and at the end of the service each of them laid his hand on the casket and "paused to say his silent goodbye before the procession could move on." As she had asked, Lillie was cremated, her little gold "5" pinned on the lace enshrouding her.

In her will, Lillie remembered Floride Green among several other individuals and left $5000 to each surviving member of the Knickerbocker Engine Company Number 5. She left $50,000 for a monument to the memory of the original Volunteer Fire Department. The residue of the estate was divided evenly among the University of Maryland, the University of California, and the City and County of San Francisco. The bequest to the University of California was for a fund to provide medical lectures to be known as The Charles M. and Martha T. Hitchcock Lectures. The gift to the city, amounting to almost $120,000, was to be expended "in an appropriate manner for the purpose of adding to the beauty of said city which I have always loved."

The monument to the firemen was erected in North Beach's Washington Square and, to add to the beauty of the city, the Park Commission proposed that a tower be built on Telegraph Hill, and named the Lillie Hitchcock Coit Tower.

Number Five's old engine, after being sold to Carson City was later discarded as being too antiquated. A few of Lillie's friends bought it and gave it to a San Francisco museum. It was to serve once more when Coit Tower was dedicated on October 8, 1933. On the last page of Floride Green's *Some Personal Recollections of Lillie Hitchcock Coit,* the Grabhorn Press added this note:

LILLIE HITCHCOCK COIT — 5

As, at the death of an officer, his sword and his reversed boots are borne by his riderless charger, so at the dedication of the Coit Tower her fire helmet and veteran's belt rested on Number 5 as it was dragged slowly up Telegraph Hill and stood there mutely speaking of the pioneer days.

Children were curious but the eyes of many old firemen and of her friends were dimmed.

It would be as impossible to duplicate such a character as Lillie Hitchcock Coit as to duplicate those village days of early San Francisco.

12

"The Jersey Lily."

The chances are that Lillie Coit and Martha Hitchcock went to see the English actress, Lillie Langtry, "The Jersey Lily," when she played in San Francisco in the late 1880s and they surely knew through the newspapers that she had purchased a ranch near the Napa County border in Lake County and had traveled from San Francisco to St. Helena in her fabulous private railroad car.

Except that Lillie Coit was ten years older than Lillie Langtry, they were contemporaries; both died in the same year. They were alike in many respects, totally unlike in others. Both were legendary characters, but Lillie Langtry was notorious, and Lillie Coit was not. Scandal was a word attached to "The Jersey Lily" wherever she went.

The St. Helena *Star* of July 22, 1887, reported that Mrs. Langtry "has had the fortune, good or ill, to be more written and talked about than any other woman of the day," and with good cause. She was the most celebrated courtesan, the best dressed and the most beautiful woman of her time. She was not a good actress, but because of her beauty and her reputation she played to packed houses. Witty, with a keen sense of humor, she disliked small talk and hated repetition. Never flustered, she was quick to make a decision, and if anyone wanted to discuss a matter further she would say: "But we have settled that already, have we not? Let us not fuss, please." Lillie Langtry had an iron will, immense courage, and was extraordinarily astute in business affairs. With her gift for mental arithmetic, she could, on the rise of the curtain, estimate the worth of the house within a few pounds. She was a fine judge of horses and winners came from her racing stables. She bet on them heavily and in all she did, she played for high stakes.

The major events in her life should be recorded before we meet her at what became known as "Langtry Farms" in Lake County. The only daughter of Emilie and William Le Breton, Dean of the Isle of Jersey and Rector of St. Saviour's Parish, she was born in the rectory on October 13, 1853. Christened

Emilie Charlotte Le Breton, she was always called "Lillie." Her six unruly brothers made her an incorrigible tomboy. She rode astride, played cricket, went swimming and sailing, and fought like a boy. And, from the start, she preferred boys to girls.

On March 9, 1874 she married Edward Langtry, an Ulsterman. The son of a well-to-do shipping man, Edward owned *Red Gauntlet,* a big white yacht. Years later, Lillie had this to say:

> One day there came into the harbor a most beautiful yacht. I met the owner and fell in love with the yacht. To become the mistress of the yacht, I married the owner.

Life with Edward was, she said "uneventful." Boredom wore her down to the point of illness. Lillie had a private talk with the doctor who prescribed a change of scene — London. Two years after their marriage, the Langtrys rented an apartment in Eaton Place.

One young artist, William Graham Robertson, crossing the road at Hyde Park Corner saw Lillie making her way past Apsley House toward the park. He had no idea who she was and he did not paint her but in his reminiscences, fifty-five years later he gives us this portrait of Lillie:

> At first glance it seemed a very young and slender girl, and dowdily dressed in black, and wearing a small close-fitting black bonnet; she might have been a milliner's assistant waiting upon a customer . . . As I drew near the pavement the girl looked up — and I all but sat flat on the road.
>
> For the first and only time in my life I beheld perfect beauty.
>
> The face was that of the lost Venus of Praxiteles, and of all the copies handed down to us it must have been incomparably the best, yet nature had not been satisfied and thrown in two or three subtle improvements. The small head was not reared on the white column of the throat, as a capital crowns a pillar, but drooped slightly forward like a violet or a snowdrop, the perfect nose was made less perfect and a thousand times more beautiful by a slight tilt at the tip. The wonderful face was pale with the glow of absolute health behind the pallor, the eyes grey beneath dark lashes, and the hair brown with hints of gold in it, the figure in its poise and motion conveyed an impression of something wild, eternally young, nymphlike . . .

One day, when visiting the new Royal Aquarium at Westminster, the Langtrys met Lord Ranelagh, who often wintered in his manor house in Jersey. Up to this time, Lillie thought she knew no one in London, but Lord Ranelagh recognized her and the following Sunday afternoon the Langtrys went, by invitation, to the Ranelaghs' garden party at their home on the Thames. The remarkable beauty of the young woman did not go unnoticed and, from then on, other invitations flowed in. Lillie became fascinated with London and London society became fascinated with her and soon the top-flight artists asked her to sit for them.

Inevitably, as Lillie edged up the social ladder, she met Albert Edward, Prince of Wales, and if one knows anything about her, one does know she became "Bertie's" first acknowledged mistress. Although others succeeded her, Lillie and Bertie remained good friends. In addition to the jewelry and the gowns he gave her, Bertie built her a house on the cliffs rising from a sandy beach at the fashionable seaside resort at Bournemouth in Hampshire. The house was to be a permanent rendezvous whenever Bertie wished but it was to be clearly identified as hers for as long as she wanted it.

In 1877, Lillie went to Bournemouth and had the mason prepare a foundation stone and cut in the letters "E.L." for Emilie Le Breton Langtry. When the house was finished, she had a painter inscribe a beam in the entrance hall "And yours, too, my friend," and on a wall in the dining room were carved the words "They say — What say they? Let them say."

By now, Edward Langtry, financially drained, had become an alcoholic and a pitiably abject man. He had withdrawn from London. Lillie gave him an allowance on condition that he would not interfere in her affairs but, in spite of Lillie's wish to divorce, he would not grant her this.

It was Bertie who introduced Lillie to his favorite nephew, the tall handsome Prince Louis of Battenberg. Louis fell instantly in love with her. They shared a bed in Marlborough House and in the country houses they visited as members of Bertie's entourage. Louis might well have married Lillie — and this would have pleased Bertie — had not Edward Langtry refused to divorce her.

When Lillie was five months pregnant, Louis was off at sea again and she was in deep financial trouble. Unpaid bills were stacked high in the house she now lived in on Norfolk Street. The sheriff served notice and the contents of the house were auctioned off. Lillie left London, rented a cottage outside St. Helier, and crossed over to France to conceal the birth of her child. The secret was well kept. Edward Langtry never guessed. Jeanne-Marie was born in 1881 and brought up mostly in the care of Mrs. Le Breton. Always introduced as Lillie's niece, the child of one of her deceased brothers, it was years before Jeanne-Marie knew her own identity.

Forced to take up some career — it was not easy in those days for a woman to do so — Lillie decided to go on the stage. After her debut in London, with only mediocre notices by the critics but to packed houses on account of being "The Jersey Lily," she signed a contract with Henry E. Abbey, a leading theatrical producer in America who had sponsored Sarah Bernhardt's American tour the year before.

Lillie arrived in New York at 4:30 a.m. on October 23, 1882. Her first appearance brought in a thousand dollars more than Sarah Bernhardt's triumphant first night. At a party afterwards, which Oscar Wilde had planned, he introduced Lillie to Freddie Gebhardt (also spelled Gebhard). A slim man over six feet tall, he had a slight mustache, prominent lips, and carried himself with a certain air of distinction. A gentleman of fashion whose clothes were made in London, he spent his time with pretty women, going to the races, gambling, yachting. The son of a Baltimore merchant, Freddie had inherited some four-million dollars which at five percent gave him an interest income of $200,000 a year. He was twenty-two years old, seven years younger than Lillie.

Freddie courted Lillie. His first gifts were a diamond necklace and bracelet to match, concealed in a bouquet of flowers. When the time came for Lillie to start on her tour she asked that he travel with her as bodyguard. Abbey protested, but complied.

On that first two-month tour that took her as far west as the Rocky Mountains, Lillie and her company covered six-thousand miles in Pullman and day coaches. She observed that some very wealthy Americans traveled in their own private railroad cars. Traveling in one would be far more pleasant. (In the 1880s, there were some 500 private railroad cars — "Mansions on Rails" Lucius Beebe called them. Most cost about $50,000 and weighed about 90 tons.)

Over the next three or four years, Lillie played in England, on the Continent and in America. On one of her returns to New York, Freddie presented her with a house on West 23rd Street, to redecorate and furnish as she wished at his expense. His next great gift was a private railroad car, especially designed by Colonel William Mann, the inventor of a railway carriage rivalling a Pullman sleeping car. Lillie likened it to Cleopatra's fabulous barge, and christened it the *Lalee,* meaning "flirt" in some East Indian dialect. The cost was a quarter of million dollars.

The *Lalee,* painted in Lillie's favorite bright Jersey-blue with a gleaming white roof, had a massive teak platform at either end. The seventy-five foot car had ten rooms, and included Lillie's bedroom, upholstered in brocade, her dressing room and a bathroom with silver fittings. There was a grand piano, bookcases and easy chairs in the roomy salon. There were two guest rooms, a maid's room with a sewing machine, a kitchen equipped to cook a full-course dinner and a pantry. There was a heavy icebox in the pantry and massive ice chests beneath the car which, as Colonel Mann boasted, were "big enough to house a whole stag." The frame was partitioned with thirteen floors and eleven ceilings and every piece of furniture was padded against injury by a sudden jolt. The rest of the company traveled in coaches ahead and the stage sets were packed in the baggage car. When Freddie accompanied Lillie on tour, he went ahead in another train to avoid the scandal-loving newspaper reporters seeing them arrive together.

In 1887, Lillie arrived in San Francisco after a highly remunerative tour. Freddie was at the railroad station to meet her. Uppermost in their minds was the problem of Lillie obtaining a divorce. On the advice of Abe Hummel, a New York attorney, Freddie either bought or rented a house for her on 21st Street. General W.H.L. Barnes, a prominent San Francisco attorney, and ex-Governor of California agreed to act for her to try to obtain a divorce. Through George Lewis, Edward Langtry's English attorney, he forwarded Lillie's offer of a large sum of money on condition that Edward would not contest the suit. Edward refused.

It was now suggested that Lillie might get a divorce in a California court, and her chances would be enhanced if she became an American citizen and a California property owner. On July 17, 1887, a federal judge in San Francisco granted her U.S. citizenship. Lillie's motives were not endearing, but in all fairness, it can be said that she liked Americans and the wide open spaces of the West she passed through in her railway car exhilarated her. And there was Freddie. Had she been free to marry him, she would automatically have become a citizen.

That same year (1887), on General Barnes' recommendation, Lillie and Freddie purchased sight unseen a portion of the Guenoc stock ranch in Coyote Valley, a few miles from Middletown. The price and the extent of the property purchased vary from one account to another, but the figures most commonly quoted give Lillie's price as $82,000 for 4,200 acres and Freddie's $32,500 for an adjoining 3,200 acres. (The *St. Helena Star* quoted Lillie's price as $75,000, but this may have not included the real estate commission.) The *St. Helena Star* of Friday, June 1st, reported that:

> Mrs. Langtry passed through here Sunday (May 27th) on the way to her lately acquired ranch. The party consisted of Fred Gebhardt, J.M. George and W.C. Abbey, capitalists of New York, James Stewart, a real estate agent of Middletown, and two servants. A large crowd had assembled at the depot to get a look at the famous beauty, but met with a disappointment as the lady saw fit to jump off the hind car, accompanied by her ever faithful Freddie, and take a short cut through Chris Deffner's saloon, and thence up Main Street, to the Windsor Hotel (now the Hotel St. Helena, 1309 Main Street). It remained for the small boy to make the discovery, but it was too late, and besides she was heavily veiled. A crowd assembled about the hotel and it was only by accident that any one got to see the lady's face, and that was when she came to lunch. She came down ahead of time, but finding the dining-room doors closed, had to wait, during which time a good view of her face was obtained. Many compliments were passed on her beauty and the manly form of the devoted Freddie. After lunch the party left for Lake County, the Lily entering her carriage at the back of the hotel, in order to escape the gaze of the curious. Gebhardt and the other gentlemen and the servants followed from the front of the hotel, in a similar outfit. Sam Kenyon and Preston Grisby with two four-in-hands, conducted the party to their destination.

> The party will return in about a week on Sunday.

Lillie, "heavily veiled," was dressed as other women travelers along the road. Stevenson, in describing the stagecoach passengers who stopped briefly at the Toll House, noted "the women swathed in veils." Dust was a menace in summer, and the veil afforded protection of the face.

On May 29, she sent a telegram to General Barnes: "Am delighted. Words don't express my complete satisfaction. Join me in Paradise."

> The *Star,* in its issue of June 8th, reported:

> Mrs. Langtry and party returned from Lake County last Monday, (June 4th) and passed through here on the way to San Francisco, from whence she will go to New York. From Mr. Stewart, the lady's agent, we learn that she is greatly pleased with her newly-acquired possessions and has laid out plans and given orders for a general overhauling and remodeling of things about her ranch. She has secured the services

of a French gardener who will lay out fine lawns etc., and otherwise greatly beautify the premises. The lady seems to take great pride in the place and aspires to make it a second Eden. She will have fine stables erected for some blooded stock she is to import. Mr. Gebhardt is also to make extensive improvements on his property, and will soon have his celebrated racehorse, Eole, sent out here. Mr. Stewart has entire charge of things during the lady's absence. Mrs. Langtry expects to be back here in about a month. The people of Lake County are very proud of their new residents. Mr. Abbey, formerly with Mr. Baldwin, a celebrated horseman, will take charge of Mr. Gebhart's ranch and horses. The gentleman is also an expert veterinary surgeon.

Lillie's plans also included making her high-framed two-story house a "really comfortable one," likewise, Freddie's smaller ranch house nearby. A Dutch oven was to be built (it took a week to complete) so that the French Chef Mezirand could bake the light bread Lillie preferred to the prevalent sour dough. A French viticulturist was sent for from Bordeaux, France to take charge of the vineyards and the wine-making. Charles Abbey (spelled "Aby" in some accounts) was to bring in a crew of laborers from San Francisco to build a mile-long race track on Freddie's ranch and thoroughbreds were to be imported from Kentucky.

Early in July, Lillie and Freddie returned to the ranch with a party of friends, this time traveling to St. Helena in the *Lalee*. Beverly, Lillie's English butler who had previously been sent ahead with "stacks of furniture" to ready the two houses, met them at the railroad station. In her autobiography *The Days I Knew* (1925) Lillie recalled:

> The "depot" was crowded inside and out, the whole countryside being massed to receive me, armed with the ubiquitous autograph books and presents of flowers, fruit and "candy," and offers of hospitality! There, also, among the quantity of queer looking wagons and buggies used in those outlandish parts, was the resourceful Beverly, with two private Wild-West coaches commandered from my ranch, each with six more or less reliable horses attached, and determined-looking drivers in waiting.

> After signing numberless autographs, and entertaining many relays of Californians to an informal reception and tea on my car, we clambered on to the antedeluvian stagecoaches which were to convey myself and party, bar accidents, to the promised land.

The seventeen miles up the corkscrew road over Howell Mountain was rough going. The stagecoach springs were leather thongs and "we felt every stone." Then as they made their way down the farther side, "the panorama opened out, and for the first time I caught a bird's-eye view of my property."

> The huge plateau appeared a dream of loveliness. Being early July, vast masses of ripe corn (grain) waved golden in the light summer breeze, dotted here and there with the enormous centenarian, evergreen oaks. It was, without exaggeration, entrancing. In the distance were the boundary hills of the far side of my land, hazy and blue as the Alps sometimes are, and on which, the mindful Beverly informed me, my numerous cattle ranged. On and down we drove, each turn of the road making us gasp with the new picture disclosed, till, threading our way through my

vineyards and peach orchards laden with fruit, which covered a great part of the near hills, we reached *home.*

Dinner was ready for the tired travelers, and consisted of trout, beef, and quail, prepared by Indian squaws, whom Beverly had recruited from the neighboring Indian reservation. From then on the squaws came in relays, "a continual coming and going of blanketed, moccasined-footed women," who, Lillie conceded, did fairly well.

> . . . when one is up at daybreak and off immediately after breakfast, dressed in cowboy style, with shirt and breeches, and long moccasins as a protection from rattlesnakes and so forth, galloping about on a cowpony exploring every corner of the land, one finds hunger a very good sauce.

There were no neighbors to raise their eyebrows at her riding astride, dressed in cowboy clothes. But when Lillie went into Middletown with Freddie driving a surrey with fringe on top, she was, as old timers remembered, beautifully dressed in city clothes. It was observed that although full-busted, she had a tiny waist and, with hair piled high, wore an enormous hat decked with plumes and feathers.

Guests came up from San Francisco. They hunted black bear in the mountains, kept "the larder full of hares, rabbits, and the partridge-like, crested quail which were extremely plentiful," and joined in corraling the cattle.

> The keyword of that ranch was "Liberty," and my cowboys, of every nationalilty, including a Chinese walked in and out of my house in search of whatever they needed. Redskins from the reservation rode over my land at will from dawn to sunset, galloping about with rifles slung on their backs, shooting the game and poaching the trout. Some of the neighboring ranchers, too, out of the kindness of their hearts, shot my deer (out of season), and presented me with them in token of welcome. Squatters annexed cows clearly marked with the brand of the ranch, in fact it was communism at its best.

It had been a "golden time" but life in the promised land could not go on forever and for the present they had spent time enough in their Eden. Lillie had to go back to the theater and Freddie grew restless for New York. When they left, both had every intention of returning.

Three summers later, just before Lillie was to spend a few months at the ranch, the train on which some of her thoroughbred mares were traveling West was derailed. Nearly all her horses were maimed or killed, and many passengers were injured. Lillie rushed to the scene of disaster. The incident disheartened her, and she regarded it as boding ill-omen. It is not known whether Lillie saw Langtry Farms again, but Freddie was there in the summer of 1890.

Writing in 1925 about the vineyard she had hoped to be so productive, she said:

> When the vineyard had to be considered it seemed impossible that anyone but a Frenchman could cope with it, so a capable man was engaged and brought from

Bordeaux to take charge, but although I am convinced that the Gascon made better wine than any ever brewed in California, a new law putting all liquor into bond for a period of years spoilt the sale of the bottles with the picture of myself on the label, and I suppose now that the country is dry my protrait still adorns the customs.

In 1963, the Magoon family of Honolulu purchased the 23,000 acre Guenoc ranch which includes what was Langtry Farms. Lillie's house has been restored and Lillie would applaud what has been achieved with her former home and vineyard.

The 270-acre vineyard is planted in Cabernet Sauvignon, Petite Sirah, Malbec, Merlot, Chardonnay, Chenin Blanc, Petite Verdot and Sauvignon Blanc. The 54,000 square foot Guenoc Winery, with its redwood exterior, is modeled after Lillie's barn. The famous portrait of Lillie Langtry, "The Dean's Daughter" by George Frederick Watts, is being used on the Guenoc Wine label by permission of The Watts Gallery in Compton, Guildford, England.

13

"Mr. Jersey"

The readers of the *St. Helena Star* presumably continued to be interested in Lillie's life after she left "Langtry Farms," partly on account of her fame but also because she did not sell the ranch until 1906. This is my reason for recording the main events in her life thereafter. Incidentally, in 1906 she sold her ranch for half the purchase price. Against Abe Hummel's advice, she reinvested the proceeds in real estate in Santa Barbara and Los Angeles, and when she sold out she tripled her money.

Lillie's *affaire* with Freddie Gebhardt lasted almost eight years. Abe Hummel had not, so far, managed to obtain her divorce decree. In 1889, against Freddie's wishes, she went to England. She had not been back for three years and was homesick. In London, she came down with influenza and became seriously ill. Daily bulletins on her health were headline news. One day, during her recuperation, the Prince of Wales came to see her. The story goes that Freddie, who had just arrived in London, rushed to see her and encountered Bertie coming down the stairs. Freddie stood his ground. After Bertie left, Lillie and Freddie had a horrendous row. Freddie stalked off and Lillie did not call him back.

Her next *affaire* was with George Alexander Baird, known as "Squire Abingdon." Partner in a Glasgow firm of ironmasters and the owner of coal mines in southern England, he had an income of around half a million dollars a year. They met at the races, standing beside the rails. The Squire told Lillie she was betting on the wrong horses. If she bet on his horse she would win, and if she lost he would pay her triple the bet. For once, Lillie hesitated. The Squire took her money to the bookmaker and placed it on his horse which easily won the race.

Squire Abingdon's greatest single gift to Lillie was *The White Lady,* a 220 foot yacht, which was twice the tonnage of Bertie's racing cutter *Britannia.* With it was a check for fifty-thousand pounds for upkeep. Another gift was a colt which won her first race. The name of the owner was listed as "Mr. Jersey," and the jockey wore her colors, turquoise and fawn.

The Squire regarded pugilism as a fine art. He arranged a championship fight in New Orleans, and went there in March, 1893. His man, Mem Hall, went down, and this time the Squire lost heavily. Soaked with sweat by his excitement and exertions at the ringside and chilled in the big drafty hall, he began to cough. Cold and feverish, he took to his bed in the Charles Hotel and died there of pneumonia on March 18.

The year of Queen Victoria's Diamond Jubilee, 1897, was also a landmark year in Lillie's life. The tireless Abe Hummel cabled Lillie that she had been granted a divorce in California, in the Lakeport courtroom on May 14. A San Francisco lawyer had produced Lillie's sworn statements, taken in England and in America attesting that she was an American citizen, and a *bona fide* resident of Lake County, where she had a large ranch bought with the proceeds of her dramatic career. The Judge, leafing through the papers, noted that Mr. Langtry had failed to answer a summons served on him. Because he had not filed a defense in the time allowed by the California court, a default was entered against him, and a divorce was granted the plaintiff. The decree was recorded in the Lake County Records on May 28, 1897.

On October 6, the newspapers reported that Edward Langtry had fallen off a train at Crewe railroad junction and was picked up staggering and delirious along the track. He was taken to an asylum near Chester pending an inquiry into his mental and physical condition.

On the 13th, a sunny, clear blue-sky October day, Lillie held her head high in public view on the racecourse at Newmarket. It was her forty-fourth birthday, and "Mr. Jersey's" five-year-old Australian horse, Marman, was entered for the Cesarewitch, England's most important long-distance handicap. As usual, Lillie backed her horse heavily, and when the bookmaker warned her that with the odds eight to one she hadn't a hope of winning, she bet ten-thousand pounds more on Marman. Ridden by her American jockey, Tod Sloan, Marman won by a neck. Lillie won over 30,000 pounds by her bet and with stake money and stud fees she netted close to 120,000 pounds on that one race.

Bertie, who had a good win earlier, congratulated her and took her into the Jockey Club enclosure which was then barred to women — women did not belong on the turf in those days. But Bertie was the Prince of Wales and his guest was "Mr. Jersey."

Two days later, on October 15, Edward Langtry died in the asylum. The newspapers trumpeted the melodrama. Only a short statement, in the back pages and inserted by Edward's attorney, now Sir George Lewis, said that Mrs. Langtry had, through her lawyer, paid her husband an adequate allowance since their separation. And that, on receiving news of Mr. Langtry's illness, she had forwarded money to the asylum authorities for his every medical care.

For a while, Lillie withdrew from the theater to supervise her string of thirty-five horses. She sold *The White Lady* for 280,000 pounds and used the money to buy more horses and a stud farm. She also bought a shabby playhouse in London, had it made over in marble, and furnished it with hangings and draperies handmade at the Royal School of Needlework. The royal box, lined with purple silk, was lit with electric light instead of gas.

It was Bertie who introduced her to Hugo de Bathe, the tall, dark, good-looking, well-dressed elder son of General Sir Henry Percival de Bathe. On the day Lillie won another big bet on Merman at Goodwood, she and Hugo were married in her father's old church on the Isle of Jersey. It was July 27, 1899; Lillie was forty-seven and Hugo twenty-eight. Bertie approved the marriage but Sir Percival was furious. He disinherited Hugo of his estate but he could not rob him of his future title.

Lillie, in spite of her age, was still a beautiful woman, her figure still slender and supple. Noel B. Gerson, in what I think is one of the best biographies of Lillie Langtry, describes at length the impression made on the press when she arrived in New York in December, 1902. She was acclaimed "still the most beautiful woman in the world," her age was of no importance. The photographers took pictures of her for half an hour on the open deck; the interview with the reporters took place in the first-class smoking room. A smoking room would not bother Lillie. She herself started to smoke on stage in one of her roles and became a steady smoker. A year or so earlier, she had met the English press on returning from her American tour, with a lighted cigarette in her hand — one of the first women in England to smoke in public.

Lillie deftly answered the reporters' questions. Asked to explain the secrets of her beauty, she replied:

> Gladly, although I wouldn't call them secrets. I've read all sorts of rubbish about a skin-peeling process I supposedly use, and about electrical massages I'm believed to take. My secret is work, plenty of sunshine, soap and water. I eat plain food, I drink very little, I inhale fresh air and I have a happy spirit.

Asked about her physical exercise, she said:

> Daily I start my day with a cold bath after getting plenty of sleep, and I do exercises for an hour. When I'm in the country I go out for long walks, but I find it too difficult in the city, where people follow me. So I make up the difference with more exercise. Any woman can do what I do.

It is also said that when Lillie was up early in a city, she jogged for two miles.

When Sir Percival died early in January, 1907, Lillie, who was playing vaudeville in Cincinnati, became Lady de Bathe. She had long since assumed a dignity, even a regal air that befitted a title either inherited or acquired — she was in her time queen of the stage, and she had been a consort of a future king.

In June of that year, she returned to her three-story house, Regal Lodge in the small town of Kentford. The Lodge had its own stable, and Sir Hugo — usually called Shuggy — stayed with her at Kentford for four months. Lillie's horses won consistently, and Bertie made several teatime visits to discuss his racing affairs.

At the end of the racing season, Lillie was too tired to return to the stage and refused all theatrical managers' offers. Instead, she spent the late autumn and winter in Monaco, and amused herself by playing roulette at the Monte Carlo casino for several hours each day. All winter, roulette-luck was against her; her losses amounted to some twenty-thousand pounds. But on her last night on the Riviera, at the end of February, she recouped her losses and even showed a profit of more than twenty-five thousand pounds. The following day JERSEY LILY BREAKS BANK AT MONTE CARLO was headline news. The bank was depleted, but it did not break.

Two of the most important men in Lillie's life died in 1910. Bertie, King Edward VII, died on May 20, and Prince Louis of Battenberg marched with the gun-carriage that bore the king's coffin through the hushed streets. Freddie Gebhardt died of pleurisy complications at Garden City, Long Island, on September 8.

After the king's death, and for the rest of the year, Lillie remained in seclusion. In 1914 she sailed for the United States to tour in vaudeville, and from then until 1917, in spite of the menace of German submarines, she crossed and recrossed the Atlantic for tour after tour, giving her salary and her profits to the British Red Cross.

Sailing from Liverpool to New York in 1916, Lillie met Somerset Maugham on the boat. As Maugham recalled in *A Writer's Notebook* (1949), neither of them knew anybody on board, so they spent much of their time together. Maugham found her beauty no longer remarkable (she was now sixty-three) but she still had her engaging smile, and she still had a fine figure.

> She made one remark which I think is the proudest thing I ever heard a woman say. The name of Freddy Gebhardt recurred frequently in her conversation one day, and I, to whom it was new, at last asked who he was. 'You mean to say you've never heard of Freddy Gebhardt?' she cried with real astonishment. 'Why, he was the most celebrated man in two hemispheres.' 'Why?' I inquired. 'Because I loved him,' she answered.

One week after the end of World War I in November, 1918, Lillie made her last stage appearance, sold her racing lodge, and went to stay at the Savoy Hotel. As she wrote in her book *The Days I Knew* (Geo. H. Doran, New York, 1925):

> After a world-shaking cataclysm such as we had just been through, ideas and plans which before had seemed of such paramount importance now seemed trivial by comparison, and for the time being I found my interest lapse in both acting and racing.

Lillie decided to settle on the French Riviera and also that she and Shuggy needed separate establishments. They could be the best of friends and remain husband and wife. Whatever romance there might have been in their marriage was brief. Eighteen months after their wedding, Hugo was seen in public escorting a chorus girl in an evening dress with butterflies painted on her bare shoulders. She was not the only girl that Hugo was seen with.

For Shuggy, Lillie bought a villa in Nice. For herself, a half-hour's drive away, she bought a bungalow, halfway down a ravine, in Monaco with a mountainous backdrop and a vista of the blue Mediterranean. The place had belonged to a croupier at the casino. Lillie remodeled it and named it Villa Le Lys, and built a small building at the rear for the servants. Her staff consisted of a personal maid, a housemaid, a cook, a butler and a chauffeur to drive her newly purchased limousine and open touring car. She moved in early in 1919, and with her was a widow, an associate in the theater, Mrs. Mathilde Marie Peat who became her faithful companion.

She entertained the permanent residents of the Riviera and friends came to stay with her. She was driven to the Monte Carlo casino usually twice a week and gambled modestly for about two hours. She kept abreast of the news of the day by reading the London and New York newspapers, visited London twice a year for one to three weeks and spent long hours working in the large garden she created. A trophy she won identified her as the best amateur horticulturist on the Riviera.

Shuggy occasionally came to see her but his publicized escapades caused her some embarassment. He had become, in his fifties, an ardent playboy. Lillie issued statements now and then that she intended to remain his wife, if only in name, and she continued to support him, as she always had done.

In the fall of 1928, Lillie, now seventy-five, became seriously ill in London. She developed bronchitis, complicated by pleurisy. She revised her will. Back home, she appeared less able; her entertaining was restricted to having friends come to tea. All over Europe, that winter was exceptionally cold and Lillie caught a chill and came down with influenza. She died on February 12, 1929, and, as she wished, was buried at St. Saviour's in the Island of Jersey. As the New York *Tribune* said: "An era has come to an end."

14

Bayard Taylor's Epic Ride

The Geysers were misnamed, but the name has stuck. In reality, they are not geysers but fumaroles. Geysers send up fountain-like jets of hot water and steam at intervals while fumaroles emit hot water steadily.

The Geysers, which were eventually to allure travelers along the road through Knight's Valley, were discovered by William Bell Elliott, a trapper from North Carolina, who had taken part in the Bear Flag Revolt and later settled on Mark West Creek on the outskirts of Santa Rosa.

In the spring of 1847, Elliott and son were hunting grizzly bear in the rugged mountainous country to the northeast. They saw what they took to be smoke from an Indian village rising from a canyon at the foot of Cobb Mountain, an extinct volcano. Coming nearer they beheld a frightening sight — steam pouring forth in high columns from a quarter-mile of hissing hot springs, vents and fumaroles. Elliott, awestruck, thought he had come upon the Gates of Hell.

The news of Elliott's discovery spread. Travelers made their way to the Geysers via Santa Rosa and Healdsburg. A short distance beyond Healdsburg was Ray's Station where saddle horses could be hired and, from there, a trail led up the steep chaparral-covered hillsides to the crest of Hog's Back Ridge. With its sheer drop-offs on either side, the ridge was a causeway connecting two mountain ranges and even a seasoned traveler might feel himself to be on the ridgepole of the world. With Mount Cobb towering above on the north and Mount St. Helena on the south, there was spread below as far as the eye could reach in that crystal clear air, a panorama of a rare, wild and spectacular beauty that was entirely and uniquely its own. On traversing the ridge, the descent into Pluton Canyon was even steeper than the grade up and when, at last, the seething fumaroles were reached, the sight and sound that met the traveler was in violent contrast to the silence and ethereal beauty along the ridge. Here was an inferno.

In the 1850s Sam Brannan was busy building his resort. Colonel A. G.

Goodwin made the trail from Ray's Station wide enough for a wagon to pass and at enormous expense built The Geysers Hotel, a two-storied frame building with a spacious veranda around it on a knoll deep within Pluton Canyon. One of the keenest observers to make the trip to the Geysers and to stay at the hotel was Bayard Taylor, the world-traveling reporter of Horace Greeley's New York *Tribune.* With him was his wife, Maria, daughter of the German astronomer Hansen.

Taylor's account of their epic ride, by buggy and on horseback, in *Home and Abroad* (second series, 1862), is important. It is the only detailed description of the Geysers to be published before they were harnessed by power plants. The account also contains the first description of Knight's Valley and the western slopes of Mount St. Helena.

It seemed an odd coincidence that years ago my husband, Bill, had lived near Kennett Square, Pennsylvania, where Bayard Taylor was born and spent his boyhood. He had known Taylor's descendants there and often had consulted reference works in the town's library named in honor of its once renowned son. Taylor's ghost was one that Bill never expected to encounter in Knight's Valley and he had to confess that he had never read any of Bayard Taylor's books nor looked into his career.

Bayard Taylor, at seventeen, was apprenticed as a printer in 1842. He printed a slight volume of his own poems. These earned him the regard of Horace Greeley, who had recently founded the New York *Tribune* and an advance on account for journalistic work in Europe. Young Taylor's two-year tour of that continent on foot cost his paper a scant one hundred English pounds, and firmly established his career as roving correspondent for the *Tribune.*

The Managing Editor of the *Tribune,* Charles Anderson Dana, later founder of the New York *Sun,* was Taylor's immediate boss. Taylor's next assignment was to California to report the Gold Rush of '49. His ensuing book, *El Dorado* (1850), sold 10,000 copies in America, and 30,000 in Great Britain within a fortnight of publication. Thereafter, Bayard Taylor's travels became worldwide and his writing output enormous.

On a return visit to California, ten years and ten days after his Gold Rush assignment, Taylor and his wife went north of San Francisco. On September 4, 1859, they left San Francisco in a little steamship for Petaluma. Bayard was to lecture in Petaluma on Saturday evening and in Napa City on Monday evening. Friends had told him he must not think of leaving California without seeing the Geysers, although he could not possibly do so in the time between the lectures, and that a guide was as necessary as good horses. "You can never find the way alone." The warning only made Bayard more determined. He would make his own way. The total distance he hoped to cover, by buggy and on saddle horse, was around 125 miles.

The lecture in Petaluma over, he and Maria set off alone, driving a rented buggy and two fast black horses through the moonlit night. After the rainless summer months, "blinding, choking, annihilating" dust rose around them. Driving as fast as his horses would go before the rising dust engulfed them, in places he could distinguish the highway only by the sound of the wheels.

After a short night's rest in Santa Rosa, Sunday breakfast at Healdsburg, a backwoodsy place but two-years-old and built in a forest of pines and firs, the Taylors reached Ray's Station at noon. A Mr. Dickinson had gone ahead with the saddle horses and he and an Indian boy greeted them. The place was more a stable than a tavern. There was a bar with bottles, a piece of cheese and a box of soda crackers in one room, a cot in the other. The best that Mr. Dickinson could offer as mounts for the hard twelve-mile ride to the Geysers was a dilapidated mustang for Taylor, a grey mare with a blind eye, a sore back, and a habit of stumbling for Maria, and a Mexican saddle apiece.

Following a trail faintly marked by cartwheels, they reached Geyser Peak 3,800 feet above sea level, saw the blue bulk of Mount St. Helena looming above a landscape "colossal in its forms, lying motionless, leagues deep, at the bottom of an ocean of blue air." Its beauty was almost unreal. "I am afraid," he said, "to describe this scenery."

Three or four miles along the ridge they began the abrupt descent into Pluton Canyon. The trail went straight down, descending a thousand feet in the distance of a mile. "It was like riding down the roof of a Gothic church. The horses planted themselves on their fore feet, and in some places slid, rather than walked."

Another two hours riding brought them to The Geysers Hotel, shaded by patriarchal oaks, and the Pluton River roaring over the volcanic rocks below. An Indian hostler took their horses, and an elegant lady in a black-velvet basque and silk skirt came forward to receive them. After a bath, lunch and a bottle of claret, Maria voted to make the tour of the Geysers — the Devil's Apothecary Shop. Mr. Goodwin, the proprietor of the hotel, offered to act as their guide through "Pandemonium" in the remaining hour-and-a-half of daylight.

After passing several hot springs they came to where the ground was hot under their feet; they could hear the bubbling of boiling springs, and were half choked by the rank steam that rose from them. Taylor wrote:

> In one place a horrible mouth yawned in the black rock belching forth tremendous volumes of sulphurous vapor. Approaching as near as we dare, and looking in, we see the black waters boiling in mad, pitiless fury, foaming around the sides of their prison, spirting in venemous froth over its jagged lips, and sending forth a hoarse, hissing, almost howling sound. This is the "Witches' Caldron."

According to Colonel Goodwin the water's temperature was about 500 degrees. Climbing up to a rocky point above the cauldron, Taylor saw the end of the canyon as "the gulf of perdition."

> The torn, irregular walls around us glare with patches of orange, crimson, sulphur, livid gray, and fiery brown, which the last rays of the sun, striking their tops, turn

76

into masses of smouldering fire. Over the rocks, crusted as with a mixture of blood and brimstone, pour angry cataracts of seething milky water. In every corner and crevice, a little piston is working or a heart is beating, while from a hundred vent-holes about fifty feet above our heads the steam rushes in terrible jets. I have never beheld any scene so entirely infernal in its appearance. The rocks burn under you; you are enveloped in fierce heat, strangled by puffs of diabolical vapor, and stunned by the awful, hissing, spitting, sputtering, roaring, threatening sounds — as if a dozen steamboats blowing through their escape-pipes, had aroused the ire of ten-thousand hell-cats . . .

The steam rushes from the largest of the vent-holes with such force, and heated to such a degree, that it first becomes visible at the distance of six feet from the earth. It here begins to mix with the air, precipitates its moisture, and increases in volume to the height of eighty feet. In the morning, when the atmosphere is cool, the columns rise fully two hundred feet. These tremendous steam-escapes are the most striking feature of the place.

Early to bed in the hotel that Sunday night and in their saddles at seven the next morning, the Taylors made the ride back to Ray's Station in three hours and 40 minutes. Maria dropped from her saddle and into a chair, unable to move. Luckily, some melons were on hand. Restored by what seemed like the food of the Gods, they climbed once more into their buggy and the well-rested pair of fast blacks was ready to go.

All through the thinly settled Alexander Valley, Taylor rejoiced to see more than one stately two-story ranch house standing, with a lordly air, in its natural park of oaks. The splendid trees, growing singly, in clumps, or in groves, were as islands of greenness projected with indescribable effect upon the yellow crop of shoulder-high, wild oats.

The oaks were hung with streamers of silver-grey moss, from one to three feet long, and resembling in texture, the finest point-lace. So airy and delicate was this ornament, that the groves through which we passed had nothing of that sombre, weeping character which makes the cypress swamps of the South so melancholy. Here they were decked as if for a bridal, and slept in languid, happy beauty, in the lap of the golden hills.

We wondered what Taylor would have thought had he come by in April, when the oaks stand out as islands in a lake of lupine-blue, and the poppies and other wildflowers are sheets of color across the hills. (Today, Alexander Valley is one great vineyard; many of the oaks, and the lake of lupines are no more.)

At the valley's end the trail threaded a narrow two-mile long canyon, deep within a labyrinth of steeply-rounded wooded hills and followed the stone-strewn, almost dry, bed of Mayacama Creek. There was hardly room for the buggy to pass. Sometimes the hubs of two wheels would graze the perpendicular bank, while the iron rims of the opposite wheels rolled the very brink of the gulf below. But where a settler's cart had already gone, Taylor reckoned his buggy and blacks could go too.

It was past noon when they emerged from the canyon, entered Knight's Valley, and saw "the stupendous bulk of Mount St. Helene," towering before them. (Taylor spelled the name St. Helene, and a reference to this comes in another chapter.) Straight on through the valley and over the wooded divide at the southern end, they found themselves at last in Napa Valley. The tired blacks trotted on, and again the road was heavy with dust: "the violet mountain, the golden fields, even the arching avenues of the evergreen oaks vanished in the black cloud, which forced me to close my eyes, and blindly trust to the horses."

At sunset the worn travelers reached Oak Knoll where they were to spend the night as guests of Mr. J. W. Osborne, owner of the 160 acre ranch. (B. B. Woodward, we remember, purchased the property after Osborne's death.) After dinner, Taylor rode with his host the five miles into Napa City, and gave his lecture on time. Later, the two men rode back to Oak Knoll in the misty night air. Taylor wrote in his journal, "I felt satisfied with the day's work — twelve miles of mountain-climbing, fifty-five in a vehicle, and one lecture equal, under the circumstances, to fiteen more!"

The Taylors were up at dawn the next morning. Mr. Osborne presented them with a basket of his choicest fruit, and gave Bayard a cheering prediction that he would make his next assignment on time. The chances are that the fruit was grown and gathered by orchardist Frank McDonald.

Bayard Taylor's account of his trip first appeared in two parts in the New York *Tribune,* then in two chapters of his book, "A Journey to the Geysers" and "A Struggle to Keep an Appointment." Thus the world became acquainted with the Geysers.

15

Napa Valley Christmastime for Richard Henry Dana, Jr.

It may seem somewhat of an anticlimax to recount the visits to the Geysers of other notable travelers, but they made their way there under quite different conditions and by another route. It does add lustre to the road through Knight's Valley to remember that Richard Henry Dana, Jr. went to the Geysers shortly after the Bayard Taylors and was followed two years later by three members of the Whitney Geological Survey. Another reason for recounting these two expeditions is that they are not referred to in the regional histories and few people know about them. Richard Henry Dana, Jr. comes first in the order of the visits.

There were many illustrious Danas in this large and influential Massachusetts family and, of them all, Richard Henry Dana, Jr. is the best remembered for *Two Years Before the Mast.*

Richard Henry Dana, Jr. (1815-1882), was born in Cambridge, Massachusetts. At Harvard, he was suspended for six months for his part in a student "rebellion." During this interlude, he developed measles, which impaired his eyesight, and he was not allowed to return to his reinstated studentship for a year. Frustrated, he obtained a berth as an ordinary seaman on a trading voyage to the California coast (1834-36). On his return home, his eyesight restored, he graduated at the head of the senior class at Harvard and entered the Dana Law School at Cambridge. After graduating, he worked in a law office, and, in 1840, was admitted to the bar. In September that same year his *Two Years Before the Mast* was published. Apparently he began to write the account of his voyage early in 1838, thinking it might bring him some maritime law practice.

The book was an immediate success. Ten-thousand copies were sold the first year. Unlike Bayard Taylor's works, Dana's book has never been out of print. To 1964, at least 91 editions have been published in the United States, 40 in Great Britain, and translations have appeared in several European countries.

For his 1869 edition, Dana wrote an additional chapter — "Twenty
Four Years After" — in which he summed up his return visit to California on his
voyage around the world in 1859. In it is a brief and provocative reference to the
Geysers. "I must not pause for the dreary country of the Geysers, the screaming
escapes of steam, the sulphur, the boiling cauldrons of black and yellow and
green . . . nor for the park-like scenery and captivating ranchos of the Napa
Valley." Dana went to the Geysers a day or so before Christmas of 1859, almost
four months after the Bayard Taylors. Why did he see no beauty in the Geyser
region which Taylor had exalted in before descending into "the gulf of
perdition" in Pluton Canyon? And how did Dana make his way to the Geysers
when the going was so arduous and the way hard to find?

The answers are found in the journal Dana kept during his second
visit to the California coast. In his journal, Dana records that on December 20,
1859, he went by steamer to see the Mare Island Navy Yard in San Francisco Bay.
On board he met Mariano Guadelupe Vallejo, who was, at the time of Dana's
first visit, Commandant of the San Francisco Presidio. Vallejo remembered the
then nineteen-year-old Dana, and repeated some of the conversation they had
together. Also on board was "old Mr. Yount, the famous pioneer, and
woodsman", who invited him to his ranch in Napa Valley, and Mr. Edward L.
Stanley, late Member of Congress from North Carolina, and also on the way to
his ranch in Napa Valley. Stanley offered to take Dana to the Geysers.

After spending the night in Vallejo, Dana took the morning stagecoach
to Napa where Stanley met him with a buggy and a pair of mules. They reached
Yount's toward night. Next morning, December 22, they breakfasted by the open
door. "Best of weather, wood fires and open doors. This is California winter."
Little did Dana guess that the winter weather, even in California, could change
so unpredictably.

Stanley and Dana then set out in the buggy, driving up through Napa
Valley and on through Knight's Valley to a turn-off at the northern end leading to
McDonnell's, who was reputedly one of the first guides to the Geysers.

Most travelers, in their letters and journals, spelled McDonnell's name
McDonald, and so it appears on Thompson's Historical Atlas Map of Sonoma
County (1877). In my text I use McDonnell — the spelling found on the small
stone marker on his grave in the Pioneer cemetery just north of Calistoga, and
also on the Department of the Interior's geological survey map, for the creek
named McDonnell for him.

Along the way, Dana observed:

Evergreen oak, and the common deciduous oak droops, almost like a willow, with
mistletoe and has long pendents of their hanging grey moss all among the leaves.
Very pretty. Trees are large and come right out of the sod, as in English parks."

They reached McDonnell's at night. He was away, but Mrs. McDonnell,
the three children and a hired man, a Norwegian called Brady, were at home. In
the stone fireplace, with its stone chimney, a wood fire with half a dozen four-

foot long logs was burning. Mrs. McDonnell was reluctant to talk about herself and the talking was left to Brady.

Next morning Stanley and Dana, with Brady as guide, set out on horseback, and made it to the Geysers in four hours and 45 minutes. The Geysers had little appeal for Dana and the weather turned against them. A heavy fog set in and the beauty of the mountainous country above Pluton Canyon was entirely obscured. Rain set in as they left the scene at 2:30. By five o'clock, it was pitch dark, raining heavily, and nothing could be seen:

> Single file, but can see neither Stanley nor his horse, nor can see the guide or the guide's horse. Call out, at intervals, not to lose each other. Several streams to ford, and occasionally a fallen tree. Guide loses the trail, — for we are on an Indian trail. He says he can follow the stream, and knows the hills — which we can see against sky, though we can see nothing against the ground. Only know we are in water by the splashing of horses feet . . . Cross stream again. Knows where he is. See light! It is McDonalds's. Get lost in the yard, as cannot see fence, or barn or shed. Glad to get to fire and lights and a change of clothes and warm supper. Mrs. McDonald nearly given us up.

It rained hard all night and it was still raining heavily the next morning. Brady reported that the streams were too swollen for a buggy to pass. But Stanley, like Bayard Taylor who had to get to Napa to give a lecture, had just as important an appointment. He was newly married. He had sent his wife to Sacramento to spend Christmas with her brother, Judge Baldwin, and he had to meet her there that day. She was unaware of Stanley's trip to the Geysers and would wonder what had happened to him.

With Brady, they walked a quarter of a mile to a neighbor, Keyes, who knew a ford not much over the buggy floor, where the buggy could cross. Presumably, it was Keyes who drove the buggy over, Stanley and Dana made it on horseback. Heavy rain, muddy roads and deep streams to be crossed slowed their progress. It was dark by the time they reached a little shop about two miles from Yount's and they decided they could go no further. Luckily there was Yount's wagon at the door that was returning. They followed the wagon and reached Yount's at 7 p.m. and again were warmly welcomed. It was Christmas Eve. Mrs. Yount, just home "from below" (presumably Napa City), was tired, so there was no special celebration.

> Sund. Dec. 25. Sunday and Christmas. But Stanley must go on to Napa and telegraph to his wife at Sacramento, or they will be in distress. Been so kind to me, and all on my account that came off here — so I accede to suggestion, and our whole Christmas, is spent on a rainy, muddy road. Afternoon, too late for Church, arrive at Napa City. Spend afternoon and evening in tavern bar-room, as no fire-place in any other room, where billiards are playing. But Stanley and I have some reasonable and agreeable conversation. All our journey, have had agreeable conversation. Stanley has anecdotes of Congressional life, politics etc. . . .

Next day, Stanley was off to Sacramento and Dana reached his rooms in San Francisco before dark.

16

The Whitney Geological Survey Surveys

Two years after the Bayard Taylors made their trip to the Geysers, three members of the Whitney Geological Survey made their way to Ray's Station and the Geysers by way of Knight's Valley. Their purpose is best explained by a brief note on the Whitney Survey.

The discoveries of gold, silver, quicksilver and tin had revealed the mineral wealth of California and, by 1860, some soberminded men in the state realized the need for a geological survey to help the direction of California's resources. Leading men of science in the East were asked to recommend a director and the choice fell on Josiah Dwight Whitney, a graduate of Yale, and author of *The Metallic Wealth of the United States*. In April 1860, Whitney was appointed to make a complete Geological Survey of the State, and was to name his own assistants. He named William H. Brewer, also a student of Yale, his Principal Assistant and put him in charge of the Botanical Department.

Brewer was primarily an agriculturist but he had also studied the natural sciences in Heidelberg and was experienced in mountain travel. He had walked six-hundred miles through Switzerland and made a shorter trek in the Tyrol. In the summer of 1860, two years after his marriage, his wife died shortly after the birth of a son, and the child died a few weeks later. Brewer was ready for a change of scene.

Like Bayard Taylor, Brewer was a voluminous writer, not a traveling-reporter but a diarist and letter writer. Unlike Taylor, he was not writing for an audience and it is doubtful that he intended any of his writings to be published. During his four years in California, he recorded in detail what he saw. His letters, based on his notes, were numbered serially and sent to his brother Edgar, with the request that, after the family and friends had read them, they should be kept until his return. These letters were published for the first time in 1930 by Yale University Press, and in subsequent editions by the University of California Press under the title, *Up and Down California,* and in

California at least, are today far more widely read than Bayard Taylor's works. Surveying the Coast Range was one season's work, and the plan was to round it off by inspecting some of the newly-discovered quicksilver 'leads' in the Geysers region and visiting the Geysers themselves. Brewer's account of this visit underscores Taylor's feat.

The Whitney Survey party were experienced in the field and, for part of the way, they did have guides. On November 6, 1861, Brewer, with Professor Whitney, Charles F. Hoffman and Chester Averill, set out from Yountville. Hoffman was a topographer. Young Averill has spent a year-and-a-half on a voyage around the world and had come to California to seek his fortune. He joined the Survey to keep the accounts and assist "in general at whatever he can do."

They rode through St. Helena to the head of the valley. Hoffman stayed in Calistoga intent on climbing Mount St. Helena. Hoffman got to within 400 feet of the top, and reckoned it about 4,500 feet high or a little less. Today, the Geological Survey gives the altitude as 4,338 feet. The party continued northward over the low divide (now known as Murray Hill) and "descended into Knight's Valley, a lovely valley watered by a tributary of the Russian River." Passing down the valley they took an obscure road over low hills to McDonnell's, where they camped alonside the creek now bearing his name.

A day was spent preparing for the field trip. On November 8, they started out on mules with blankets and provisions. White tin cups, pistols, knives and hammers swung from their belts. McDonnell as guide, was on foot. The going was so rough, like McDonnell, the three surveyors had to walk most of the way. "The ascent was steep, the trail very obscure, and we would never have found it alone, even with all our mountain experience."

McDonnell accompanied the surveyors as far as what I believe was Ray's Station, so close is Brewer's description of the locality and the place itself to that of Bayard Taylor's. After unloading and picketing the mules to feed, they made their way into an adjoining canyon to a quicksilver claim that was being worked. Returning to the cabin they found two other men had followed with pack horses. They, too, had quicksilver mining interests. They all had supper together; the Professor and Brewer then spread out their blankets under a fir tree, while the others slept indoors.

By early dawn the next morning they struck a trail leading to the Pioneer Mine. There, welcomed by the foreman, they spent the afternoon looking around. The mine was remarkable for its native quicksilver ore — quicksilver mixed with the rock that, in places, was completely saturated with the fluid metal. One had but to shake a lump of rock and a silver shower of the glittering metal fell from it.

That night was spent in a mine cabin. The Geysers were less than four miles away by crowflight, six or seven by trail. With rain threatening to mark the late beginning of the rainy season, the next day was perhaps the last chance

Brewer and his companions had of reaching their goal before returning to their winter quarters. It was Sunday, November 10, and the foreman and another man from the mine offered to act as guides. Riding along Hog's Back Ridge, Brewer marveled at the view.

Heading downward, the grade into Pluton Canyon, was so steep, that they had to dismount and lead their mules. Brewer's description of the Geysers is more factual, less dramatic than Taylor's, but the impact of the roaring, rushing, hissing steam they had heard a mile away, and the seething, steaming Witches' Cauldron was the same.

The Geysers Hotel, busy only during the summer, was unprepared for guests, and there was a tedious wait for the midday dinner. When the meal was finished, the men went out to saddle their mules. The sky suddenly became dark, and the ridge, when they reached it, was shrouded in fog. Dripping wet, they got back to the mine, built a big fire in the cabin just before the rain began to come down in torrents. But the rain and the wait they had at the Geysers Hotel was a small price to pay for their visit to the Geysers. Brewer had seen what Bayard Taylor had seen, and what Dana had apparently missed on account of bad weather — he had seen the view from Hog's Back ridge. Taylor, who often wrote so exhuberantly, said he was afraid to describe the beauty of the scene. Brewer, who usually was factual in his writing said "The scene was not merely beautiful, it was truly sublime." Besides, he and his companions had reached "the goal of our summer's hopes."

17

With Clark Foss
To The Geysers

Brewer's poor opinion of The Geysers Hotel was not entirely due to being an out-of-season visitor. The summer trade had fallen off, Colonel Goodwin's wagon road had deteriorated, descriptions of the Geysers had been grossly exaggerated and the prices the hotel charged were exhorbitant. The trip was too arduous for most people and was not worth the cost.

But enterprising Colonel Goodwin was not about to abandon the hotel in which he had invested so great a sum. In 1862, the year after Brewer's visit, he and two associates financed the building of a toll road from Ray's Station over Hog's Back ridge. Clark Foss, a native of New Hampshire, started the first stage line out of Healdsburg over Goodwin's road in 1863.

Two years later, Foss established his own stage line out of Calistoga which, by now, was attracting hundreds of tourists. He bought a tavern at the southern entrance to Knight's Valley and converted it into a wayside inn that was well up to Calistoga's hotel standards. The place was known as Foss's Station or Fossville. The inn contained twenty-five guest rooms and its big main room had red plush draperies and crystal chandeliers.

In 1868, three years after Foss opened his hostelry, Sam Brannan brought the railroad to Calistoga, and with Calvin Holmes, who owned a large ranch in Knight's Valley, Brannan and others soon extended the scenic road through Knight's Valley to Healdsburg. The road from Calistoga now became the main road to the Geysers and this in turn gave Clark Foss the monopoly of the Geysers tourist trade. From then on, the wayside inn entertained guests from all over the world — princes from Europe, members of the British Parliament, a one-time President of the United States, generals, millionaires and troups of circuses. And as many people came to ride behind the Old Chieftain, as Foss was known locally, as to see the Geysers themselves.

Robert Louis Stevenson later immortalized him in *The Silverado Squatters*. He saw Foss once, and twice talked with him — the second time by

85

telephone from Cheeseborough's Magnolia Hotel in Calistoga when Foss was at Fossville. "It was an odd thing," Stevenson remarked, "that here, on what we are accustomed to consider the very skirts of civilization, I should have used the telephone for the first time in my civilized career." By repute, Stevenson learned that:

> Along the unfenced, abominable mountain roads, he launches his team with small regard to human life or the doctrines of probabilities. Flinching travellers, who behold themselves coasting eternity at every corner, look with natural admiration at their driver's huge, impassive, fleshy countenance. . . wonderful tales are current of his readiness and skill.

Teamster Billy Spiers, who became a fine stagecoach driver too, vouched that R.L.S. "wasn't laying it on none to thick." Foss, he said, handled "four or six horses like you'd handle that many cats. He would lift them right up off their feet and swing them round the corners so fast you couldn't see the leading team." Maggie Turner, who lived across the road from the hostelry as a child, summed him up as "rough and gruff, a great giant of a man" (he stood six feet, two inches tall and weighed 265 - some said 300 pounds). "The way he drove his horses was enough to make your hair stand on end." Maggie continued. "I rode behind him many times, scared as I was."

It was 68 miles by boat and train from San Francisco to Calistoga. The trip to the Geysers started from the Magnolia Hotel early in the morning. The first stop was Fossville, and the distance from there to the Geysers was 26 miles. A team of good horses could make the journey in five-and-a-half hours.

Then Foss, like Colonel Goodwin, built a road that cut up into mountainous country at the northern end of Knight's Valley; along an upgraded seven-foot shelf of the mountainside, unprotected by wall or fence, with drops of several thousand feet to the valleys below. He bypassed Ray's Station, traversed Pine Flat (a bustling mining community) and linked up with the Hog's Back Ridge road. This cut the distance by six miles, and Foss's driving skill and fast horses almost halved the driving time.

The last terrifying descent into Pluton Canyon and the cry "All Out" as Foss drew up at The Geysers Hotel made the "mouth of Hell" spouting steam with a continuing roar, sheer anti-climax. One of the Goodwin family recalled that the last abrupt descent often compelled the ladies to dive under the seats, their bonnets awry or off their heads. Some passengers were so sick they had to be put to bed to recover their balance.

The stage line to the Geysers did not operate during the rainy winter months because the dirt roads were too deep in mud. The flow of guests did not begin at Fossville until April, reached full-stream during July and August and dwindled again to a trickle in November with the late autumn rains.

During the dry season, Foss made the round trip daily, and won a small fortune and undying fame. His fare, one way, was twenty five dollars, fifty dollars for the round-trip, or more than one thousand dollars if reckoned in today's money. The round-trip fare included a sumptuous dinner, that Mrs. Foss had ready for the travelers on their return to Fossville. There was lamb, chicken, game, fresh and preserved fruits and numerous vegetables (no doubt from Frank McDonald's nursery orchard-garden); desserts, coffee, tea, milk, buttermilk and pure mountain water.

The Fossville Register records that Tom Thumb and party of Philadelphia were among the first notables at the hostelry. Thumb was the world's most acclaimed midget, and he may well have relayed to Foss some of the wisdom of Phineas T. Barnum of "The Greatest Show on Earth." Possibly it was sheer coincidence that, after Thumb's visit, Foss added yells and curve-rounding on two wheels and his reputation as a master showman as well as a king of the reins grew rapidly.

The new tactics paid off. The world of travel became aware of a rare new thrill for those of good nerves and stomach. How the hooves pounded along the Knight's Valley road, mingled with the roars of Foss, the barks of his yellow dog running between the rear wheels, and the cries of the occupants of the lunging stagecoach. Guests' comments written in Spencerian hands multiplied. By May 1868, some were addressing him as Captain Foss; by June, it was Colonel Foss. By July, a party headed by the wealthy Floods of San Francisco inscribed their testimonial, "We shall not soon forget the trip with Genl. Foss. Most magnificent ride of our lives." And for good measure, the men noted the driving time. "Left 6:05 A.M. Arrived 8:40 A.M." while the ladies put down a special note: "Charmed with Genl. Foss."

Colonel H. W. Freedley and Captain C. D. Mahaffey, U.S. Army, fighters in the Civil War, wrote for the record in October: "Foss must stand acknowledged while these hills do stand as the most accomplished and capable driver as ever cracked the whip or held the ribbons."

By 1871, the Crockers, the Hopkinses, the elite of California and their guests, as well as travelers from New York, Boston, London, Rome, even Peking, were making a point of having ridden with Foss, parodying Tennyson "Out of the jaws of death, Back from the mouth of Hell." Other notable travelers were the North's great cavalry hero, Gen. Phil Sheridan and wife, U.S.A.

Mrs. Foss's busiest day was probably October 6, 1876, when Cooper's Great International Circus and Menagerie, mercifully minus the menagerie but with its Royal Jap Troupe, thirty-four hungry souls in all, checked into Foss's Station, all eager to shake the hand of the reinsman to the Geysers.

A month later, according to the register, Foss's coach bore as catholic a company as any one might try to conjure. It was made up of the princess of Montenuovo and of Liechtenstein, both of Vienna; Mr. Chim Linn Pim and party of the Chinese consulate, San Francisco; Miss Jennie McGeorge, of Scotland, and a pair of whiskery miners heading for Mule Canyon. Another day, one California Joe rode elbow to elbow with one Chas. Julius Augustus Casius Caiser, while the Honorable Judge Boone of Kentucky, and his lady, shared their seat with Lord

Snodgrass, M. P. Dover, England.

One may wonder how Felix Adler, philosopher and founder of the ethical culture movement, made out, rounding some ferocious hairpin turns, between fellow passengers Miss Dora D.L.D. Byron of England, and William R. Hearst, then age 15.

The banner-raising entry was one on October 7, 1878, and the page was no less ink-spotted than many others, the pen used evidently the same terrible hotel pen used by the miners and the millionaires. Midway on a page in the Register were the names of Geo. N. Grant and Miss Sophie B. Grant of Oakland. Following in a schoolboy scrawl, the name Gen. U.S. Grant.

Towards the end of his stage-driving career, while driving a team of young colts, Foss's speeding stage plunged into a canyon on the way from Pine Flat to Fossville. Seven, including Foss, were badly injured; one young lady was killed, and another maimed for life. From then on, the blustering stage-driver became more reserved. In 1881, a full year after Stevenson's visit, he handed the reins over to his son, Charlie, and moved into town. The St. Helena *Star* reported in the August 28, 1885 issue that he died at his home in Calistoga, and was buried in St. Helena cemetery.

Charlie's fame was overshadowed by that of his father and, in stature, he was slighter, standing just over six feet and weighing 190 pounds, but his reputation was untarnished. He was well-trained, for he grew up as a driver among the coast mountains, then spent several years in Southern California and Arizona, graduating in the Sierras. At the time he took over the reins of the Fossville-Geysers run, he was driving over the Yosemite road.

In contrast to the Old Chieftain, he was a less spectacular but entirely safe driver. Clark Foss's lead horses carried no bells, as was common practice for all other vehicles on the road — his terrific yells and the clatter of his horses could be heard half a mile ahead. Charlie's lead horses did carry bells and, instead of running his horses down the Hog's Back at a run, as his father did, he drove down at ten miles an hour.

One traveler writing for the *Overland Monthly* (1898) of his ride to the Geysers with Charlie had this to say of him:

> . . . he was one of the gentlest and most polite fellows I have ever known . . . he made the thirty-five mile stagecoach drive every day, and never had an accident or a breakdown . . . he invariably halts at the summit (of the Hog's Back) where may be seen a landscape that has few superiors. Mountain, valleys, orchards, and villas may be seen for a hundred miles when the atmosphere is clear and rare . . . he has no superior in the world, probably, in his line.

By car and on foot we tried in vain to retrace Clark Foss' cutoff into the hills northeastward of the Spy-glass. But only bears, deer, and mountain cats travel much of that old road today. During the San Francisco earthquake of April 1906, boulders crashed down upon it and Charlie was unable to clear it and make it fit for stagecoach traffic again. Instead, he drove the first road to the Geysers, the road out of Healdsburg.

18

Postscript To The Geysers

This postscript serves to round out briefly the story of certain people and of place names that appeared in the preceding chapter but are not marked on today's maps. It also explains how we learned about the Fossville register.

What was once Fossville was around a bend in the road about half a mile from our house. Mr. Frank Turner, who had a prune orchard and a sizable vineyard, lived in a modern ranch house on a knoll above the site of the hostelry and, across the way, his tractors were housed in what had been Clark Foss's stables. He was Maggie Turner's son, and orchardist Frank McDonald's grandson.

When Clark Foss moved into town, Frank McDonald took over the hostelry and eventually Frank Turner inherited both the family ranch house and the hostelry. Both needed a lot of repair. He took them down and used the wood to build his new house. Goodness knows what happened to the red plush drapes and the chandeliers but Frank Turner did have one irreplaceable item — the Fossville Hotel Register that he kept in a kitchen drawer. All this we learned from our intervening neighbor who was, romantically it seemed to us, a stagedriver's daughter.

One morning I caught Mr. Turner on his doorstep, just as he was setting out to his vineyard. Knowing he was busy, I lost no time in asking about the register. He went indoors, and after a moment returned with a big, somewhat battered leatherbound book. "I don't usually let it out of my sight. Some people, strangers, I lent it to once, tore several pages out of it. Keep it a couple of days, if you want to."

Ray's Station, more stable than tavern, was, naturally enough, another vanished place name. Where was it?

We reasoned it must have been somewhere about the northern end of Alexander Valley, and one day we asked at a roadside auto repair shop. The young man listened to our question, shook his head and looked at us as if we might be wandering in mind as well as wondering. But an old man emerged from the shadows, said "Yes, there had been such a place once upon a time, somewhere along the Old Red Winery Road. O'er thataway," he pointed.

The Old Red Winery Road yielded no signs. Again we stopped. This time we asked a young woman mowing the well-kept grass outside a trim modern home.

No, she had never heard of Ray's Station. As we turned to go, I mentioned that it had been a place where people had changed horses on the way to the Geysers. She thought a moment, and said she had heard there once had been a stabling place on neighboring Mr. Dana's land. Mr. Dana's mailbox and the entrance road leading up the steep hillside to his house were half a mile down the road.

The entrance road was steep indeed but broad and well-kept. A great iron gateway introduced the big ranch house atop a foothill. A housekeeper in uniform told us Mr. Dana was probably down at the stables, just off the road we had climbed.

Behaving like some persistent reporter, I asked how he happened to have come to this spot. He replied that he had two homes, one near New York City, the other this ranch of 50,000 acres. No one had directed him here, but after looking the country over for a place where he could best enjoy his hobby of raising and showing cow horses, this had proved to be that place.

Taylor's ghost would hardly be flattered by William Dana's lack of recognition, but would have perhaps smiled at the coincidence that brought this descendant of his famous editor to raise cow horses at Ray's Station. Bayard Taylor and William Dana did, however, have two things in common. Both had traveled widely and both loved what we called our part of California. Taylor, writing of it after traveling across "all zones of the earth with the exception of the Antarctic," saw our countryside as one of singular beauty, as an altogether new variety of landscape:

> Even in California, where Nature presents so many phases, there is nothing like it elsewhere. Fancy a country composed of mounds from one to five hundred feet in height, arranged in every possible style of grouping. . . covered with a short, even sward of golden grass and studded with trees — singly, in clumps, or in groves. . .

What the travelers wrote in the Geysers Hotel register we shall never know, for both hotel and register burned years later. It could very well have contained the signatures of the French-born, English writer, Hilaire Belloc, the landscape painter, Thomas Hill and one of photography's pioneers, Eadweard Muybridge. All are known to have visited the Geysers.

A mystery surrounds Thomas Hill's paintings of the Geysers. Art historian, Mrs. Marjorie Dakin Arkelian, who did the research for the Thomas Hill exhibition at the Oakland Museum in 1980, told me that one painting, "The Geysers" was exhibited at the San Francisco Art Association in January 1873, and one critic declared it to be as natural as the Geysers themselves.

This picture is of the Devil's Teakettle and Indian Sweat Bars, and the surrounding hills, which in reality furnish but poor material for the picture; but still, what with the sun shining down the canyon, lighting up the scrubby oaks and lovely madronas with brilliant gold and crimson, and the singular color of the earth and the steam, the effect is really very fine.

This painting may have been destroyed in the San Francisco earthquake and fire of 1906. However that may be, Hill was a prolific painter, and it is hard to believe that he painted but one picture of the scene when the trip to the Geysers was not an easy one.

The Geysers today present a vastly different appearance, rather they make no appearance at all. They are capped, and their thrusting power harnessed — making the Geysers the only presently operating geothermal energy producer in the United States, and the largest in the world. The Union Oil Company of California, in an equal partnership with Natomas Company (which acquired the interests formerly held by Thermal Power Company and Magma Power Company) conducts the exploration of the Geysers geothermal field, drills the wells, constructs the pipe lines, and produces the bulk of the steam from which the Pacific Gas and Electric Company generates the electricity.

P. G. & E. in 1981 derived from the Geysers between seven and eight percent of northern California's electricity needs. The Geysers' present electrical generating capacity is 936,000 kilowatts, enough to supply the needs of a city of some one million people. It would require eleven million barrels of fuel oil per year to generate this amount of energy. Two new generating plants will begin operation in 1983 which will increase capacity by 228,000 kilowatts, and there are indications of steam available for further expansion of this natural energy source. Dr. Carel Otte, president of the Union Oil Company's Geothermal Division has pointed out that:

> For years, mankind has dreamed of capturing the earth's natural elements — the sun, the wind and tides and the heat of the earth for his own use. Scientists tell us that energy from the sun, wind, and tides are still a long way off — but geothermal energy, nature's own boiler, is a reality. It's here today.

19

Indicted For Murder

Few, if anyone, who traveled the Knight's Valley road made such headline news in the local and San Francisco newspapers as did Eadweard Muybridge in the fall of 1874. Four years earlier, on July 1, 1870, he had visited the Geysers to record the scene with his camera — almost eleven years after Bayard Taylor's epic ride. It may have been on this occasion that he also photographed the newly-discovered petrified forest near Calistoga.

He was already a famous photographer and was to become as prolific in picture-taking as Taylor was in writing. His fame has outlasted Taylor's and rests not only on his landscape views of the West but in being acknowledged as "the Father of the Motion Picture."

His purpose in coming to Calistoga in the fall of 1874 had nothing to do with photography. He came to seek out and kill his wife's lover and he found him in a ranch house, high up on the mountainside above Knight's Valley. At his trial various episodes in his life were cited in the argument for insanity.

There was a good deal of drama in Muybridge's life and much of his work focused on dramatic scenes and subjects. Aside from newspaper reports, what I have learned of Muybridge is from the biographies by Gordon Hendricks and Robert Bartlett Haas which appeared in 1975 and 1976 respectively, the one in London, the other in New York. He was born on April 9, 1830 at Kingston-on-Thames, England, and was christened Edward James Muggeridge. In due course, he changed his name to Eadweard Muybridge. He was twenty-two years old when he came to New York and set up as a commission merchant, binding and selling unbound books imported from England. Three years later, in 1855, he established a bookstore in San Francisco, became a leader in the book-selling trade and was elected to the board of directors of the prestigious Mercantile Library.

When Muybridge made his first visit to Yosemite Valley, his first glimpse of it was from the spot which early travelers referred to as the

"Standpoint of Silence." Like so many contemporary artists and early photographers, notably Carleton E. Watkins who began his great series of Yosemite in 1861, he was captivated by the valley's spectacular wild beauty, and determined to make photography his career.

In 1860, he set out for England to buy the latest equipment. Traveling by the overland mail stage from San Francisco to the East Coast, the stage brakes failed in Texas. Muybridge went hurtling through the luggage carrier at the rear and was thrown headlong against a boulder and knocked unconscious. He had a wound on top of his head and, for a time, lay ill and unidentified in a hospital. When able, he continued his journey by railroad and spent two months in New York before sailing for England. For several months he was plagued by deafness and a loss of taste and smell.

By the mid-1860s Muybridge was back in San Francisco with his new equipment. He spent June to November 1867 in the Yosemite and the photographs he took launched him on his career. He now described himself as a landscape photographer and assumed the pseudonym, "Helios."

Important commissions now came his way. The War Office appointed him official photographer on General Halleck's mission to survey the newly-acquired territory of Alaska. He recorded each new lighthouse on the Pacific Coast for the Light House Board.

Apparently, Muybridge had a showroom at the entrance to Woodward's Gardens where he photographed the eight feet, three-inch tall Chinese giant with his wee wife and a group of Japanese musicians and acrobats, among the first Japanese to come to America following Commodore Perry's visit to Japan. He also took a photograph of a "petite but voluptuous young woman with a sweet face and large lustrous eyes." This was probably Mrs. Flora Shalcross Stone who was to become his wife.

Muybridge first met Flora at a studio where she was employed as a photographic retoucher. She left the studio to work at a Dollar Store, and there met Lucius Stone, a well-known saddle-maker. She was sixteen years old when she married him. In due course, Flora left the store to work for Muybridge, again as a retoucher. The upshot of that move from store to studio was Flora's divorce from Stone, with Muybridge paying the divorce costs. In 1871, Flora and Muybridge were married; she was twenty, he forty-one.

During the first year of the marriage, Muybridge's work kept him in San Francisco, but the year following, he was away a good deal. The summer was spent in Yosemite. Most important, there was work to do in Sacramento.

Sometime previously, Muybridge had met Leland Stanford, a former governor of California, and one of the "Pacific Quartet" credited with the spanning of the continent by the iron horse — the railroad. Stanford was enormously wealthy. He commissioned Muybridge to photograph the interior of his palatial Sacramento mansion and his horse, Occident.

Stanford was a great lover of horses and had an eye for a good one.

He had bought a horse named Wonder that he saw drawing a wagon in the Sacramento streets, rechristened him Occident and trained him to be a record-breaking trotter. This revived the old argument as to whether a horse trotting at top speed ever had all four feet off the ground at once. James Keene, president of the San Francisco stock exchange, and other sportsmen on the East Coast believed it did not. Stanford believed there were moments when it did.

A story went around that Stanford bet Keene $25,000 that he was right. There is some doubt about the credibility of the story, but true or not, Stanford engaged Muybridge to take a series of photographs of Occident going at full speed. None of these showed the horse's four feet off the ground at one instant (that Muybridge would show five years later) but one negative did show Occident in full motion.

Although this picture was not published until 1877, its existence was reported and the results of the experiment described in the press. *The Daily Alta California,* under the heading, "Quick Work," declared the successful negative to be "a great triumph as a curiosity in photography — a horse's picture taken while going thirty-eight feet in a second." Muybridge's achievement did, in fact, mark the beginning of motion photography.

Another momentous year was 1873 — for Muybridge, Flora and Harry Larkyns, a newcomer to town. Recently, Muybridge had begun his association with Bradley and Rulofson, San Francisco's largest photographic establishment, and one day when he was there with Flora, Harry Larkyns came by. Flora, who had met Larkyns previously, introduced him to Muybridge. Larkyns lost no time in calling on the couple, and soon was given permission to escort Flora to the theatre. "Helios" was glad for Flora to have company; he was about to journey to, what was then, far-off northern California to record the Modoc Indians' stubborn stand in the Lava Beds against the Army's determination to dislodge them and drive them from their homeland. He was also commissioned to photograph portions of the Central Pacific and Union Pacific Railroads.

As The *San Francisco Daily Morning Call* later wryly summed up:

> The remainder of the story may be condensed into a few sentences. Muybridge was away from home frequently and bestowed more care on business than domestic affairs. Mrs. Muybridge was vivacious and young enough to be his daughter; Harry Larkyns was gay, dashing and handsome, and having permission to escort Mrs. Muybridge to the theatre, he did not neglect the opportunity and abused it.

When Muybridge was away, Flora joined Larkyns in his rented rooms nearby, Larkyns explaining to his landlady that Flora was his wife, that she was staying with relatives in the city and that soon they would be living together.

On April 15, 1874, Flora gave birth to a son. He was christened Florado Helios Muybridge. Apparently it never occurred to Muybridge that his attractive young wife would philander. However, he did send Flora and the two-month old Florando to stay with her relatives in Oregon, thinking perhaps that Flora needed some company, being so much alone with the baby. Harry

Larkyns, in due course, went to Calistoga to write an account of the neighboring quicksilver mines for the San Francisco Stock Report.

Six months after Florado's birth, on October 14, Mrs. Susan Smith, the midwife who had attended Flora, went to court for payment of her services, and was awarded a $107 judgment against Muybridge. Two days later, the unsuspecting Muybridge met Mrs. Smith at the attorney's office and, in the evening, went to her home. Seeing his baby son's photograph on the wall, he turned it over and saw "Little Harry" written on it. Mrs. Smith then showed him some incriminating letters.

Next day, Saturday, October 15, Muybridge went to see Mrs. Smith again. She recalled her warning to Larkyns to go slow. His reply was "Flora and I have fooled the old man so long that we can keep it up still longer."

That afternoon Muybridge called at Bradley and Rulofson's. Rulofson, alarmed by his ashen pallor and strange behavior, thought he had gone crazy. Emotionally distraught, tears and perspiration running down his face, Muybridge eventually told his story. He had, he said, no thought of suicide but wanted to vindicate his honor and in doing so knew he might lose his life. It was not difficult to track Larkyns down. That summer he had gone on Clark Foss's stagecoach to Pine Flat to map the area and get the facts he needed for the Stock Report. Now he was reportedly staying at the Magnolia Hotel in Calistoga.

Rulofson, aware that the boat left at four o'clock, tried to delay Muybridge by talking against time, but suddenly Muybridge "looked at his watch; and said time was up, and tore away from me . . . it was 4 minutes to 4 o'clock P.M. when he left me; my office is 10 minutes walk for me, 12 blocks from the boat; my watch was very near city time."

Muybridge made it to the ferry, caught the evening train from Vallejo up Napa Valley to Calistoga. Larkyns was not at the Magnolia Hotel but Muybridge learned at a livery stable that he was at the house of the superintendent of the Yellow Jacket Mine, on the mountainside above Knight's Valley. Muybridge hired a rig and young George Wolf to drive him. Being coatless, he flung a buggy robe around his shoulders and off they went into the night.

Along the way, Muybridge talked about highway robbery, said he was unsure whether or not his pistol was in order. He asked whether a shot would frighten the horses. No, said George, and Muybridge fired one shot.

Midway in Knight's Valley they took the turn-off leading up the steep two-mile long road to the mine superintendent's house. Wolf brought his rig to a stop outside the kitchen door. Muybridge got out, knocked, introduced himself and said he wanted to see Major Larkyns.

Larkyns, who was playing cards with some of the ladies in the parlor, got up and went through the kitchen to the open door. He asked who wanted to see him.

"I can't see you," he said.

"Step out here and you can see me," was the reply.

Larkyns stepped outside the door.

"My name is Muybridge and I have a message for you from my wife."

One shot from the pistol, aimed at the heart, and Larkyns reeled back into the house, staggered through the kitchen and the parlor and out of the door. He fell dead at the base of a great oak tree beside the front entrance. Muybridge, who had followed Larkyns into the house, was disarmed. He offered his buggy for a doctor to be brought from Calistoga and calmly awaited his arrival. The doctor arrived about ten o'clock and pronounced Larkyns dead. Muybridge, feet tied, was put on the back seat of a wagon with one man beside him and taken to Calistoga to stay in custody at the Magnolia Hotel until Monday when he was taken to Napa, the county seat. Larkyn's body was taken to San Francisco to lie in state in a rosewood casket with silver-plated screws and handles and given a martyr's funeral.

1. Mount St. Helena seen from Frank McDonald's ranch house in
Knight's Valley. Oil on wood 20 x 27″ by William S. Dutton, 1962.

2. Robert Louis Stevenson in his smoking cap
at Grez-sur-Loing, France, by Fanny Osbourne.

3. Mrs. Annie Schram.

4. The Stevensons in the assay office. Frontispiece to the first edition of *The Silverado Squatters,* from a drawing by Joe Strong at Silverado in 1880.

5. The Sea Fogs from Stevenson's viewpoint, by Joan Parry Dutton.

6. Road from Knight's Valley to
Great Western Mine by Virgil Williams.

7. Virgil Williams' painting, "Cabin in the Woods" of his cottage on Mt. St. Helena.

8. Fossville, from *Historical Atlas Map of Sonoma County, 1877*.

9. The Geysers. View up the Canyon
from the Witches' Cauldron,
by Eadweard Muybridge.

10. Ruins of Jack London's Wolf House, Glen Ellen, in the Valley of the Moon.

11. Drake's Bay by Philip Hyde.

12. California Sea Otter, with red sea urchin, near Point Lobos by Scott Ransom.

13. Aleuts hunting in their baidarkas, from Litke's *Voyage Autour du Monde*.

14. Fort Ross, from *Historical Atlas Map of Sonoma County*, 1877.

15. Residence of Cyrus and Rufena Alexander, from *Historical Atlas Map of Sonoma County, 1877*.

16. Pomo basket. Plain Twined. Fort Bragg.

17. Pomo basket with red woodpecker scalp feathers and quail plumes.

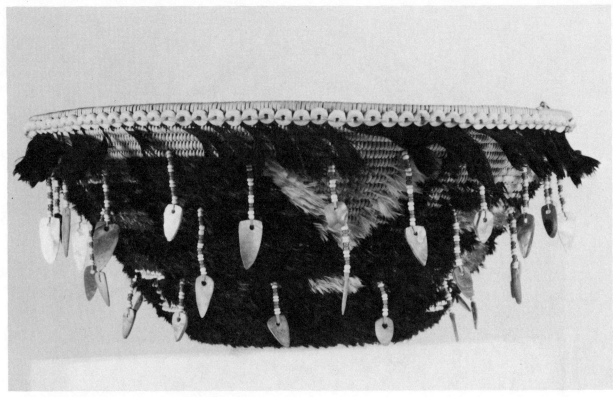

18. Wappo basket; coiled, feathered, truncate-cone shape;
beads, pendants, string-bead handle. Alexander Valley.

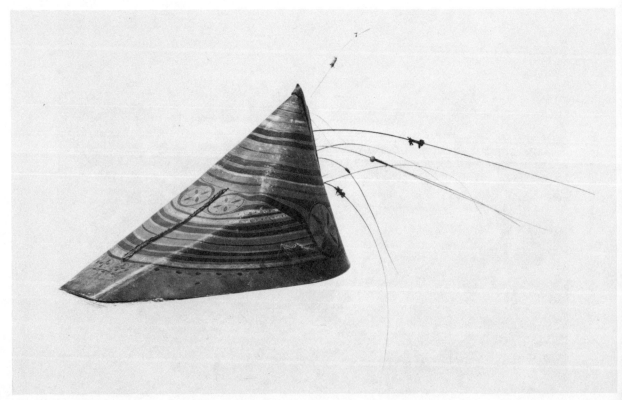

19. Aleut wooden rain hat with sea-lion whiskers.

20. Obsidian arrowhead, 1¼″. Sacramento.

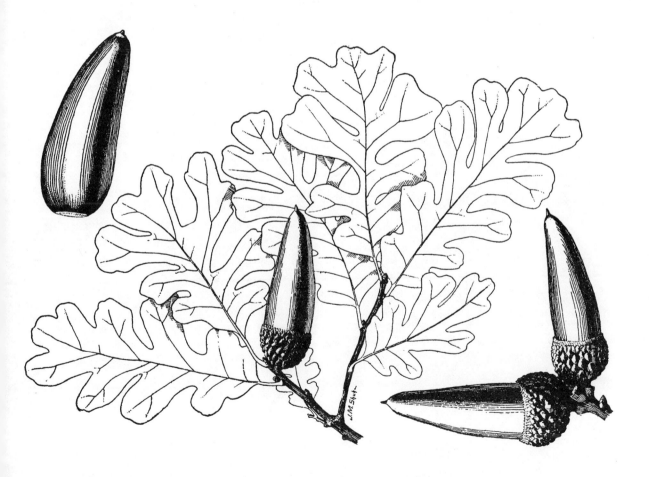

21. Valley oak *(Quercus lobata)*

20

Father of the Motion Picture

Muybridge, comfortably lodged in prison, was allowed books and papers and writing materials, and meals were brought in from a hotel across the street. Early in December, a few days before he was indicted for murder, Flora returned from Oregon, filed for divorce but was denied alimony. Muybridge was brought to trial on February 2, 1875.

Opinion was that the prosecution handled by the Napa County district attorney and a county judge, Stoney, would be outmatched by Muybridge's defense team, Wirt Pendegast of Napa, a handsome young attorney who was serving his fourth term as a state senator, Cameron King and another attorney from San Francisco.

The trial was headline news, reporters filling column after column in the daily papers. King opened for the defense and, in pleading insanity, gave the 1860 stagecoach accident as the basic cause. Rulofson, perhaps persuaded to bolster the insanity plea, said that after the stagecoach wreck, Muybridge was careless with money and refused to take a picture which did not suit his artistic taste, no matter how much money he was offered. And no sane man would sit on the brink of Contemplation Rock in Yosemite, as Muybridge had done, to be photographed 3,400 feet above the valley floor. Others testified that Muybridge was, at the time of the murder, cool and collected, and the doctor of Stockton Lunatic Asylum said nothing would convince him of Muybridge's insanity. The killing was, he declared, premeditated and the prisoner was well aware of the consequences.

On the third day of the trial, when the case was expected to go to the jury, the courtroom was thronged long before the hour of opening and crowds gathered in the street outside. King again made the opening address for the defense, adhering to their policy to admit the killing, establish the seduction of Muybridge's wife and plea that the discovery of it drove him to temporary insanity and, under the influence of an uncontrollable impulse to slay Larkyns.

King quoted at length from the Bible: "Let no man commit adultery." And "thou shalt not covet thy neighbor's wife. On these two commandments rest all the law. The man that committeth adultery with another man's wife, even he that committeth adultery shall surely be put to death. So shalt thou put away evil from Israel. Though this is not the law of California, I believe it is the same moral guide."

Cameron King's address was the prelude to Senator Wirt Pendegast's impassioned oratory. He spoke for two uninterrupted hours. In pleading that Muybridge committed justifiable homicide, he said, "It is the weakness of the law that there is no adequate punishment for the seducer." He closed with a stirring appeal:

> I cannot ask you to send this man forth to family and home — he has none. Across the arch of his fireplace where once was written the words "Home, Wife, Child, Content and Peace," there now appears as a substitute for all, in black letters, placed there by the destroyer, the single, awful word DESOLATION. But I do ask you to send him forth free — let him take up the thread of his broken life, and resume that profession which is now his only love. . . Do this, but this, and from every peaceful household, and from every quiet home within the state there will come to your verdict the echo of a solemn and a deep Amen!

The jury retired shortly before 10:00 p.m. and returned to the courtroom around noon the next day. The one holdout finally agreed with his fellow jurymen when someone pointed out that at that very moment another man might be with his wife. When the verdict "not guilty" was pronounced, Muybridge sank forward in his chair, weeping convulsively, and Senator Pendegast carried him from the courtroom and laid him on a lounge in his office. In a short while, his emotion subsided, and he was able to go out on the street where the waiting crowd acclaimed him.

So ended one of the greatest trials of early California. The press unanimously applauded the verdict:

> Mr. Pendegast said in his speech, 'Larkyns staked his life on a desperate game and Muybridge held the winning hand.' The enforcement of this stern rule will mark out a new lesson in man's philosophy 'that the price of happiness is virtue' and gives a new force to one old one that 'the wages of sin are death.'. . .The brilliant defense of Mr. Pendegast was such an effort as is seldom heard twice in a lifetime. . . he has added new laurels to his crown of oratory and given utterance in that overwhelming appeal to words that should be embalmed in the pages of history, and go down to posterity as one of man's greatest appeals for man.

Muybridge, back in San Francisco, mingled freely with his friends and set about making plans for a photographic survey of Central America and the Isthmus of Panama that had been under discussion the previous summer. Flora's divorce action put his property in jeopardy but again he held the winning hand.

He had his equipment packed in cases marked "Bradley & Rulofson", secretly taken on board the *Montana*. The following evening, February 27, the *Montana* moved out into the bay, slowed her engines as a long boat came alongside and Muybridge went aboard and sailed to Central America.

Flora, who had again appealed for alimony late that March, fell ill. Paralysis set in and she died in mid-July. Florado, left in the care of a French family, was later placed in an orphanage. When he was nine years old, Muybridge had him apprenticed to a harness-maker. Later he turned to gardening and was a garden laborer in Sacramento, where, in 1944, he died after being knocked down by a car.

Muybridge returned to San Francisco from Central America in November 1875 and shortly produced some magnificent panoramas of the city from the turret of Mrs. Mark Hopkins' still unfinished house atop California Street. But the work that was to bring his greatest fame lay ahead.

In August 1877, Leland Stanford asked him to take photographs of all stages of a horse's movements on the trotting track at his Palo Alto farm. The following summer, by means of twelve especially equipped and electronically-triggered cameras, one photograph taken of Abe Edginton, another of Stanford's trotters, showed a moment when all four feet were off the ground. Reproduction of the photograph appeared in many publications. The *Scientific American* of October 19, 1878 reproduced on its cover a series of drawings after Muybridge's photographs of a walking horse and a trotter. By December, news of the experiments was widespread in Europe.

Muybridge's fame as an early exhibitor of motion pictures rests on the instrument he developed, and which he called the zoo praxinoscope. It combined for the first time the projecting lantern, the revolving disc, and a counter-revolving slotted disc that acted as an intermittent shutter. He used this instrument for the first time at a private party at Stanford's house, Mayfield Grange, in Palo Alto, in the fall of 1879. On January 16, 1880, Muybridge presented his latest motion pictures on a screen in the ballroom of Stanford's San Francisco house before a group of the city's elite. Other showings followed in March and May. These marked the official beginning of motion pictures on the screen in America, which earned for Muybridge the title "Father of the Motion Picture."

Muybridge's biographers point out that it was a chance circumstance in the history of photography that Muybridge was the first in the field of motion pictures. Stanford was the patron and Muybridge the executer. Stanford wanted the work done and had the means to buy the equipment and have it perfected. Another rich man in another country and another gifted photographer would have achieved the same end — but probably no better man for the job would have been found.

Muybridge made several visits to England and Europe to exhibit his moving pictures and, from the summer of 1884 until early in 1886, his work was at the University of Pennsylvania in Philadelphia. In all, he took about 30,000 motion pictures of men and women, animals and birds. Out of these, 781 plates were chosen for his eleven-volume *Animal Locomotion* printed in 1887.

As Senator Pendegast predicted, after the trial, Muybridge's only love was his profession. He was remembered in Philadelphia as a recluse, a stocky man about five feet, eight inches tall, with a flowing beard. His clothes were almost too decrepit for him to go out of his studio and he usually wore a black felt hat almost the width of his shoulders, his hair protruding from a hole in the crown.

His work made an impact on realistic painting. His influence can be traced in the work of Thomas Eakins, Frederick Remington, Meissonier of France and, most recently, the English artist, Francis Bacon.

In 1894 Muybridge returned to his birthplace, Kingston-on-Thames, England. Except for one last visit to America in 1896-97, he lived there for the rest of his life. Two books appeared, the proceeds from which probably were his mainstay: *Animals in Motion* (1899) went into five printings; *The Human Figure in Motion* (1901) into seven printings. He died on May 8, 1904. His books have recently been reprinted by Dover Publications Inc., New York.

To put Muybridge's place among the early photographers in perspective, it is only fair to mention Carlton E. Watkins (1829-1916) again. Both he and Muybridge were born within a year of one another. The son of a hotel-keeper in New York, Watkins was twenty-two years old when he came west seeking fortune. One of his jobs in 1854 was to fill in for a studio photographer. He proved so able that his emloyer kept him on until, in 1861, he went into his own business. In the late summer of that year he made the first of his many visits to the Yosemite.

By the time Muybridge made his first visit to the Yosemite, six years later, Watkins had achieved universal acclaim as a landscape photographer. He had received awards in Europe and South America and, in 1867, had won an international award at the Paris Exposition for his landscape pictures. Artistically, his work surpassed that of the many other photographers in the West.

Admirers of his work included Asa Gray, botanist at Harvard, (for whom Watkins made a series of portraits of trees), Brewer and Whitney of the California State Geological Survey, and the landscape painters, Albert Bierstadt, Thomas Hill, Virgil Williams and William Keith. Bierstadt ordered and received six-hundred dollars worth of Watkins' pictures but to his shame refused to pay for them. Muybridge's influence on painters was on their portrayal of men and animals and birds in motion — on the anatomy of their subjects. Watkins' appeal to the western landscape painters was a recognition of artistry as well as techinques. Today he is acknowledged as the "Master of the Grand View."

Watkins, on his fiftieth birthday, married Frankie, who came to work for him in San Francisco after meeting him when he was in Nevada photographing the Comstock Mines. She was nearly thirty years younger and bore a son and a daughter.

It was, apparently, a happy marriage, although Watkins was away from home a great deal and was continually impoverished, partly through bad luck and partly by being utterly unbusinesslike. He lost, or rather forfeited, a number of his landscape negatives through his bankruptcy which was touched off by the failure of the Bank of California in 1874. By the 1890s he was physically worn out. His work had taken him all along the Pacific Coast and across the Southwest and his eyesight began to fail. By 1903, he was almost totally blind. His studio in San Francisco and all its contents, including a trunk full of his rare daguerreotypes awaiting removal to Sutter's Fort Historical Museum, were burned in the earthquake and fire of 1906. After the San Francisco earthquake, he went to live on a small ranch at Capay, which Collis P. Huntington had deeded to him. In 1910, his family had him committed in Napa State Hospital, where he died in June 1916.

Watkins, Muybridge, and those many other landscape photographers in the West, were as remarkable in their way as were the mountain men. They had to transport their cameras and glass plates, dark-tent, chemicals, and the rest of their gear on the back of pack animals and work in the field under immensely difficult conditions. Whitney records that, on one occasion, Watkins was going into the Yosemite "with material for a big 'take' there and back, over 2000 lbs. of baggage, glass for over 100 big negatives . . ." They were not pathfinders but they were pioneers in landscape photography. The fact that the landscape painters "freely employed Watkins' vision" tells us that they regarded landscape photography as an art in itself. And one advantage the painter had over the photographer was that he did not have to carry the amount of equipment with him or work in the field under harsh conditions. Some of the early landscape photographs are as valuable today as the early landscape paintings. In a New York auction in 1979, fifty-one of Carleton Watkins' photographs were bought for $100,000.

Some nineteenth-century artists also tried their hand at photography, presumably to use it as a tool. In a letter to Frank McDonald, Virgil Williams said he was sending him some photographs he had taken in Knight's Valley and Louis Comfort Tiffany shared with Muybridge, the distinction of being one of the first to take instantaneous photographs of animals and birds.

21

Hilaire Belloc's Honeymoon

Coincidences often follow one another. During time off from ghost-hunting and because of a love for his writing, I read *The Life of Hilaire Belloc,* by Robert Speaight, published four years after Belloc's death in 1953. Among all that I found of interest was an arresting fact. On a June day in 1896, after their marriage in Napa, Hilaire and his bride had come along our road on a honeymoon visit to the Geysers. Belloc's ghost was one I never expected to encounter in Knight's Valley.

Through his books, I'd known him since I learned to read. His *Cautionary Tales for Children,* "designed for the admonition of children between the ages of eight and fourteen years," was published the year before I was born. Once, in my teens, I heard him lecture and, in my mind's eye, I can see still the square-set, bulldog-like figure, dressed in a dark suit. Many of his books — his verse, his essays, his travels, and his historical biographies — have been on my bookshelves since I've owned books.

Hilaire Belloc was born twenty years after Robert Louis Stevenson and, another coincidence, his story was in many ways that of Stevenson's. He loved landscape, hills and the sea, and to walk the open road or sail a boat. Born in France — his father was French, his mother Irish — he became an English subject and lived to the ripe age of 83.

Lifelong friend as he was, I knew nothing about his California days until — for old times sake — I read his biography in Knight's Valley. The story of those days began early in 1890, when three Americans were traveling in Europe: Irish-born and widowed, Mrs. Joseph Smethwick Hogan of Napa, California, and her two young daughters, Elizabeth and Elodie. As good Catholics, the travelers were on a pilgrimage to Rome, although Mrs. Hogan did not then know that Elodie was already inclined to become a nun. The pilgrimage accomplished and crowned by an audience with the Pope, the trio made a leisurely tour of Europe that ended in London before returning home.

There, in June, a friend took the Hogans to have tea at 11 Great
College Street, Westminster, the home of the widowed, Madame Belloc. During
teatime, her young son, Hilaire, walked in and was introduced. He was still a
Frenchman and of course bowed longest before the beautiful, blue-eyed Elodie
with her polished auburn hair.

Soon afterward, Mrs. Hogan, unexpectedly, had to return to America,
and left her daughters under Madame Belloc's supervision in the ground floor
rooms in Great College Street, then unoccupied. Elodie, encouraged by the
constant letters from a priest she had met in Rome, was still considering a
religious life and was indifferent to what soon became Hilaire's complete
devotion. Elodie was a few years older than he. To her, he was simply a
companionable guide about London.

When the Hogan girls left London, Hilaire, nearing tears, threatened to
follow Elodie to California. Back home, the Hogans moved from Napa to San
Francisco, where Elodie was still undetermined which way to turn. The religious
life beckoned, but now six thousand miles away, she missed Hilaire's
companionship. Gertrude Atherton, the novelist and a family friend, recalled
finding Elodie sitting on the edge of her bed one morning, crying into a cup of
cocoa, wanting and not wanting to become a nun, praying that Hilaire would
not come out to her and hoping that he would.

To Hilaire, his threat became a pledge. Telling his mother that he
wanted to visit his cousins in Philadelphia — rather incredibly, she believed him
— he sold the books he had won as school prizes, borrowed twenty pounds
from a friend of his mother's and bought a passage in the steerage from
Liverpool to New York.

Both in New York and in Philadelphia, where he paid his cousins a
brief visit, Hilaire could not fail to notice the placards that advertised California
fruits, wines, preserves, even California flour. And one street vendor in New York
had California violets.

Traveling as light as any itinerant, a sketchbook in his pocket, young
Belloc set out on foot for San Francisco. He had little money left, but certain
talents served him well. He gambled in the widely spaced saloons, and for a
while his luck held. Named for his grandfather, a noted French painter, he had
long practiced sketching and now put it to good account. Over a quarter century
later he recalled the journey in his book, *The Contrast:*

> I was free in those days; and during the months that followed I took my way as I
> would: very often for whole weeks on foot, sometimes riding or driving, here and
> there, then cutting out great spaces through the railway, and then on foot again for
> weeks in the lonely places of the west. I handled the salt dust of the deserts and I
> watched the faces and the gestures of these new men . . . I drew the mountains in
> sepia for my pleasure and their snows. And by the way, having lost my very small
> stock of money at cards (playing against more cunning and older men in a deep
> valley of the hills) I cheerfully procured my further progress by the selling of these
> pictures to mountain men. I would make a good little sketch in sepia of some peak,

and this a lonely fellow on a ranch was very glad to have, giving me in exchange my supper, my breakfast and my bed; and I would go on next day to another, and draw another picture and sell it for another lodging.

A letter written long afterwards to a friend gives us another glimpse of the traveler, as he made his way on foot, for lack of a railway ticket, along the Denver and Rio Grande;

> through the deserts and threading odd and deep canyons by way of the railway embankment, seeing trains go by with people in them and sleeping out and trudging on next morning and marvelling at the rocks and the new sights and sleeping in unexpected houses and so on . . . Wondering about things that don't matter and writing verses in one's head . . . limping into Canyon City and then getting money again and walking over the shoulder of Pike's Peak down on to the Florente and landing up at night in a goods wagon — and so on to the end.

He summed up:"I crossed the great plains, I lingered in the mountains I had granted to me the miracle and vision of California. I looked at last upon the Pacific."

However hard the going, he would ever remember that miraculous moment when the world about him changed. The desert lay behind him and there was a sudden vision of Europe glorified, "It is the cascade of dense forests downward and still downwards and, below, into the paradise of California."

Mrs. Hogan did not fail to show her displeasure when the travel-stained Frenchman, without a cent in his pocket, turned up uninvited on her doorstep in San Francisco, and impertinently it seemed, asked for her daughter's hand. But she had, after all, accepted much hospitality from Madame Belloc in London, and she could hardly refuse to admit Hilaire to her house.

Gertrude Atherton had mixed feelings about Elodie's suitor. He was not an impressive figure, she remembered, when she came to write her *Adventures of a Novelist* and therein included the up and coming and the famous. Hilaire's "hair was long and dusty," she wrote. "His hands and linen were never clean, and his clothes looked as if they had been slept in." One evening Hilaire came to call on her alone, and stayed until four o'clock in the morning:

> He sat huddled over the fire, his hands hanging between his knees, his shoulders above his ears, and talked and talked and talked. Such a flow of words I have never listened to, and every one of these sparkled. From his passion for Elodie and his determination to marry despite Church, Mothers, Youth and Poverty, he passed on to the affairs of the world, and never before or since have I heard anyone discourse so brilliantly . . . I still wondered how Elodie could have fallen in love with him, but when he turned on that extraordinary mind of his at full blast, I could have listened to him for ever. He almost convinced me that he knew more than any statesman in Europe.

Hilaire stayed at the Hogan home only a few weeks. Mrs. Hogan opposed any idea of marriage and, under her domination, Elodie hankered more and more for the religious life. Hilaire took the railroad eastward:

Gertrude Atherton surmised that Mrs. Hogan may have lent him his return passage-money, wanting to get rid of him at almost any price and counting on Mrs. Belloc to repay.

Back on the eastern seaboard, just before sailing for England, Hilaire received Elodie's final "No." Mrs. Hogan perhaps watched over her daughter's shoulder as she wrote and maybe mailed the letter herself. Deeply hurt, Hilaire sadly summed up California "as Paradise, and Paradise never lasts long."

Straightway, Hilaire decided to complete his legal term of service with the French army, though an Englishman by rearing and at heart. Away on service, he asked his mother to send a few extras that would soften the austerity of his service and "If anything comes from America, pray send it on at once." He did not then know that his mother had written to Elodie asking her to stay with her in London, arguing that if she really loved Hilaire there was every good reason why she should marry him now.

He grieved over the loss of a pocket photograph which he had carried with him, and the face he saw when he wrote of the bivouac under the stars was the face of that lost photograph:

> You came without a human sound,
> You came and brought my soul to me
> I only woke, and all around
> They slumbered on the firelit ground,
> Beside the guns in Burgundy.

From time to time some news came in occasional letters from Elodie, from which he learned that Mrs. Hogan had died in 1891, and that Elodie intended to enter a convent in Maryland in the fall of 1895. A month later, having made no vows, she decided finally that she had no call for that life, and quit the convent of her own accord. Late in the January following that news, Hilaire sent a cable: "Elodie write plans won't wait." He had completed his legal years of military service and had spent three years at Oxford. Meanwhile, Elodie evidently had not yet given her final answer on their marriage.

Early in March, Hilaire sailed for New York with his mother. Again he had to borrow the money for the journey, at an interest of five percent. He lectured at various eastern cities before setting out for San Francisco alone, Madame Belloc staying behind in Philadelphia.

The frantic anxiety on this second journey was Elodie's sudden silence. No letter awaited Hilaire in Philadelphia and though he had sent her way-stop addresses across the continent, there was still no word. Elodie had been dangerously ill, but was convalescent by the end of the month and eager to welcome him.

"I had no conception till I got here of what those five years had been," Hilaire wrote to a friend. "My soul had frozen — a little more and I should have done nothing with my life. Thank you for the 100 Dollars. They will form the most useful of wedding presents for I fear the little estate over here in the hills is mortgaged past all hope (and in the present decline of values) and my work does not begin till October."

On June 16, 1896, Hilaire and Elodie were married in Napa —Elodie's birthplace. Although the little estate in the hills was mortgaged, the Hogans were a prominent pioneer family and some of the Hogan cousins owned a good deal of land (they were established in Napa and on the Silverado Trail by 1852). If Elodie's mother had never any use for the young groom, the family as a whole could be proud of him. He had, after all, crossed the plains; not as cousin Ed Hogan's grandparents had crossed, in an ox-cart, but mostly on foot.

Hilaire was now twenty-six. Certainly he had proved his devotion and more besides. As he recalled later in life:

> When one is young then is the time to learn the world . . . I have always been glad that I left school at 17, learnt to plow, reap and sow, shot a lot, went off to America from east to west, walked all over California and Colorado, went into the French artillery and got into Balliol all before I was 22.

He might have added that he won First Class Honors at Balliol, Oxford. His was a proud record for any young man.

Whatever the Hogans and their Napa friends really thought of him, they put on a sumptuous wedding breakfast — Hilaire sent his mother a piece of the wedding cake. Headed for the Geysers, the couple hurried off to take the morning steam train to Calistoga. Along the way through the Napa Valley they would have seen great fields of oats ripening under a warm spell of weather; never was there a season when the grain had grown so rank as that summer, some six feet high. Haying had just begun.

Whether they stayed a day and night in Calistoga before continuing on by stagecoach to the Geysers, I do not know. Nor do I know whether either Elodie or Hilaire had read Stevenson's *The Silverado Squatters.* If so, they would be aware of the many changes in the little town since R.L.S. was there on his honeymoon in June, sixteen years before.

Calistoga had burned almost to the ground. The Springs Hotel had gone along with the rest of the buildings but the town was once again doing a thriving tourist trade. Indeed, the week Hilaire and Elodie arrived, travel was so heavy that Bill Spiers, who now owned a stagecoach line, found it necessary to put on an extra four-horse stage up Mount St. Helena. The newly-built, three-story Magnolia Hotel was a model of convenience, its tables furnished with the best the market afforded, its clerks and waiters attentive and obliging to the guests. The bar was stocked with choice wines, liquors and cigars; hot sulphur baths and a large swimming pool were at hand, as well as good livery and feed stables. The town band gave concerts on the Magnolia's veranda in the evenings.

We often wondered whether Hilaire Belloc knew how alike his own story was to Stevenson's. Both of them had crossed the continent almost penniless to claim their brides, both had gone to San Francisco, both had begun their honeymoon in Calistoga. One thing is certain. Elodie kept a scrapbook and in it was a portrait of R.L.S.

Hilaire and Elodie had several sons and daughters. She died in February 1913. Toward the end, as her speech wandered before she lost consciousness, it was touched with the old California accent which Hilaire had "cured" her of in the first years of their marriage — one thing I did not admire him for doing. Hilaire dressed in black broadcloth for the remaining forty years of his life, until his death at the age of eighty-three in July 1953. In his old age, he would talk much of the beauty of the land he saw in youth, the land he called Paradise. "I sometimes wish I'd remained in California," he said on one occasion.

One of his sons, Hilary A. Belloc, a civil engineer, fulfilled that wish and came to live on de Silve Island in San Francisco Bay. And a grandson, a London architect, who spent a twelvemonth in San Francisco, chose to marry his bride, a granddaughter of one of Hilaire's old school friends, in the same church in Napa where Hilaire and Elodie were wed sixty years earlier. Ed Hogan, a guest at the June wedding of 1896, was too old to attend.

It is surprising how little is known in detail about Hilaire Belloc's time in California, in particular in Napa Valley, and where he and Elodie went besides the Geysers on their honeymoon. Letters to me from his family show they regret this also: "we were too young to question him when we could."

In October 1962, I did hear an echo of both Belloc's and Stevenson's moving footfalls. I had read *Vines in the Sun — A Journey Through the California Vineyards* by Welsh-born, Idwal Jones (1888-1964), who became a California writer, and his book seemed to me to resemble in style and spirit Belloc's most famous book, *The Path to Rome*. Shortly after reading *Vines in the Sun,* I copied down this verse inscribed on one of the display wine barrels at the Buena Vista Winery on the outskirts of Sonoma.

> Back of the wine is the Vintner,
> And back through the years, his Skill;
> And back of it all are the Vines in the Sun
> And the Rain
> And the Master's Will.

Had the poet worked the words of the title into the verse, or had Idwal Jones taken them from the verse for his title? I wrote to ask him, and made some mention of Belloc's *Path to Rome*. He replied:

I had all but forgotten that vineyard book which is juxtaposed, on your hospitable shelf at least, with Belloc's magnificently Anglo-Saxon account of his tramp to Rome. No doubt you are aware that he was also a haunter of St. Helena whilst wooing the lady he married.

The title of *Vines in the Sun* was original with me. About two years after the book was published, Mr. and Mrs. Bartholomew, who found it to their liking, worked the title into the rhyme affixed to the exhibition barrel in their wine-cellar. The lines are charmingly wrought. And they were kind enough to send me a photograph of the barrel.

I was in Napa Valley but two or three times, and then only for brief visits, and the impulse was my admiration for *Silverado Squatters,* which I think incomparable, and have read thru a hundred times or more. But the first visit left a deep impression on me, and enough to carry me through a couple of books in which I made it a setting.

For some reason or another I did not follow up the statement that Belloc was "a haunter of St. Helena whilst wooing the lady he married." Two years after he wrote to me, Idwal Jones died, just short of his seventy-seventh birthday, in Laguna Beach, where he had lived since the 1930s.

22

Jack London's Wolf House

We should have known. But each valley in the Coast Ranges is so much a world of its own and so distinct, one from another, that it came to us as a surprise to discover — casually as we did — that we had another ghostly neighbor who ranks with Stevenson as a writer of adventure stories.

Jack London, author of *The Sea Wolf, The Call of the Wild* and many other books, had lived near Glen Ellen, overlooking the Sonoma Valley, also known as the Valley of the Moon. The newspaper announced that the state was about to dedicate a park in his memory.

We went there one day in late fall. All around Glen Ellen the leaves of the native grape vines were clear yellow, a cascade of sunlight pouring over the staircase of the supporting trees. The village extended an atmosphere of a quiet backwater with its modern eating place on one corner. A faded frame building with an old-time facade on another corner housed a general store and the post office.

The way to the park leads up a side road by the post office to a high plateau in a circle of hills, with the Valley of the Moon spread below. The park comprises forty-eight acres of the vast ranch Jack London gradually acquired. From 1905 to September 1911, he lived nearby at Wake Robin Lodge. Then he moved to the ranch. Included within the park boundaries are the ruins of his dream, Wolf House, which burned before he could complete it, as well as the house of Happy Walls built by his second wife, Charmian, three years after his death, and now furnished with mementos of his life and work. In a nearby hillside grove of trees, beneath a big red lava rock, is his burial place.

We went first into Charmian's spacious, stonewalled house to find in the big living room (twenty-five by forty feet), the story of Jack London's life, the behind-the-scenes view of his phenomenally successful writing career. Looking at one exhibit after another we pieced together the story of the hectic years.

Born in San Francisco in 1876, of a quite ordinary family, the boy took early to romantic reading, borrowing every dime novel he could get in his hand. Later, living in Oakland, he discovered the free reading room of the public library. Growing older, he sailed a skiff on San Francisco Bay, frequented the harbor saloons, and became acquainted with an opium smuggler. He worked in a cannery, a jute mill, as a pinsetter in a bowling alley, as a school janitor and as a fish patrolman for the State of California. Between times he adventured as oyster-pirate and, at seventeen, as a boat-puller on a seal-hunting schooner bound for Japan and the Bering Sea. Home again, he was soon off "riding the rods" to Omaha, thence across the middle west and the east as a common "hobo" and then to the Klondike in search of gold.

He began to write. There is the famous letter he wrote in 1900, when he was twenty-four years old, in which he defined his writing ambitions:

> I am writing for money; if I can procure fame, that means more money. More money means more life to me. I shall always hate the task of getting money; everytime I sit down to write it is with great disgust. I'd sooner be out in the open wandering around most any old place. So the habit of money-spending, ah God! I shall always be the victim.

All around in the House of Happy Walls is evidence of his early progress as a writer. "Lord, what stacks of hack I'm turning out!" Night and day, working on a rented typewriter, he wrote tramp stories, sea stories, fish-patrol stories and Klondike stories with which he battered editors all across the country.

First acceptances were meager: five dollars each for two tales Bret Harte published in the famous San Francisco magazine he started, *The Overland Monthly.* Then seven dollars and fifty cents a tale. The first pay-dirt strike of two cents a word was elsewhere. His determination and drive was brought home to us when we looked at one exhibit: fifty rejection slips on one manuscript alone.

In 1903, with *The Call of the Wild,* Jack London became a best-selling author. From then on he went up and up — and so did his expenses. "I wonder if ever I'll get clear of debt."

Keeping open house to a retinue of ten to twenty relatives and tramps who stayed for long periods, went hand in hand with turning out up to four-thousand words a day. Divorce, a second marriage, travels as a newspaper correspondent, other restless and incessant wanderings, the building of *The Snark* — a forty-three foot ketch, rigged like English boats on Dogger Bank, named from Lewis Carroll's *The Hunting of the Snark* — then the buying of a farm of 129 acres near Glen Ellen in 1905, and constant additions that brought the total to thirteen-hundred acres before he died, are all part of the London story. That story is of a young man who joined the Socialist Labor Party and backed revolutionary causes but enjoyed living as a capitalist with, as his wife put it, "a princely ego."

The cream of the extraordinary accumulation of Jack London's treasures, his "gear" as he called it, was all around us. There was a complete set of first editions of all his works. Jack London summed up his works when, after

110

completing *The Human Drift* on what proved to be his last birthday, he said: "I celebrate my fortieth birthday, my fiftieth book, my sixteenth year in the writing game."

Along with the books on exhibit is a collection of original illustrations, letters and manuscripts. The walls around present a strange assortment of treasure-trove he brought back from his travels: South Sea Island curios, a cannibal chief's full dress of bright-colored bird skins, Melanesian weapons, Colombian pottery, Tahitian Kava bowls, a Solomon Islands carving set, Egyptian cats, Indian weaving, oriental enbroideries, a shrunken head, tusks, all representative of a giant inventory and revealing how acquisitive a poor boy become rich can be.

There is no hint of extravagance, however, in a small side room. Once Charmian's library, it is now refurbished into a duplicate of Jack London's workshop in the nearby ranch house which is not a part of the park. The tools of his trade are assembled here: a typewriter that by today's standard would be pronounced unusable, fit only for the dump, and chairs that look about as comfortable as wooden stools. The roll-top desk, a fine one, was especially made for him from the wood of the California Laurel, grown in Oregon and there called the Oregon Myrtle.

From here, we walked the half-mile trail to the Wolf House. On either hand, groups of tall redwoods stood out as sentinels above the lesser maples and madrones. Some of the one-hundred thousand eucalyptus trees from Australia Jack London had planted had grown into a rag-and-taggle army of ill-nourished conscripts beside the noble native trees.

We came upon the Wolf House suddenly, in a clearing of one of the redwood groves and hidden from any passing view. The tall chimneys, so tall that even the redwoods scarcely diminish them, stand above massive fireplaces, stone arches, loggias, and a central reflection pool. The whole confronted us so abruptly we felt as if Jack London himself stood in the pathway wondering why we were trespassing and invading his privacy. But the stark ruin of the giant house was mute.

All through 1912, story by story, he had watched his dream taking shape as four-horse wagons hauled the redwood logs and his big draft horses, four by four, hauled the great red-amethystine boulders up the mountain from a quarry three miles across the valley.

"The stone house grows," London exulted. So did the cost.

London needed fifty-thousand dollars to meet the cost of construction the following year and mortgaged everything in sight, including his own and his sister's cottage. August 18, with but three-hundred dollars in the bank and large obligations pressing, he negotiated another mortagage so that he could push on and complete the Wolf House before winter set in.

On August 22, 1913, three nights later, flames and smoke were seen rising straight in the windless night when the Londons were aroused. Jack drove unhurriedly to the scene. "What's the use of hurry?" he asked. "If that is the big house burning, nothing can stop it now." By the time he reached the scene, the beautiful red-tile roof had clattered down inside the massive stone walls and the walls were no more than a shell.

"Why don't you cry, or get excited, or something?" a neighbor asked as Jack London walked quietly about, directing the firefighters. "What's the use?" he answered. "It won't rebuild the house . . . though it can be rebuilt." It is now thought that the Wolf House probably burned by spontaneous combustion, however Jack always believed that some unknown hand or hands had fired it.

Hardly were the ashes cooled that disastrous summer night before he had work crews cutting and stacking redwood logs against the day when the logs were properly seasoned. Before that day came, on November 22, 1916, he died.

Today the Wolf House personifies Jack London. It is as much his portrait as the one that looks down from the walls of Charmian's house. Like so much of his writing style, the theme of the Wolf House was the strength of felled redwoods and enormous hand-blocked stones, of the struggle of the individual to build a castle from rough-hewn native material.

Charmian, asked so often why Jack London, a socialist and friend of the common man, should build so large a house, explained it clearly. He liked large and enduring things. He wanted a spacious place for himself and for his friends to breathe in. Also, he wanted a place for the permanence of his treasures, his curios, blankets, books, his "gear." With a foundation measuring roughly eighty feet from corner to corner, with a two-story living room and gallery, guest rooms, a sleeping tower for himself, quarters for Charmian, a library, servants' quarters and a "stag" room for men to lounge and play billiards below the high hall or living room, he wanted his house to be the most beautiful house in the west. As Charmian summed up: it should be thought of, in relation to Jack, not as a mansion, but as a big cabin, a lofty lodge, a hospitable tepee, where he could stretch himself and beam upon the world that gathered by his log fires.

We explored the ruin. We came across the splendid retaining-wall of mossy gray stone on one seemingly disused driveway, a wall which Jack London had his entire crew building on the Monday following Friday's fire. None of those who came to see the Wolf House while we were there saw this way in, to their loss.

The driveway's entrance to the house is flanked by two sky-high redwoods, each growing as two trees in one — two straight columns from a broken bole in youth now become a two-pillared gateway of a height and majesty unsurpassed.

We stayed there until the light was going. There was still time to go up to the knoll a short way from the Wolf House where Jack London's ashes are buried, near a small paling-fenced cemetery enclosing the graves of little David and Lily Greenlaw, children of a former occupant of the ranch. The little boy had died in 1876, the year Jack London was born. London had once said to Charmian, "If I *should* beat you to it, I wouldn't mind if you laid my ashes on the knoll where the Greenlaw children are buried. And roll over me a red boulder from the ruins of the big house. I wouldn't want many to come."

The big red rock which marks his grave was one that had been hauled across the valley for the Wolf House, but which the contractor had discarded as being too porous. "Leave it here — we'll find a use for it," Jack London had said, and there it was left until six horses drew it up the steep knoll to the grave site, and the ranch hands rolled it into place.

Our visit to Glen Ellen brought home another coincidence. Two great storytellers of their time, by a freak of chance and within a few years of each other, came to what was still a rather remote area. It was no Left Bank or Greenwich Village, but undeveloped country, sparsely populated by plain, hard-working farmers, woodsmen and hunters. Stevenson came from his father's home in Edinburgh — the home of a successful and respected engineer — to the Napa Valley. Jack London came from the waterfront and oyster flats of San Francisco Bay to the Valley of the Moon. Jack London's ranch is only about twenty miles by crowflight from Silverado. His bestseller, *The Call of the Wild,* was published just twenty years after Stevenson's *Treasure Island.*

Jack London came along our road to the Geysers just after the 1906 earthquake to survey the damage in the countryside around. Once he went up the mountain on pilgrimage to Silverado, for Stevenson was one of his heroes; "as a story-teller there isn't his equal," he wrote. One of the main exhibits in Charmian's dining room at the park is a set of the Stevenson's dinnerware, a quite simple pattern, with a green border on a white background that Jack brought back from Samoa.

There were things other than writing the two men had in common; one so frail and one so husky. Both loved the sea, both died around the same age —Stevenson at 44, London at 40. Both were Socialists and espoused the cause of the underdog.

The politics of these men are of little account now they themselves are dead and gone. They live on in their books. The world beats a path to the site of the assayer's office at the Silverado mine and to Jack London's Wolf House ruin — more than 106,000 visitors walked through the woods to see it the year after we did and the number increases year after year.

23

The Mountain

As our neighbors had foretold, the mountain became part of our lives. We came to know it as one knows a near yet aloof friend of inscrutable countenance. We learned that by geological reckoning it was a young mountain, a mere 500,000 years old; to us it was as old as Time.

Until the coming of the gold-seekers to California, it had been left almost entirely to the Indians and to nature but since then great changes have taken place. Repeated fires destroyed much of the virgin forest that once covered even its upper slopes, so that only a scattering of the lofty sugarcone pines that once crowned its summit remain. Its steep, rocky sides have been looted by loggers and mined for whatever prospectors could find of value. Even the Indians found use for cinnabar, the ore from which mercury is obtained; it gave them ceremonial vermillion body-paint. Later, its pinkish-grey stone, ryolite, which a fiery sunset can warm and deepen until it glows rose-red, was used to build the bridges and the early dressed-stone wineries. Luckily, man's pounding fist against the mountain has left few visible signs of disgrace. Time and new growth have largely obliterated the scars of old.

The mountain has had a different meaning for many different men: so has its outline. To Robert Louis Stevenson, the immense silhouette along the eastern horizon, as seen from Knight's Valley, resembled a ship. To Andy Tajha, our carpenter-builder, it was the form of a woman lying on her back, face upwards to the sky.

"You can't mistake it," he declared, tracing the figure from left to right with his hammer handle. "It was the Russians who named her Saint Helena — ask any old-timer in the valley, many say it was a Russian princess who named it. They left a plaque to prove they reached the top, it's near the fire lookout tower on the north peak."

Sometime we would have to make our own ascent of the mountain to see the fire tower — the modern Spy-glass — and the Russian marker,

114

by driving up the Forest Service road that leads from the northeastern slopes — on the other side of the mountain from the trail the Russians would have followed. It is no road for the timid, we were warned, though an improvement over the old saddle-road. But first we had to have permission and then get the keys to the gate that bars the road from casual passersby.

One midsummer day we set out. We got permission and the keys from Mr. Claude Russell, whose mountain holdings included the land around the lookout tower. We found him, a big, kindly man, at his trout farm amid the firs and redwoods at the northeastern base of the mountain. Readily he lent us the keys to the doubly padlocked gate and told us that it was six miles from gate to peak. And, to our surprise, we learned that a young woman, Mrs. Kit Horn, was the firewatcher.

"I've telephoned Kit and she's expecting you. She'll be right glad to see you. It's a bit lonely up there you know."

Shortly, the nose of our car pointed up, we were scraping around turns barely wide enough for us to pass, gaping over ledges that dropped hundreds of feet below. The road would seem to vanish: a chasm yawned on one side, a sheer cliff above on the other, but we rounded those hairpin bends, the car's wheels spewing rocks and dust, and kept on climbing.

The radiator was boiling when we gained the summit, a level space, bare of trees and strewn with rocks and windlashed manzanita bushes. The fire-tower, stark and white, faced the gale-like winds.

Kit Horn hailed us from a turret of glass high above, and we climed three long flights of wooden stairs to her perch. Trim in pressed dark trousers, surrounded by maps, direction finders, plotting instruments, a telescope, shortwave radio, small electric stove and refrigerator and a loaded rifle to ward off bears and other intruders, Kit Horn looked a highly competent fire-guardian of our region.

"Of course, I know you," she said in greeting. "You live in the house with the new terra cotta tile roof." And she showed us, through the telescope, the speck of roof far below that made us her neighbors and wards. But we needed no telescope to see the view.

Our own valley and Napa and Sonoma valleys spread out below us with their vineyards, orchards and pasture land. Southward, beyond the valleys' wooded rims, was San Francisco, the Bay burnished by the sun. Eastward was Clear Lake, and beyond it, beyond the jumbled panorama of hills and mountains, lay the rich Sacramento Valley, the great basin of California, framed by the Sierra Nevada and the Coastal Ranges. Westwards and northwards was the Redwood Empire: there was the great horseshoe of the Russian River and beyond, bounding the Empire on the west, lay the Pacific Ocean. On some rare crystal-clear days, Kit Horn told us, one might pick out, far to the southeast, the jagged outline of the High Sierra; and far to the north, that of the Cascades' snow-capped Mount Shasta and Mount Lassen.

We asked about the Russian marker and Kit told us that it was a replica of one found on the north peak by a physician from Petaluma in 1853. The doctor had "lifted" the original, taken it home, made a paper rubbing of the surface and then placed the plate in a San Francisco museum for safe-keeping. Like so many relics, the plate was lost during the earthquake and fire of 1906.

Luckily, the paper rubbing was preserved in a drawer of the doctor's desk. A replica was made from it and placed on the north peak of the mountain in 1912, as a part of the ceremonies marking the centennial of the Russian founding of Fort Ross, their settlement on the Sonoma coast. Another version of the removal of the Russian plate is found in Robert A. Thompson's *Historical and Descriptive Sketch of Sonoma County* (1877). This states that the plate was discovered in 1853 by Dr. T.A. Hylton and a copy of it preserved by Mrs. H.L. Weston of Petaluma.

Kit Horn directed us down to where the plate was set in a block of tufa rock. Engraved on it in Russian characters was the inscription

June, 1841

Russians

I. G. Voznesensky and E. L. Chernykh

But who named the mountain? And was it named after a saint, a ship, or a princess?

24

A Thought-Provoking Label

Although there are traditional stories about the naming of Mount St. Helena, place-name authorities say flatly that no evidence has yet been found to show when and why and by whom the mountain was so named. We did not expect to come up with any solution to the puzzle but, in comparing fact with fiction, we did discover some things that are little known and of which historians seem unaware.

According to tradition, the mountain was named thrice, on three separate occasions. Each name-giver spoke a different language, but all three bestowed the same name.

First, there was the Spanish monk. Padre Jose Altimira, a Franciscan trained in Europe, who (according to tradition), on his journeying, carried a bag of mustard seed with a hole in it. As he jogged along on his burro, a trickle of seed dropped through the hole and he traced his way back a few months later by a ribbon of growing gold.

History records that in 1823, Altimira reconnoitered the as yet almost unknown valleys north of San Francisco in search of a site for a new mission. He chose the Sonoma Valley and founded a mission — the last of the line — at what is now the town of Sonoma.

During his reconnoiter, Altimira is known to have traversed the Napa Valley. If the traditional story has any truth in it, he must have continued northwards through Knight's Valley too. Only from there could he see the long silhouette that, so the story goes, for him instantly recalled the effigy of Sainte Helena in the Abbey of Hautvilliers, near Rheims, France. Was not the mountain a gigantic natural reproduction of that ancient effigy, and the foothills as the folds of her drapery. "Sainte Helena!" he cried.

The second claimants are the Russians. The story current in the 1840s was that Count Alexander Rotchev, Governor of the Fort Ross colony, and his wife Helena, née the Princess Gagarin and a niece of the Tsar, also climbed the

mountain along with Voznesensky and Chernykh, and it was the
Princess who named the mountain after the Russian Empress. When it was
realized that the name of the empress in 1841 was Alexandra, the story was
changed — the princess named the mountain after Russia's patron saint.

     This, the most popular story locally, has grown with the telling and
become a highly romanticized tale that is pretty wide of the mark. Alexander
Rotchev was never a count, although he was a nobleman. It seems doubtful that
Princess Gargarin was a niece of the Tzar since the Tzar and his two brothers all
married foreigners, two Germans and a Pole. One sister married a German
nobleman and the other was sought by Napoleon, who was rejected. The
Princess' father was Prince Sergie Gagarin, Director of St. Peterburg's theaters.
And Russia's patron saint is not St. Helena but St. Nicholas.

     Lastly, tradition makes a claim for the Yankee sea captain, Stephen
Smith. The records show that three years after the Russians withdrew from Fort
Ross, the Mexican governor granted Smith a large portion of their former
holding, near the present fishing port of Bodega Bay. Along with land,
presumably, went a surplus ship the Russians left behind; its name the *Saint
Helena*. The rest of the story is self-evident. Smith named the mountain he could
see from the ridge above Fort Ross after the Russians' ship.

     However, Russian ships named after saints did not prefix the name
with "Saint." Hence the Russian ship *Helena* was in fact *Saint Helena*.
Incidentally, the ship which Rotchev took to America via the Horn in 1835 was
the *Helena*.

     Let us turn now from tradition to known facts, to coincidence and
surmise. The fact that the names of Count Rotchev and his wife were not
engraved on the plate surely rules out the romanticized story that they ascended
the mountain with Voznesensky and Chernykh on that June day in 1841.

     Ilya Voznesensky was a naturalist and an artist. He was twenty-four
years old when he was sent to Russian America by the Zoological Museum of
the Imperial Russian Academy of Sciences in St. Petersburg (now Leningrad) to
collect for the Academy's museums. Taking the usual route around the Horn to
Sitka, he left there on the first of July aboard the same ship Rotchev had sailed
on — the *Helena* — and thirteen days later reached Bodega Bay. On the first of
August he proceeded to Fort Ross and began "to collect a rich harvest of
acquisitions in all branches of natural science and ethnography."

     Egor Chernykh was a Moscow-trained agronomist sent to Fort Ross
four years earlier to expand the settlement's agricultural frontier inland. His
small ranch house, ten miles inland from Bodega Bay, was stark, but had the
customary Russian bathhouse. His plantings included fruit trees and some two-
thousand grape vines, and the agricultural and meteorological records he kept
over the four-year period were the first and the best of the kind in pre-American
California. (Voznesensky's memoir raises a question as to whether his explorer-
companion was Chernykh, the agronomist, or another: the memoir refers to

"Afonasii Chernykh" yet the initials on the metal plate are E.L.)

In May 1841, the two men explored the Russian River and named four of its tributaries; two after themselves, the other two after Commandant Rotchev and Olkhovka (meaning "alder" creek). In June they made the ascent of Mount St. Helena, "one of the highest mountains, which has never previously been climbed," Voznesensky noted. The plate they left at the summit was, no doubt, made at the Fort Ross forge.

Voznesensky's memoir suggests that the ascent was made in early June. The choice of the name for so important a landmark may well have been decided upon after the explorers' return to Fort Ross. Since the Russians, like the Spanish, often named land forms on the feast day they were discovered or traversed, the mountain could have been named after Saint Helena, whose feast day, according to the Russian church calendar, falls on June 3rd (Old Style). Or the mountain may have been named after Governor Rotchev's wife, Helena. The names of the only other important personages at Fort Ross were already given to the Russian River tributaries.

One thing is certain. Before Voznesensky left Fort Ross, the mountain was known as "m. St. Helenae." Voznesensky's "rich harvest of acquistions" included a collection of plants. This collection came to light in the 1930s and although some well-informed botanists are now aware of its existence, historians and place-name authorities seem to have overlooked it.

The story of Voznesensky's plant collection is told by John Thomas Howell, botanist for many years, and now botanist emeritus of the California Academy of Sciences, in an article "A Collection of Russian Plants," published in *Leaflets of Western Botany*, Vol. II. No. 2 (April 1937, San Francisco).

Some time in the mid-1930s, Soviet scientists came across a box in the basement of the once "Imperial" Russian Academy of Sciences in Leningrad. The box contained Voznesensky's dried plants collected during his stay at Fort Ross and Bodega. The forgotten herbarium specimens were sent from Leningrad to the Arnold Arboretum in Massachusetts, with a request that the plants be identified. Some of the dried plants were labeled in faded Russian script as having been gathered in California. Accordingly, the Arnold Arboretum forwarded the bundle to botanist Howell.

It was a rare occurrence in itself, wrote Howell, for a collection of herbarium specimens to encircle the earth in order to be named: from California to St. Petersburg via Alaska and Siberia, and then back to California via Western Europe and across the Atlantic Ocean and the North American continent. Moreover, the dried plants were back to less than one hundred miles from where they were collected nearly one hundred years ago.

Next, Thomas Howell rounded out perhaps the longest homecoming of any plants by noting that the dried specimens were fairly representative of the flora of present-day Sonoma County. A number were obviously from the coastal hills and mesas in the immediate vicinity of Fort Ross and others were from the chaparral of the interior hills and mountains, some certainly from Mount St. Helena.

A few of the specimens bore labels indicating exactly where they were found. There was, for instance, a buckwheat from Bodega and an everlasting from "fl. Slavjana" (Russian River). A mariposa lily, two snapdragons, an Indian pink and other plants were marked clearly in Latin script: "m. St. Helenae et desertum St. Rosae." This, as Thomas Howell noted, is a thought-provoking label.

Such evidence suggests, but provides no positive proof, that the Russians named the mountain. Voznesensky and Chernykh's ascent postdated Father Altimira's reconnoiter in 1823. The Russians at Fort Ross were on friendly terms with the Mexican soldiers at the Sonoma garrison, and the padres at the Franciscan mission there, and may well have heard about Altimira's explorations.

Lastly, there is Bayard Taylor's description of the mountain when he passed through Knight's Valley on his way back from the Geysers in September 1859. This is as thought-provoking as Voznesensky's label, for he repeats the story of the Russians' naming the mountain, yet saw it through Altimira's eyes. Taylor's is, perhaps, the oldest reference to the Russians' naming:

> The pass opened into a circular valley, behind which towered, in the east, the stupendous bulk of Mount St. Helene. This peak received its name from the Russian settlers, as a compliment to the Grand-Duchess Helene. It is generally called St. Helena by the Americans — who, of all people, have least sense of the fitness of names. The mountain, 5000 feet high, rises gradually above all the neighboring chains. As seen from this point, its outline strikingly resembles that of a recumbent female figure, hidden under a pall of purple velvet. It suggests to your mind Coreggio's Magdalen, and a statue of St. Cecilia in one of the churches of Rome. The head is raised and propped on the folded arms; the line of the back swells into the full, softly-rounded hip, and then sweeps away downward in the rich curve of the thigh. Only this Titaness is robed in imperial hues. The yellow mountains around are pale by contrast, and the forests of giant redwood seem but the bed of moss on which rests her purple drapery.

In September, when Taylor saw the mountain, the grass was dry and straw-colored, hence "the yellow mountains." It is hard to imagine that he could possibly have written as detailed a description without stopping his horses to take a long look at the scene, and make notes of what he saw. Had he heard the story about Altimira and, finding Altimira's impression valid, used and embroidered it, and changed the resemblance of the mountain to a European effigy he himself had seen? Was it, after all, Altimira who had given the mountain a name which was obviously an entirely appropriate name for the Russians to retain?

One day, perhaps, somebody will find *the* answer either in the archives of Mexico City or in those of Leningrad. *California Place Names,* edited by Erwin G. Gudde, states that the first mention of the name, "as far as could be ascertained," is in a report on the Geysers in the *American Journal of Science and Arts,* November 1851. Voznesensky's plant label now outdates that statement and sets it back ten years to June 1841.

      "m. St. Helenae et desertum St. Rosae." *Desertum* — desert also means wilderness. Which had Voznesensky in mind? The land was then wilderness. Also, for one accustomed to the countryside around Fort Ross, protected from the heat by summer overcast and buffeted by ocean winds, the shadeless plain about Santa Rosa would, in June at least, be in striking contrast, in comparison as hot and dry as a desert. Inland, the carnival of wildflowers would be over; the grass on the foothills already golden, but a handful of flowers still to be found here and there. Every time I came across a snapdragon or a scattering of the lovely sunlit-yellow mariposa lilies on our sunburnt foothills, I thought of Voznesensky and that bundle of dried plants that had for so long been forgotten.

25

The Sea Otter Fur Trade

It was Voznesensky's ghost that beckoned us to Fort Ross — not once, but many times. The fort, a somewhat incongruous structure, stands alien and alone on a bluff above the sea. For the twenty-nine years it served as headquarters for Russian activities in Northern California it was a thought-provoking citadel that Spain, Mexico, England and the United States of America wished to erase.

If the sequence of events had been different, if the sea otter had not been hunted almost to extinction, if Spanish officials in Mexico had been willing to trade, the chances are that the Tzar of Russia would have had far more territory than Alaska to sell to the United States at a later day.

Why, in that momentous year of 1812, when Britian and American were at war with one another, when Napoleon was in retreat from Moscow, and Moscow itself was in flames, did the Russians establish a settlement so far from home?

The answer is best comprehended in a brief review of the sea otter fur trade and the race for possession of the Northwest Coast. This was the name given by the British and Americans in the late eighteenth century to that part of the western coast of North America extending from Northern California to the Bering Strait and inland from the Rocky Mountains to the Pacific Ocean.

Long before Fort Ross was founded, Russia had entered the North Pacific being the first to do so. Vitus Bering, a Dane in the service of the Russian government, made two exploratory voyages from Siberia to Alaska and the Arctic. On the first, 1728 to 1730, he found the passage later named the Bering Strait. On the second voyage, eleven years later, he discovered the Aleutian Island chain, but his ship was wrecked on an island during a December storm and Bering did not survive.

The survivors, forced to winter there, trapped the docile sea otters that teemed in the offshore shoals. Their pelts gave extra protection against the Arctic cold. When spring came, the ships were repaired, loaded with bundles of blue fox, fur seal and some nine-hundred sea otter skins. By August they were safely back at their home base.

Furs were one of the items that Russia traded with China, for the Chinese had no wool: the poor wore layers of cotton clothing, the rich wore silk and furs. The black-brown, silk-soft, shimmering fur of sea otter was recognized as the finest of all. Chinese mandarins were willing to pay exhorbitant sums for what became their symbol of wealth and status. Sea otter pelts were made into robes for the men and capes for their wives. The fur was also used for hats and gloves, for sashes and belts decorated with precious gems, and as trimming to silk garments.

When the Russians realized that the otters' stronghold was in the kelp beds of the Aleutian Islands, the stampede to the rich hunting grounds was on. Ships and men were lost but no hardship stopped the advance. Private fur-trading companies were formed, and the sea-faring Aleuts, brothers to the Eskimo and naturally skilled in hunting sea otter, seal, sea lions, ivory-tusked walrus and whales, were forced to work for them.

To the Aleut, sea otter pelts were ordinary and were used as bed coverings and clothing for the women. The men wore two garments, winter and summer: an undershirt, a seabird feather parka that dropped below the knee, and over it a long one-piece sealskin jacket. Their peaked or conical wooden rain hats were quite stylish, painted with magic designs, decorated with sea lion whiskers and sometimes further adorned by a small carved ivory ornament. Four sea lion whiskers stood for one sea lion killed. The hide of a sea lion was used in covering their baidarkas (kayaks), the blubber for oil, the sinew for cordage and the bladders were made into waterproof parkas, and containers in which down feathers were stored, and sent to Sitka.

The Aleuts' two-man baidarkas were made of a large sea lion skin stretched over a light framework of whalebone fitted together and tied with gut. There were two circular holes for the double-bladed paddles and these also were carved out of driftwood. To prevent water from washing into and swamping their craft, the hunters attached their clothing to their baidarka. The Aleut and his boat were one, and the Russians enslaved him.

To turn now from the North to the South. More than two centuries before Bering discovered the Aleutian Islands, the Spaniards had entered the South Pacific and claimed sole supremacy of the Pacific Ocean. After the conquest of Mexico City (1521) and subjection of the Aztec Empire, Spain turned her attention to the mainland of North America.

In 1534, the Bay of Paz in Baja (lower) California was discovered. Eight years later, Cabrillo entered San Diego in Alta (upper) California, and in 1542, Spain's first Viceroy of Mexico instructed him to explore the California coastline. He sailed some sixty miles north of San Francisco, but made no landfall there.

Reports of Russia's activities in Alaska, following Bering's discoveries, made Spain aware that her claim to the entire Pacific Ocean was being challenged. The Viceroy of Mexico was ordered to draw up a plan for the colonization of Alta California. This was threefold in design: the establishment at various points of a presidio, a fort or garrison; a mission to care for the religious life of the colonists and to convert the heathen *Indios* and train them in various skills; and a pueblo for the civilian population.

Gasper de Portola and the Franciscan father, Junipero Serra were joint commanders of the colonizing expedition. The first presidio and the first mission were established in 1769 at San Diego. That same year Portola discovered the Bay of San Francisco (by land and not from the sea) and ten years later, in 1780, construction of a strongly fortified mission was begun at Monterey.

The Franciscans, in their zealous quest for souls to be saved, made the mission by far the most effective arm of the threefold plan. Under the Spanish regime, four presidios, but two really effective pueblos, and twenty-one missions were established. Spain now occupied Alta California as far north as San Francisco. Reassured for the moment that her province was secure, she did not pursue her colonization further north, although navigators were sent to explore the northwest coastline.

Among them were two explorers who anchored in what were to become strategic ports of call. Juan Perez Hernandez anchored in Nootka Sound on the west coast of Vancouver Island in 1774. The following year, Juan de la Bodega y Quadra reached Alaska, and on his way back, put into the bay that was named after him, Bodega Bay, some forty-five miles north of San Francisco.

Spain's failure to colonize north of San Francisco left the way open for rival nations to challenge her claim to the Pacific. Her most formidable rival was Great Britain. England was hardly likely to forget that Sir Francis Drake, on his around-the-globe voyage, spent five weeks in June and July, 1579, on the Northern California coast. He claimed the land for England and named it New Albion. The name appeared on contemporary maps and the Russians perpetuated it well into the nineteenth century.

Two-hundred years after Drake's exploit, England, intent on western expansion, offered twenty-thousand pounds to any British subject who found a navigable passage leading from the Pacific into the Atlantic Ocean. In 1776, Captain James Cook left Plymouth, commissioned to lead an exploratory expedition to the Northwest Coast. He discovered the Hawaiian Islands, proceeded north and during a storm took shelter in Nootka Sound. Continuing north when the storm abated, he reached the Bering Strait, but found no "Northwest" Passage. On the homeward voyage he put in again at the Hawaiian Islands where he was killed by the natives in February 1779.

The many accounts, official and otherwise, of Captain Cook's expedition told the world of the existence of uncounted numbers of sea otter in Pacific waters and the fabulous profits to be had from marketing sea otter pelts in China.

It was soon common knowledge that the range of sea otters extended along the coastline from the Aleutian Islands southward to central Baja California. Nootka Sound, where Captain Cook had seen the greatest concentration of sea otters, became the scene of international rivalry. Great Britain, Spain and the United States made efforts to occupy the port and lay claim to the northwest coastline.

Esteban Jose Martinez was dispatched by Spain's viceroy in Mexico to occupy and fortify the port of Nootka. The fort was completed in June 1788 and Martinez took formal possession in the name of the King of Spain. Two months later the British arrived at Nootka intent on doing what Martinez had already accomplished. Fighting was averted and the issue peacefully settled by the Nootka Convention of 1790 and ratified five years later. The terms provided that Spain surrender Nootka Sound to the British, thus relinquishing her claim to the Pacific which she had held for almost three-hundred years. Nootka Sound was declared open to all nations and became the headquarters for the Northwest Coast traffic.

The United States, having won her independence from Britain, now entered the scene. American merchants had the monopoly of the Northwest Coast lucrative fur trade for some time to come.

New England ship captains set out on what was a two-to-three year voyage. Sailing from Boston they rounded Cape Horn and proceeded some 6,600 miles northward to Nootka where they traded their manufactured wares for sea otter pelts. Having secured their haul, they sailed south to the Hawaiian Islands to obtain fresh foodstuffs, fill their water tanks and take on sandalwood. The Chinese prized sandalwood for its close-grained fragrant hardwood used in ornamental carving. The New Englanders then crossed the Pacific to Canton where they traded furs and sandalwood for spices, silks and porcelain, then set course for home across the Indian Ocean and around Africa's Cape of Good Hope.

Meanwhile, the Russians had broadened their trade with China. In the year the account of Captain Cook's voyage was published, they began to establish fortified settlements in their fledgling Pacific Empire. Traders, organized into private companies, amassed great fortunes from the sale of sea otter pelts. Fort Kodiak, a base for hunting sea otter, seal and fox, became the center of Russian America.

In 1799, the Russian-American Company was formed; Tzar Paul I granted a charter that gave the company sole right of trade and settlement in the territories of the Pacific Ocean from 55 N.L. to the Bering Strait. The private trading companies were taken over and Alexander Baranov was appointed Chief Manager (in effect, Colonial Governor of Russian America).

To secure his territory, Baranov extended the Russian settlements to the sourthern boundary of his dominion and, in 1804, transfered his headquarters from Kodiak to the new fortified settlement at Sitka (New Archangel). He also made a peaceful collaboration with the Americans who had been trading for furs with the seafaring Indians at Nootka Sound for the past several years. He contracted to supply a New England shipmaster with Aleut hunters in return for a share of the spoils. Similar joint expeditions were arranged and for some years the hunters ranged as far south as the kelp beds of the Santa Barbara Channel.

As the outposts in Alaska increased, and with the ever-uncertain arrival of supply ships before winter closed in, the colonists of the Russian-American Company were too often running short of food. Incessant hunting, to meet the insatiable demand for furs, was also causing a growing scarcity of sea otter and fur seals.

The Company's problem had to be solved somehow. Geographers in St. Petersburg — at that time rated second only to Paris as a center for intellectual activity — reasoned that California, at best only nominally controlled by Spain, might be the answer.

In 1802, the wife of Nikolai Resanov, the Company's chief envoy, died twelve days after the birth of their second child. The Tzar, who had a great affection for the grief-stricken Resanov, decided to send him on a mission to Japan, to the colony of the Russian-American Company and to California. On the eve of Resanov's departure for Japan, the Tzar awarded him a new title, His High Excellency, Grand Chamberlain, the highest rank at court.

The mission to Japan was a failure, and the inspection of the Alaskan colony disquieting because of the conditions that prevailed there. After spending the winter of 1805 with Baranov in Sitka, Resanov purchased an American ship from a New England captain and in March 1806, anchored in San Francisco Bay.

Arguello, commandant of the presidio, was with the Governor Arillaga in Monterey, but his twenty-one-year-old son was in command at the presidio and his sister Maria del al Concepcion, nicknamed "Concha," was with him. On being informed that a strange ship had anchored in the bay, the young Arguello rowed over to investigate and returned to the presidio as fast as he could to tell Concha there would be guests for morning chocolate.

Resanov, a forty-two-year-old handsome man, a head taller than most Spaniards, was splendidly attired. Maria was a rare fifteen-year-old beauty. A week went by before Arguello returned to the presidio, where Resanov had visited daily. During his six-week stay in San Francisco, Resanov made a deal for wheat despite Spain's prohibition against trade with foreign countries. He also obtained Arguello's consent to wed Maria providing that the Vatican grant a dispensation, and the King of Spain gave his approval. One of Resanov's gifts to the Spaniards was a piano originally intended for the Japanese Mikado. This wound up at the Sonoma mission, Altimira himself playing it during the services. As far as is known, this was the first piano in California.

Resanov expected to return in two years to claim his bride. Crossing Siberia on his way home, fatigued, drenched and chilled by freezing winds, he fell ill. Insisting on forging ahead before he was fully recovered, he fainted one day, fell from his horse and was struck on the head by a hoof. He died early in March 1807. The course of California history might have been different if Resanov, the Grand Chamberlain of Russia, had married Maria, the daughter of the Spanish commandant at the presidio in San Francisco.

Baranov was now left with full responsiblity for colonizing what Resanov referred to as "the one unoccupied stretch of California." First of all, he must develop a plantation in New Albion that would supply Sitka with foodstuffs and serve as a base for hunting the sea otter in relatively new waters. This he entrusted to Ivan Kuskov, his chief assistant.

Navigators were sent south to explore the Northern California coastline. One, Shvetzov, in 1807, was the first Russian to anchor in Bodega Bay. The following year, another navigator set up a stake imprinted with the Imperial arms on the Bodega shoreline and claimed the territory for the Tzar.

Next came Kuskov. Although he wore a peg leg he was himself a hunter, navigator and an able administrator. Over a three-year period he made several visits to the Bodega area, and while the Aleuts who accompanied him went to work in their *baidarkas,* Kuskov set out to look for a site for a hunting base, a plantation and a fort. He explored some fifty miles of the Russian River he named "Slavianlea," and by August 1811 was ready to report to Baranov at Sitka.

On the coastline twenty-four miles north of Bodega and seventy-five miles north of San Francisco, he had found a promising site for what was to become the Russian-American Company's farthest outpost; a promontory, a strip of bare tableland about two-miles long and almost half as wide. There was an abundance of timber nearby and a good water supply. Below the promontory was a small cove where cargoes could be loaded and unloaded. It was also suitable for shipbuilding. The open sea off the promontory being too rough for safe harborage, Russian vessels would continue to lie at anchor in Bodega Bay.

Kuskov and a work force of ninety-five Russians and about eighty Aleuts returned to Bodega the following spring. The coastal strip to the north was purchased from the friendly Indians (the Pomo) for three blankets, three breeches, two axes and some beads. On a day the Romans called the Ides of March, March 15, 1812, the construction of Fort Ross began.

26

Fort Ross

Fort Ross — "Ross" was an old form of the word *Rossiia* (Russian) — was formidable for its time. Its thirteen foot high palisade of stout redwood timbers enclosed a quadrilateral of three acres. A seven-sided, two-story blockhouse on the north and a two-story octagonal blockhouse on the south had gun ports on all sides on both upper and lower levels. Each blockhouse was mounted with cannon, and smaller calibre cannon were placed at the entrance gates and within the stockade, perhaps twelve to fifteen pieces in all. Some of the cannon had been abandoned by Napoleon's Grand Army during the retreat from Moscow and transported to Fort Ross by way of Alaska. Sentries with flintlock guarded both gates and blockhouses. Facing the Pacific and backed by steep timber-crested hills, with a cannon and musketry sweep in all directions, the fort was secure from surprise attack.

The settlement contained a number of buildings when completed, including the chapel, the commandant's house, barracks, warehouses, and a bell house.

Outside the palisade were the little houses of some sixty Russian colonists, redwood cabins for the Aleuts, and just beyond the cabins were the the cone-shaped huts of the Pomo Indians. There were kitchens, bathhouses and a number of workshops. At the foot of the bluffs fringing the cove was a small wharf for ships' carpenters, and sheds for storing lumber and the Aleuts' skin boats.

From the blockhouses, and the flagstaff on the bluff above the cove, fluttered the Russian-American Company's flag. Fort Ross was a symbol of Russia's advance in the Pacific and the world regarded it as such.

No attack was ever made upon the fort. The colonists concerned themselves with hunting, raising stock and growing crops, and engaged in various industries vital to their needs.

From the start, Kuskov continued the friendly relationships that

Nikolai Rosanov had established with the Spanish in San Francisco and, in spite of Spain's veto on trading, deals were made and gifts exchanged. As early as 1813, the Spaniards presented Kuskov with horses and cattle, the first to be brought to Fort Ross, and small fruit trees — apple, cherry, peach, pear and bergamot — were acquired at Monterey. Some apple trees apparently came from the homeland.

But as that first decade drew to a close, far-reaching changes were taking place all across the Pacific. Baranov died in 1819. Kuskov, after thirty years in the Company's service, nine of them at Fort Ross, was replaced by a younger man. Mexico won independence from Spain in 1822 and promptly announced that land in California that was unoccupied by Mexicans belonged to her.

Mexico made a gesture that implied so far but no further. The last of the Franciscan missions, the only one that was established under the Mexican regime, was founded at Sonoma in 1823. That same year, the American President proclaimed the original Monroe Doctrine that checkmated any further European colonization on the North American continent.

In the two years following, Russia concluded a treaty first with the United States, and then with Great Britain whereby she agreed to abandon her expansionist policy on the Northwest Coast. No provision, however, was made for a withdrawal from Fort Ross. For a while longer the Russians held on to their farthest outpost.

Fort Ross, was a long way from either Mexico City, London or Washington, D.C. Treaty signing did not put a stop to clandestine trade and social visiting. Nor did it limit Russian hospitality to travelers from afar, drawn by the allure of the unknown, or by their own government's curiosity about so remote an outpost. Even before the founding of Fort Ross, scientists aboard various other foreign expeditions were eager to learn about the flora and fauna of California and the Northwest Coast. Some dropped anchor at Monterey, others in San Francisco and Bodega Bays.

The Russians themselves sent out an expedition in 1815 under Captain Otto van Kotzebue in the *Rurik*. Two scientists accompanied him; Adelbert von Chamisso, poet as well as botanist, and Johanan Friedrich Eschscholtz, a naturalist and a specialist in entomology. In the following year they were in Monterey, San Francisco and Bodega.

The California poppy was one of the plants Chamisso collected and few plants have suffered such international confusion in name-giving as has this lovely flower. The Spaniards called it *Copa de Oro,* cup of gold, but by luckless chance it fell to Chamisso, who was of French parentage, but born and reared in Germany, to classify and give the plant its botanical name. His muse forsook him. He named the poppy for his friend Eschscholtz and the new land, and gave it, in part, a botanical tongue-twister, *Eschscholtzia californica.*

Von Kotzebue did not visit Fort Ross in 1815. Kuskov met him at the San Francisco Presidio, but on his second visit to the Northwest Coast in 1824, he was received there, and Eschscholtz accompanied him. They entered San Francisco Bay toward the end of September, and a small number of Spanish attendants from the San Rafael Mission rode with them on horseback to the Sonoma Mission in November. From there they rode to Bodega and northward along the coastline to Fort Ross. Von Kotzebue stayed for two or three days, but Eschscholtz stayed a week collecting insects, and returned by water. He left Bodega Bay in a baidarka manned by Aleuts and was escorted by a small flotilla. A violent storm near Point Reyes forced the Aleuts ashore to bivouac on the naked rock and make do as best they could with the scant provisions they had with them. When the storm abated, Eschscholtz and the flotilla of twenty baidarkas entered San Francisco Bay.

Von Kotzebue noted that the sea otters were almost exterminated. Domestic animals had, however, steadily increased. Duhaut-Cilly, a French visitor, reported four years later that farming and lumbering were foremost. The slopes around the fort were divided into fields of corn, French beans, oats and potatoes, and surrounded with palisades as protection from wild and domestic animals.

Logging extended over many acres. In Fort Ross cove, California's first shipyard, four two-masted vessels were built. Ranging in size from 160 to 200 tons, they sailed southward as far as San Pedro and northward to Siberia. Long boats, skiffs and rowing boats were also built. Some were sold or traded to Mexicans in the San Francisco Bay area. Entire houses were built, taken apart, carefully numbered section by section, and tranported to Alaska — forerunners of the prefabricated houses of today. Planks of redwood and Douglas fir were also sold to the Californians.

Bricks and domestic pottery made from the local clay were fired in kilns. Soap and candles were made from animal fats. Flour mills were worked by windmills. The master tanner, a Kodiak Aleut, turned hides and skins into boots and shoes and the softer Russian leather. Combs, powder horns and lanterns were fashioned from the horns of steers and oxen. Sheep's wool was carded, spun and woven into clothing and blankets.

Wool, tallow, hides, butter and wood products were the prime exports to Alaska. One visitor to Fort Ross in 1828, recorded that the colony obtained more butter and cheese from its sixty cows than the Spaniards obtained from their numberless herds throughout Alta California. Down feathers from the Farallon Islands packed thirty pounds to each sea-lion bladder container were sent to Sitka; nine such containers in 1827 and eleven in 1828. Thousands of sea birds were killed annually, dried and salted as provisions for the Russian settlements. Even in the first year of settlement, Aleuts had been sent to the Farallons to kill the birds and the sea lions and collect fresh gull and cormorant eggs during the spring season.

No amount of industry, however, made up for the decline in the fur trade. Year by year, the Company was faced with increasing deficits and foreign settlers were edging closer. The situation at Fort Ross became precarious although this was not reflected in life at the fort itself.

In 1838 Alexander Rotchev, who had visited Fort Ross three years earlier, was appointed Commandant. A noted poet and translator, described as a "very good-looking man, in the prime of life," brought his wife (who as already mentioned was the Princess Helena Gargarin), and their three children with him.

Accustomed to life in St. Petersburg, Rotchev and his wife softened the austerity of the Commandant's house and gave it an air of sophistication. White linen sailcloth covered the walls and ceilings. Tapestries and fine carpets were brought in from abroad, and a piano was placed in the parlor. Bowls were filled with flowers from the garden and from the conservatory the Princess had built. There were gay parties. Even the Mexicans helped celebrate the Princess' birthday, thirty of them riding all day from Sonoma to dance the night away.

During the last year of Commandant Rotchev's office, and the last year of Russian occupation of Fort Ross, the French government sent Eugene Duflot de Mofras to report on Mexico and California. A tour of the outlying farms from Bodega to Fort Ross showed each farm had its bathhouse, commodious quarters for the Indians, windmills, handmills, sawmills, granaries, and rooms for drying tobacco. De Mofras noted that the Russians treated the Indians with the utmost kindliness, paid them fair wages in kind, and never abused them. He had this to say of the fort itself, and the hospitality he received there:

> Fort Ross, with its gardens has a superb location. Nothing can surpass the picturesque and spectacular setting which the forests of mammoth pines that form its background supply.
>
> From a personal standpoint, appreciation of the amicable welcome that was invariably accorded our party by the Russian officials during our visits in 1841 cannot be too warmly expressed. The governor of Ross, Alexander de Rotchev, his wife, nee Princess Gagarin, M. Kostromitinov, head of the counting-house, at Sitka, Captain Sagoskin, commander of the sloop *Helena,* and M. Wosneseki (Vozesensky) scientist of the Academy of St. Petersburg, exerted themselves at all times to make our visit at their settlements agreeable.
>
> In addidtion to our reception, which was almost European, they materially assisted in the exploration of various parts of the country by placing at our use numerous relays of excellent horses. . . travelers who have passed long months of privation. . . can fully appreciate the joy of a choice library, French wines, a piano, and a score of Mozart. . . regal hospitality.

Du Mofras would surely have known of Russia's intention to withdraw from Fort Ross before his arrival on the coast, for back in March 1839, the Company had petitioned the Tzar for permission to relinquish the colony. Two weeks later Tzar Nicholas I gave his order: the colonists were to return to Sitka and the fort sold. Rotchev opposed the decision, but to no avail. Offers for sale, first to the Hudson's Bay Company, then to Mexico, were turned down.

Next, John August Sutter was approached. Sutter, a Swiss immigrant, was to become one of California's great adventurer-agriculturists and founder of its capital city of Sacramento. He had received a grant from the Mexican Governor of an enormous tract of land at the confluence of the American and Sacramento rivers. He could use the buildings, livestock and farm implements in his New Helvetia, and also several cannons to strengthen the defense of Fort Sutter. The equipment could be shipped by schooner and the cattle driven overland.

The contract was drawn up at Bodega Bay in September 1841 and the papers signed on December 13 in San Francisco. Rotchev and about a hundred colonists sailed on the last ship for Sitka two weeks later.

It was the end of an era. The hunt for sea-otter fur had begun just a hundred years ago with the death of Vitus Bering in December 1741. In less than a hundred years, the otter herds had disappeared from the kelp beds off the California coastline. The Aleuts, too, had dwindled and those that were left no longer owned their land. As the Russians moved out of Northern California, the first wagon train bringing American settlers climbed over the Sierra Nevada.

Before she left, Madame Rotchev, as the Princess was known to the colonists, wrote to Sutter begging him not to destroy the garden house in which she had spent so many happy hours. But when Sutter's men began dismantling, they had no understanding of the workmanship of Russian carpenters. The twenty-foot square conservatory, with glass windows and doors, was taken in sections to the Sacramento Valley but never reassembled.

After Sutter had shipped all he wanted, only the Russian chapel, the commandant's house, and a few other buildings remained. Probably a number of smaller outbuildings were soon destroyed by grass fires. Eventually, after a successive ownership, Fort Ross and the adjacent land became the property of Sutter's Fort Trustees — later to become the State Park Commission — on March 23, 1906. Twenty-seven days later, the earthquake of April 18 shook the nearby San Andreas fault. The walls of the chapel collapsed. Oddly, the roof and its distinctive cupola survived. Built like the inside walls of a round tent with sixteen naturally bent limbs from madrone trees as rafters, the roof settled down upon the ground intact, like a hen upon her nest.

In due course, the work of restoration began; over the years the commandant's house, the chapel and the stockade were rebuilt. Another disaster occurred in October 1970. The chapel burned to the ground and its one surviving bronze bell that had been cast in a St. Petersburg factory, was destroyed. Again, the following summer, a fire attributed to arson destroyed the roof of the commandant's house. Thanks to various agencies and the generosity of private individuals, restoration of the chapel and the commandant's house was completed in 1974, and the melted chapel bell recast in its original form.

As the fate of Fort Ross was eventually settled by negotiation, so was that of the sea otter. In 1911, an international treaty was signed by Great Britain, Russia, Japan and the United States, protecting fur seals, sea otters and polar bears in the North Pacific from haphazard hunting.

The gentle, frolicsome sea otters were all but exterminated from California water, but in 1916, thirty-one were sighted south of Catalina Island. And as only the Fish and Game Department's personnel knew, there were a few survivors along the rugged Big Sur coastline. In 1939, a newly opened highway gave access to this hitherto inaccessible stretch of the coast, the public discovered a herd of otters at Bixby Creek twenty-five miles south of Monterey. The official count then was about three hundred. As wards of the U.S. Government, the sea otters have slowly increased. The 1976 California Fish and Game census, made by air and from land, tallied 1,561 sea otters distributed over 160 miles of coastline between Shell Beach, San Luis Obispo County to Pigeon Point, San Mateo County, a few miles south of San Francisco. In the Aleutians, they are numbered in the thousands.

27

The Russian-American Company's Flag

I remember two visits to Fort Ross in particular for widely different reasons. One was to retrace Duhaut-Cilly's journey of 1828 by the coast road from Bodega, the other to see the Russian-American Company's flag fluttering on one unique occasion above the blue Pacific.

Duhaut-Cilly, like most of Fort Ross's visitors, came by sailing ship to Bodega Bay, and from there rode on horseback along the road the Russians had built. Its worst difficulty was its steepness, but it was a steepness that horses in relays, and oxen hauling heavy loads, could manage.

It was the first week in June when Duhaut-Cilly arrived at Bodega, in time to see the last flourish of spring flowers and before the chilling summer fogs roll in. Horses, an Aleut guide and several Russians awaited him as he disembarked. Mounting their horses they proceeded northward, and Duhaut-Cilly rejoiced to see the ground

> . . . carpeted with grass mixed with strawberry plants loaded with their fruit, and enameled with a multitude of flowers of all colors. The sea was breaking at the foot of the rocky cliff, where it opposed its snowy foam to the dark color of the rocks, and to the rich verdure of the fields which our horses were treading, without making more sound than if they had walked upon eider-down.

On reaching the Slavianka (the Russian River, now spanned by a steel-concrete bridge) the party was ferried over one by one in a baidarka that only had room for one Aleut and one passenger. Not wishing to remain idle during this precarious passage, Duhaut-Cilly seized a paddle and "dabbled" with it skillfully enough. The horses, relieved of their saddles, swam over as if by habit.

Safely across, the party rode on uneventfully. Presently, the road ran steeply upwards. Duhaut-Cilly wrote:

> We climbed a road so steep that we could hardly understand how our horses were able to hold themselves on it without falling over backward upon their riders . . .

The mountain, whose top we reached not without difficulty and even some danger, was covered with enormous firs, mixed with sycamores, bay trees, and various species of oaks. At a height of three hundred fathoms, we commanded a view of the sea which came beating its base, and whose waves, for us silent, appeared only as little whitish spots, scattered on an azure cloth.

Part of the old Russian road that Duhaut-Cilly traveled, including the steep climb to the crest, is marked today on the map as Sea View Road. It runs parallel to, but high above the modern highway which was blasted and bulldozed from the rocky hillsides lower down and opened in 1925, and it does have advantages that the highway lacks. It is solid, well-drained and less subject to earth and rock slides during the torrential winter rains — slides which can close the lower road for hours, even days. The highway is also narrow with tortuous curves, while the upper road though as steep as a road can be, is comparatively straight and of ample width. On clear days it affords a panorama of seascape and landscape that ranks as one of the most beautiful in all California.

Modern grading and surfacing make Sea View Road incomparably easier for present-day travelers. Even so, we too, in our well-powered automobile, were glad to stop when we reached the crest where Duhaut-Cilly changed horses. Everyone who went that way in the old days stopped there too.

This was a part of the earliest road made by white men between San Francisco Bay and Alaska. Along it came Russians driving their heavily laden ox-drawn carts and wagons. Here, in 1822, the Franciscan Father Payeras, and Canonigo Fernandez, head of all the California missions, rode on mustangs escorted by Captain Don Luis Arguello (later Governor of Alta California) and rested on their way to an official state visit to Fort Ross. Here, on Passion Sunday, April 4, 1824, traveling from north to south, the down way, came Russians bearing gifts of mass bells for the dedication of the Sonoma mission. The bells were, perhaps, from China and similar to those used at the Fort Ross chapel. Other gifts included a hammered brass or copper ewer and basin, wrought iron door hinges, and picture frames.

Continuing on along the crest all was, as Duhaut-Cilly described: the land on either side is not so densely forested, but there are still some enormous oak and bay trees. We stopped again where there was a clear view out over the ocean and Fort Ross appeared as a speck on the coastline. It was almost eerie to stand so high, so immediately it seemed above the sea, without hearing any sound from the impounding waves below.

Duhaut-Cilly said nothing of the inland view; of hill upon hill rolling inland, seemingly endlessly, and far away on the horizon — thirty-three miles by crow-flight — rose the mountain *Sainte Helene.* It was as familiar a landmark to the Russians as it was to us, and a reminder that the ocean was in view of the Spy-glass.

Sea View Road continues some way north of the fort, to descend to the highway by decent grades. But following Duhaut-Cilly, we took what is still today hardly more than a logging road, unmarked on road maps. Duhaut-Cilly said it was "as cruel an incline as the first." We found it more so.

For the only time we could remember in our many years of driving, we had not only to drop into low gear but use both hand and foot brakes as well. Around every curve we prayed we would not meet a logging truck. Only once were we able to pull off the road where it widened a trifle, to cool the hot brakes and our nerves. Below us "through the trees, or above their tops" we could see the Russian fort.

The landscape about the fort is not as Duhaut-Cilly saw it, when the marine terraces were under cultivation. It is more as the Russians knew it in 1812, the year of settlement, than when they left in 1841. The rugged coastline country proclaims itself pretty bleak for farming. Scattered along the level stretches of the coast road is an occasional farm building, ramshackle and paint-peeled. Cultivated acres are rare. Old and beautifully weathered split fences zigzag across the face of the land as witness of later ranchers' holdings. It is an empty, wind-battered country where only sheep move across the barren slopes and only the ospreys, the ravens and the bobcats know what is going on in the brush-choked ravines.

Measured in miles, Fort Ross is not remote but it is so in climate, being either fog-bound or swept by heavy, steady, cool winds much of the year. The bright days in between are miracles of deep blue seas; of rocky, inlet-studded coves, beaches of white sand between bold promontories as far as the eye can see.

Inland, early in spring, the wind-cropped turf is literally carpeted with flowers; lupin and iris and the wild pink and the white wild radish and scores of bright diminutives grow acre by acre along the coastline.

The second visit I remember in particular was made on August 13, 1962, which was one of the rare bright summer days. We went there that day to witness the celebration to mark the 150th anniversary of the completion and dedication of the stockade in August 1812. This time we traveled the roads due west of Mount St. Helena, across the Santa Rosa plain, to join the coast road by the bridge which spans the Russian River where the river flows into the ocean through a narrow strait in the great sandbar.

From there, a little more than half way between Bodega and Fort Ross, the coastal highway, though lower than the Russians' coast road, climbs steeply upward, winding tortuously around rocky hillsides and ravines. Every year the engineers widen and improve this narrow ledge above the sea, but it is never an easy road to drive on foggy days or at night. As the rugged sea-cliffed coastline rises, mountainous ridges rise abruptly from the ocean, and a driver has no time to get more than a risky, cheating glimpse of either the near or the far, except by drawing off the road at one of the turnouts and getting out to look.

Some six miles of horseshoeing in and out along the edges of the steep slopes led us out onto a coastal terrace. Ahead in the distance we saw the sun glinting on the windshields of a congregation of cars, parked between the redwood stockade and the sea.

The wind was blowing so hard down on the point when we got there that we could hardly stand without support. But once we were within the stockade, the wind seemed to go over our heads. Some fifteen-hundred persons were already assembled, waiting quietly until a small boy in blue jeans rang the chapel bell for silence — the bell that had been cast in St. Petersburg and destroyed in the chapel fire of 1970.

Below us was the Pacific, an intense blue; inland to the north, the rolling timber-crested hills. Three flags fluttered in the wind: the Stars and Stripes; the Bear Flag of California; and the Russian-American Company's flag with the black eagle emblazoned on the yellow ground.

In this extraordinary setting, a moment or two after the bell called for silence, six bearded priests, in long gold robes, emerged from the chapel to group themselves on the entrance platform around John, Archbishop of the Russian Orthodox Church of the Western United States. He was robed in purple; his face, a face I shall remember always, smiling, spiritual, beautiful rather than handsome, and on his head the miter, the headdress of his office.

It was quite a feat for the priests in their gorgeous vestments to enact their ceremonious role upon the tiny platform, the chapel's doors open to display its altar to the hushed crowd without. A small acolyte alternately swung the censer and rearranged the Archbishop's robes whenever a gust of wind blew them awry. It was not a long sevice, but included bursts of song in Russian from a robed choir. We did not, of course, understand a word of it except the short address one of the priests gave in English, the kind of address which signaled him out as a diplomat as well as a priest. He said that nowhere else in the world could such a service, a memorial to the old Russia, occur.

Around us, white Russians and people of Russian descent followed the ritual with tears in their eyes, joining devoutly in the prayers and responses of the mixed-voiced choir. Finally, Archbishop John gave his blessing. Then it was over, save for the civil cermony and speeches by American officials to mark the dedication of Fort Ross as a National (as well as a State) Historical Landmark.

28

Nova Albion

In exploring the coastline south and north of Fort Ross we became familiar with the Point Reyes Peninsula about eighteen miles south of Bodega Head, and with the bay immediately south of the point that is marked on the maps as Drake's Bay. Eventually, it dawned on us that Sir Francis Drake is the most famous mariner ever to come within the view of the Spy-glass.

England remembers her most illustrious Elizabethan sea-rover for his several superb exploits; above all for his voyage around the world (December 1577 to September 1580), and his defeat of the Spanish Armada off the coast of England eight years later. Drake was the embodiment of the spirit of his age.

Before Drake, Spain's Magellan had been sent to find a passage to the Moluccas. Magellan was killed in a skirmish with the natives on the Philippines and only one of his vessels, under del Cano, had continued westward and circumnavigated the globe. For del Cano and for Drake, this was, in its time, as great a feat as twentieth-century man landing on the moon.

Outside of England, Drake is probably better remembered in Northern California than anywhere else in the world, chiefly for one event, but an event that was crucial to the success of his greatest voyage. He spent five weeks on the Northern California coastline to careen and repair the *Golden Hinde*. Before heading for home westward across the Pacific, Drake claimed the land for the Queen and named it Nova Albion (Albion was the Greek name for England). This was the first New England on the American continent — twenty-eight years before the founding of Jamestown, Virginia, and forty-one years before the *Mayflower* anchored off Plymouth, Massachusetts.

There are other reasons why Drake is so well-remembered here. For years, just which harbor Drake put into has been a matter of ardent controversy, and the finding of a plate of brass fueled the flames. Until recently, the plate was displayed as the original Drake is known to have left on the shoreline to establish his claim to the new land. Both conundrums have recently been satisfactorily explained.

To put Drake's California sojourn in its proper context is to trace very briefly the course of the first part of his voyage. It is a story of adventure that outshines that of Stevenson's *Treasure Island*, and the treasure that was stowed away in the *Golden Hinde*, unloaded while the ship was careened, then reloaded, was probably worth more than all the precious metals mined from Mount St. Helena.

The expedition of 1577 was on a larger scale than any other Englishman's voyage of trading and exploration. It was financed by several of the most influential men at Court, including the navy treasurer. The Queen, fully informed, neither gave nor withheld approval. Drake's instructions were to pass from the South Atlantic through the Magellan Straits to the South Sea the Spanish named the Mare Pacificum, explore the American-Pacific coastline not under the obedience of any Christian prince; prospect for minerals, spy out a place for marketing English goods, and *to return by the way he had come* (the italics are mine).

The Magellan Straits afforded a shorter route than going around the Horn, but no navigator had done this since its discovery by Magellan when he was sent on his epic exploratory voyage by the Spanish crown in search of a strait to the Spice Islands (the Moluccas). The given latitudes for Drake's exploration meant Chile, possibly Peru, for it was not then known how far south the Spanish had settled.

Drake assembled his small flotilla consisting of five ships in the summer of 1577: the *Pelican*, his flagship; the *Elizabeth* and the *Marygold;* the victualling vessel, the *Swan*, and the pinnace, *Benedict.* On board the *Pelican* was Francis Fletcher, the chaplain, Drake's youngest brother, Thomas, and his nephew, the fourteen-year-old John Drake, who probably served as his cabin boy.

There were fiddlers for entertainment, silver vessels for the table, and fine oak furniture in Drake's cabin. In addition to an armament of eighteen guns, the ship carried an ample store of firearms, ammunition, swords, and bows and arrows. A number of prefabricated pinnaces were stowed away in sections in the hold which could be quickly assembled for use in exploring inshore harbors. And there was Drake's drum to accompany the fiddlers and for signaling the crew.

The flotilla sailed out of Plymouth Sound on December 13, and proceeded southward off the coast of Africa, then west across the South Atlantic. Early in July 1578, Drake put into the Brazilian Port St. Julian, the harbor Magellan had used sixty years before. Here he spent six weeks reorganizing his supplies and refitting his ships. To free himself of all that might hinder him, he broke up the *Swan* and the *Christopher*, a pinnace he had captured off the coast of Morocco, exchanged for the *Benedict*, and renamed "Christopher" as a gesture to Sir Christopher Hatton, the Queen's minister and Drake's chief advocate at Court.

On August 17 the ships weighed anchor and in three days reached the opening of the dreaded Strait of Magellan. No one since Magellan had passed through those straits. It was here that Drake changed the name of the *Pelican*, renaming her the *Golden Hinde*, after the Hatton crest.

For sixteen days, to the beat of the drum, the ships crept through the straits , and, on September 6, entered the Pacific Ocean. America's southwest coast was a new and untouched source of plunder. Spain's treasure house was within reach at last.

The next day, a gale arose and lasted two weeks. The ships were scattered; the *Marygold* foundered, and the captain of the *Elizabeth*, believing Drake was lost, returned to England the way he had come. Drake waited, then sailed northward, hoping the ships might join him off the coast of Chile. Unknowingly, he and his crew were to pursue their course alone.

In Chile's great harbor, Valparaiso, Drake captured a ship and took her gold, cedar wood and wine. Ashore, he ransacked a warehouse and a church — the chalices, silks and altarcloths were handed over to Chaplain Fletcher for use on the *Golden Hinde*.

It was in mid-February of 1579 that Drake slipped into the Peruvian port of Lima, from where Spain's treasure ships sailed for Panama. Following his usual tactics, Drake surprised ship after ship, grappled, boarded and plundered. But the great ship, known locally as the *Cacafuego*, well-armed and capable of considerable speed, had already left, laden with gold.

Drake pursued and overhauled his great prize on the first of March. The *Cacafuego* surrendered with scarcely a shot being fired. The next day Drake had breakfast aboard her. It took three days for a pinnace to transfer the treasure to the *Golden Hinde*.

Now, Drake could loiter no longer. Since ships all along the southwest coast would be on the alert for him, he knew he could not return home the way he had come. If he could not find the fabled Northwest Passage (no one knows whether he sought this or not), he would have to sail across the Pacific and the Indian oceans, past the Moluccas and around Africa's Cape of Good Hope. On April 15, he put into Guatalco, a small Mexican seaport. This was his last port of call in settled Spanish America. Next day, he struck out into the Pacific and headed for the Northwest Coast.

Chaplain Fletcher's narrative records the sequence of events. Somewhere off the coast of southern Oregon, contrary winds forced Drake to run inshore. But, as Fletcher wrote, "in this place was no abiding for us." It was bitterly cold, the winds at gale force were against them, and instead of exploring any further north, Drake coasted south in search of a safe harbor, where he could repair and caulk his ship before embarking on the long voyage across the Pacific. The *Golden Hinde* was leaking from the weight of her heavy cargo and his water supply was low.

It was chilly and sunless when the *Golden Hinde* entered "a conuenient and fit harborough, and June 17, came to anchor therein: where we continued till the 23 day of July following." To the Indians she must have appeared a phantom ship looming up out of the mist. Quickly they gathered along the shoreline.

A single Indian paddled out in a boat-shaped tule balsa, stopping short some distance from the ship to deliver a long and tedious oration. He repeated the ceremony three times, each time coming closer, the third time bringing with him a bunch of black feathers tied in a round bundle, and a little rush basket full of *tobah* (tobacco). He threw these into the ship but refused all trinkets offered him in return, accepting only a cap thrown down into the water for him. This was the first meeting between Englishmen and the North American Indian.

The immediate coastline, and some distance inland, was the Coast Miwok Indians' territory. Point Reyes Peninsula itself was uninhabited, the Miwoks believing it to be the abode of the dead. The Indians, all during Drake's stay, showed submission and respect. By their repeated wailings and self-laceration, their burned "sacrifices" of feathers, they plainly regarded the white man as the returned dead.

> . . . they came down unto us, and yet with no hostile meaning, or intent to hurt us: standing when they drew neare, as men ravished in their mindes, with the sight of such things as they neuer had seene, or heard of before that time: there errand being rather with submission and feare to worship us Gods, than to have any warre with us as with mortall men.

On June 21 some of the crew went ashore to prepare a camp. Two days later the *Golden Hinde* moved up the channel leading from the bay to the estero, and readied for repair — first by unloading her fabulous cargo of silver and gold, chests of plate, China dishes of white earth, great store of China-silk, "a fawlcon of golde, with a great emeraud in the breast thereof," great riches, jewels and precious stones.

The Miwoks ran "very swiftly and long," and the news of the white men's presence ran like wildfire "as it seemed a great way up into the countries." On June 29 a great asembly of men, women and children appeared on the bluffs above the bay and descended in ceremonial order to the beach below. This was the day Drake received his Indian crown, "a cawle of feather decorated knitworke" set upon his head, disk-bead necklaces hung around his neck, and the title of *Hioh* — chief or friend — was bestowed upon him with a song.

For the Miwoks it was a day of painted faces. Every man's face was painted black or white or another color. They wore plumes of feathers and flicker-quill headbands, and coney skins on their ordinarily naked bodies. In the hands of every man and woman were gifts; strange assorted foods and baskets trimmed with shells and woodpeckers' red scalp feathers that customarily were made and destroyed in honor of the dead. It was a day of speeches, of singing and dancing; of women moaning, shrieking, with fingernail-torn faces, bruised and lacerated bodies self-inflicted beforehand, in honor of the white gods.

The Indians continued to come to the beach as the work on the ship went forward. If there was any one phrase of Indian speech which the English were to remember it was *notcato mu - nocharo mu,* meaning keep away or touch me not. It may have been a phrase often repeated because, except for the single occasion of Drake's crowning, when Indians embraced their guests, the red men avoided touching the whites. Bodily contact with a dead person or spirit was to be shunned as a fatal touch.

Shortly after repairs on the ship were in hand, Drake led a party to explore the region. The coastline was windswept moorland, the grass had lost its winter greenness, but inland was "a goodly country and fruitful soyle, stored with many blessings fit for the use of man . . . "

> Our Generall called this Countrey, NOVA ALBION, and that for causes: the one in respect of the white bankes and cliffes which lie toward the sea: and the other, because it might have some affinites with our Country in name, which sometimes was so called.

From a distance, the cliffs and banks of Drake's Bay appear white, and instantly recall the chalk cliffs of the English Channel. However, they are made up of a kind of shale, often miscalled "chalk-rock" and are not so strikingly white as the chalk cliffs of England. At a closer view they are a warm sand color and resemble more nearly the cliffs of Sidmouth in Drake's native Devon.

The climate at the encampment was infinitely worse than the worst of English summers. Fletcher's fingers must have been half numb when he wrote:

> . . . notwithstanding it was in the height of summer, and so neare the sunne, yet were wee continually visited with like nipping colds as we had felt before; insomuch that if violent exercises of our bodies, and busie employment about our necessarie labours, had not sometimes compel'd us to the contrary, we could very well have been contented to have kept about us still our winter clothes; yes (had our necessities suffered us) to have kept our beds; neither could we at any time, in whole fourteene dayes together, find the air so cleare as to be able to take the height of sunne or starre.

Nor could the food have been particularly appetizing, even when washed down with Chilean wine, and some of it was shared with the Indians:

> During their Stay here they usually brought Sacrifices every third Day, till they clearly understood the English were displeased, whereupon their Zeal abated; yet they continually resorted to them with such Eagerness, that they oft forgot to provide Sustenance for themselves, so that the General, whom they counted their Father, was forced to give them Victuals, as Muscles, Seals, and the like; wherewith they were extremely pleased . . .

As the repair work neared completion, the Indians sensed Drake's departure. The joy they had shown at the gods' arrival changed to sorrow; they refused all comfort, accounted themselves as castaways whom the gods were about to forsake, wringing their hands and tormenting themselves as they moaned and wept.

> Before we went from thence, our Generall caused to be set up a monument of our being there, as also of her maiesties and successors rilght and title to that kingdome; namely, a plate of brasse, fast nailed to a great and firm post; whereon is engraven her graces name, and the day and year of our arrival there, and of the freegiving up of the province and kingdome, both by the King and people, into her maiesties hands; together with her highnesse picture and armes, in a piece of sixpence currant English monie, shewing itself by a hole made of purpose through the plate; underneath was likewise engraven the name of our Generall, etc.
> The Spaniards never had any dealing, or so much set a foote in this country; and utmost of their discoveries, reaching only to many degrees Southward of this place.

On July 23 the Miwoks took a sorrowful leave of their gods, and

> . . . went to the top of the Hills to keep sight of them as long as possible, making Fires before, behind, and on each side of them, wherein they supposed Sacrifices were offered for their happy Voyage.

Within twenty-four hours Drake reached the Farallon Islands about thirty miles offshore of San Francisco, and now included as part of the City and County of San Francisco. Here the *Golden Hinde* was revictualed with sea-lion meat, wild fowl and their eggs, "such provisions as might completely serve our turns for awhile," and then set out across the Pacific.

Drake bypassed the Moluccas (the Spice Islands) on account of hostile Portuguese, then cleaned ship and rested his crew at Ternato, the most northerly of the Molucca Islands. At another island to the southwest that has never been identified, he again careened his ship. Putting into port at Java he revictualed, bartering for hens, a whole ox, rice, and several fruits including sago. From there he crossed the Indian Ocean. On June 18, he cleared Bon Esperance, Africa's Cape of Good Hope and in July replenished his water supply at Sierra Leone. On September 26, 1580 he sailed into Plymouth Sound after two years, ten months and some few odd days spent "in seeing the wonders of the Lord in the deep, in discouering so many strange adjentures, in escaping out of so many dangers, and ouercoming so many difficulties in this our encompassing of this neather globe, and passing round the world." Thus Drake became the first Englishman to achieve this feat.

In October, Elizabeth I summoned Drake to court. Hero that he was, Drake's presence did cause some embarrassment in diplomatic circles. The Spanish clamored for the restitution of the Spanish treasure; this was taken to the Tower for safety and on the advice of her statesmen, the Queen caused a rumor to be spread around that Drake had not brought that much plunder home.

On New Year's Day, Elizabeth wore Drake's gift in her crown, an emerald from Peru. Early in the spring she ordered that the *Golden Hinde* be brought to Deptford, and on April 4, 1581, Drake entertained her at a banquet on board the ship. Elizabeth handed a sword to Monsieur de Marchaumont, a

French envoy sent by the brother of the King of France, authorizing him to perform the ceremony of knighting Drake for her.

The King of Spain, infuriated, swore that "England shall smoake." In 1588 he sent forth his mighty Armada.

England's defeat of that huge Spanish fleet, due largely to Drake's leadership, smashed Spain's power as the world's leading nation, and established the supremacy of England's fleet. In celebration of the epochal victory, great bonfires were lit high on the cliffs of Dover. Did Drake remember that other time when he had watched the Miwok's fires along the white cliffs of Nova Albion?

29

The Plate of Brasse

Why has Drake's harborage on the Northern California coastline been a mystery for so long? Noel B. Martin, Jr., a student of that mystery points out that the fundamental reason is because Drake's own record of the voyage has not come down to us. It was probably handed over to the Queen, and doubtlessly regarded as a top-secret document. To publish it would have revealed Drake's exploits off the Pacific Coast of Spanish America at a time of tense relations between England and Spain.

The first published account of the voyage appeared in Richard Hakluyt's, *The Principal Navigations, Voyages and Discoveries of the English Nation* (1589) and was based on Francis Fletcher's narrative. So was another early account by an unknown compiler, generally referred to by the first three words of its long and grandiloquent title as *The World Encompassed* (1628). This is the fullest and regarded as the most reliable account. But Fletcher was a chaplain, not a navigator, and his description of the scene on the California coastline is not explicit enough to determine which harbor Drake put into to careen and repair his ship.

Captain George Vancouver, another famous English navigator, almost two-hundred years after Drake, came within view of the Spy-glass and anchored in Drake's Bay in November 1792. In his, *A Voyage of Discovery to the North Pacific Ocean and Round the World,* Vancouver noted that the Spaniards believed it to be the bay in which Drake careened his ship, and so marked it on the charts.

In the late 1800s, George Davidson, a leading geographer of the United States Coast Survey in the Pacific, made a special study of Drake's California and concluded that Drake's harborage was Drake's Bay. Accordingly, the bay was officially so named, and the shallow estuary that opens from it, Drake's Estero.

But San Francisco Bay still had its advocates who maintained no mariner would fail to use so magnificent a harbor. When a young clerk, Beryl Shinn, picked up a metal plate while picnicking on a ridge along the shoreline of San Francisco Bay, in the summer of 1936, the old controversy became headline news.

Shinn used the plate to cover a hole in his car. Some months later, when ready to repair the hole, he cleaned the plate, saw an inscription on it that he could not read, and took it to Dr. Herbert Bolton of the University of California, at Berkeley. Dr. Bolton believed it authentic beyond all reasonable doubt, but to be doubly sure, sent it to two metalurgical and electrochemical experts who pronounced the plate to be genuine. The discovery was announced by the California Historical Society at a banquet held at the Sir Francis Drake Hotel in San Francisco on April 6, 1937. Shinn was presented with two-thousand dollars, and the plate was acquired by the University. From then on it became a treasured exhibit of the Bancroft Library.

William Caldeira, a chauffer, now came forward to say he had picked up the plate about five miles from the Estero Cove while waiting for his employer who was hunting quail. He kept it for a while, and then one day when driving along the San Francisco shoreline, flung it out on the roadside below the ridge where Shinn had found it. Who moved the plate from the roadside to the ridge above has never been revealed.

The finding of the plate gave no conclusive answer as to the identity of Drake's harborage, and there were experts in the U.S. and in England who expressed their doubts about the plate being genuine. Among them was Samuel Eliot Morrison of Harvard, himself a navigator and the nation's leading naval historian. He not only believed the discovered plate to be a fake, but discounted any chance of Drake having entering San Francisco Bay. Years later he set forth his argument in *The European Discovery of America: the Southern Voyages* (1974). This may be summed up as follows.

The entrance to San Francisco Bay is through a narrow opening, named the Golden Gate by Fremont in 1849. Navigators can sail almost to the Golden Gate without realizing there is an opening; the headlands and the surrounding hills on either side appear as a continuous land mass. Spain's exploring voyagers never sighted the entrance, nor did the Manilla galleons returning annually to Acapulco.

The bay was finally discovered in 1769 (from the land and not from the sea) by an overland expedition led by Gaspar de Portola. The first known ship to have entered the bay was the paqueboat, *San Carlos*, commanded by Juan Manuel de Ayala, who was sent to explore the bay's numerous arms and channels in 1755. In the days of the gold rush, in the 1850s, sailing ships coming from Cape Horn frequently missed the Golden Gate and ended on the rocky shore nearby. Morrison said that, when he was sailing along the coast on a clear May day in 1973, he could not see the Golden Gate when eight miles away. Approaching it from the north, the Golden Gate cannot be sighted even three

146

miles away. With George Davidson's conclusion, and both state and nation officially naming Drake's Bay and Drake's Estero, "I see no reason to disagree."

The finding of the plate of brass was probably the greatest single impetus in arousing local interest in Drake. The Point Reyes Drake Navigators Guild was formed in 1949 for the express purpose of identifying, if possible, Drake's harborage, so that the site might be preserved as a National Historical Monument to the first New England in the western world, and the first place where Englishmen had camped on the North American continent.

As a result of the Guild's long and intensive quest, the mass of material its members tracked down, and the anthropologists comparing Francis Fletcher's description of the Indians with what later became known about the Coast Miwok, most people now acknowledge that the bay and the estero were rightly named. The Guild went a step farther than George Davidson in pinpointing the site. They contend that Drake anchored first in Drake's Bay, and after a pinnace had explored inshore, the *Golden Hinde* was moved up the narrow channel leading to a cove just inside the estero. Anchorage in the bay is difficult, but the estuary provided perfect shelter. The channel is now silted up but was navigable up to the early part of this century when coastal schooners used the estero as a refuge.

In 1977, forty years after the finding of the "Plate of Brasse," the Bancroft Library disclosed that it was indeed an elaborate and scholarly fake — one that for Californians at least ranks second only to that of the Piltdown skull. The question remains, who did it?

Dr. Bolton, who died in 1953, was beloved by his students and constantly urged them to keep a lookout for Drake's plate. He believed absolutely in the validity of the plate that was discovered. Whoever did it probably intended to reveal the hoax in due course and thereby raise a good laugh. Later, realizing that such a revelation would crush the professor's spirit, decided to keep the faking a secret. Had the fake never been perpetrated, the Drake Navigation Guild might never have come into being, and the world would know far less than it now knows about Drake's sojourn in Northern California.

Besides the Plate of Brasse, other Drake memorabilia include the name Francis Drake Boulevard in Marin County and in San Francisco the well-known Sir Francis Drake Hotel. Also, in the north aisle of Grace Cathedral, is John de Rosa's wax tempera, five-panel mural (1949), commemorating Drake's landing and Chaplain Francis Fletcher conducting the first English-language and Anglican service on the mainland of North America. The mural shows Drake (as he appeared in contemporary portraits), his crew, Francis Fletcher and the Miwok indians (shown as Europeans of the time *imagined* they looked); the Tudor flag (the Tudor rose), Drake's arms, the world globe and sails of the *Golden Hinde.*

30

The Californios

At first, as newcomers to California, the term, "the Californios" was confusing. It does not mean those who are or were California-born. The Californios were that mixed company of soldiers and settlers of the old Spanish regime who, in 1822, when Mexico declared her independence from Spain, and California became a province of the new republic, in turn became citizens of Mexico. Among them was a sprinkling of foreigners, some English and Swiss, but mostly Americans, including the Mountain Men, members of bands of trappers who were the first Americans to come overland. Many of them learned to speak Spanish, a language that the California Indian also obtained a smattering of.

Those Mountain Men who retraced their way back to Missouri reported the far-off Mexican province to be a near paradise, rich in game, a land of perpetual spring. Through their reports they were the unwitting heralds of undreamed of change to come in California life.

The chance came in 1833 for citizens and foreigners alike to own their land individually. That year the Mexican government confiscated the vast lands of the Franciscan missions. The padres left. With so much released land on their hands, Mexico's colonial governors could afford to be generous. Land grants "by the league" were bestowed on soldiers and civilians of good record, and on favored foreigners who qualified for Mexican citizenship. Joining the Catholic Church was a prime requirement. Marrying a Spanish or Mexican-born girl helped. The government favored unions creating home bonds not readily broken. If the foreigner married a Mexican girl of influential family, the California paradise, by way of a land grant, was at his feet.

The land grant system in California was similar in many ways to the land grant system in the thirteen British colonies along the eastern seaboard. It was, of course, the best means of planting a colony. But those who were given land grants in California were, with but few exceptions, a different breed of men from the landowners in the southern states.

148

With the exception of Georgia, many of the South's plantation owners were the younger sons of cultured English families and many more of them whose origin is unknown were of English stock. In Virginia, in particular, whatever their social standing "back home," once they had acquired land and cultivated enough tobacco, they strived to mirror in the Virginia wilderness the manners and lifestyle of the English country gentleman. To this end, in exchange for tobacco, they imported English goods wholesale: clothing of the latest London fashions, furnishings, and all sorts of household goods. In the late seventeenth and early eighteenth centuries they brought skilled carpenters and woodcarvers over from England to build their plantation houses. They saw to it that their children were brought up with the manners of the English gentry and they sent their sons at a surprisingly young age to be educated at Oxford or Cambridge and to study law at the Inns of Court in London.

A century later, in California, the Californios had little in common with the planters in the southern states, except an appetite for land with which to derive wealth. Many of the land grants went to the mountain men. Few of them had the cultured background and the polished manners of the southern planters but they were the finest type of men. The historian, Robert Glass Cleland, described "The fur trader, trapper, beaver-hunter, or mountain man" as "a peculiar product of the American frontier."

> He belonged to a calling that had no counterpart. He started from frontiers at which more cautious pioneers were glad to stop. He was an adventurer to whom danger became a daily commonplace, an explorer who took tribute of the wilderness and wandered through the reaches of the outer West with all the freedom of the lonely wind. He was the predecessor of the missionary, the gold-seeker, the cattle-man, the settler, and all kindred pioneers. The feet of a nation walked his half-obliterated trails, the course of empire followed his solitary pathways to the western sea.

The era of the western fur trader was from 1820 to 1840, and when it closed, it closed forever.

> The mountain man, unlike the prospector, cattleman, or frontier-settler, left no successor; his brief day had no tomorrows.
> But in his few allotted years the trapper set his impress forever upon the map of North America and the fate of the United States. He affected the destiny of nations; he changed the future of a continent; he bequeathed to later generations of Americans a tradition of heroic exploration comparable to that of the seamen of Elizabeth or the conquistadores of Spain.

To carry on their arduous, risky trade, the mountain men had to be self-reliant, courageous and willing to endure hardships. Those who became frontier-settlers and rancheros did have two things in common with the planters, a boundless hospitality and a well-ordered, disciplined way of living. Few gentlemen drank deeper than some of the Virginian and other southern plantation owners but the successful among them kept a check on themselves and did not become befuddled, at least in public. Isaac, one of Thomas Jefferson's slaves, recalled "Isaac never heard of his (Jefferson) being disguised in drink." One of the problems of the eighteenth-century planters was keeping the negro servants sober and they had to set an example. The same applied to the successful settlers in the west who were dependent on Indian labor. And a trapper, and a hunter who shot grizzly bears with a rifle had to have a clear eye and a steady hand.

North of San Francisco Bay, Mariano Guadelupe Vallejo (1807-1890) was the first to receive a land grant. He was an exceptional grantee. His parents came of old Spanish aristocracy. Born and schooled in Monterey, Vallejo was twenty-four years old when he became Commander of the Presidio at San Francisco in 1831. Three years later, Jose Figueroa, the wise and perceptive Mexican Governor of California, appointed him Military Commander and Director of Colonization of the Norther Frontier and charged with the changeover from Church to civil authority at the Sonoma mission. As a further encouragement, the Governor made Vallejo a grant of ten leagues of land (forty-thousand acres) in the adjoining Petaluma Valley to develop as a private rancho. During the next several years, Vallejo increased in size his highly productive Petaluma Rancho and acquired another vast rancho and other lands. By 1846 his land holdings came to more than seventy-five thousand acres.

He surveyed and established the Pueblo of Sonoma, set his adobe home, La Casa Grande, on the plaza at Sonoma and became one of the wealthiest and most influential men in California. As Military Commander and Director of Colonization of the Northern Frontier, Vallejo was virtually the undisputed ruler of the country north of San Francisco Bay and the dispenser of the Mexican Government's land grants.

31

George C. Yount
A Peer of Pioneers

One of Vallejo's first land grants was two square leagues in Napa Valley to George C. Yount (1794-1865). He named it the Caymus Rancho after the Kaymus (Caymus) group of Wappo Indians living in that part of the valley. George Yount, one of a large family, was born in North Carolina and at the age of ten trekked out with his parents to Missouri. On his eighteenth birthday he enlisted as a soldier in the War of 1812, and helped to protect the small Missouri settlements from the British-inspired Indian attacks.

When the fighting was over, Yount married and took to hunting and farming. Through some misplaced trust he lost most of the money he made, and with a growing family to support he tried to recoup his losses in the Commerce of the Prairies, as the bartering of goods for furs was called. St. Louis, founded by French fur traders and named for the sainted Louis IX, king of France, was the *entrepôt* or warehouse of the fur trade. Caravans set out carrying merchandise from there to New Mexico's frontier post in Santa Fe, returning with the mountain men's beaver and otter pelts.

Yount and his goods reached Santa Fe by caravan in the summer of 1826, but a large caravan had sapped Santa Fe of hard cash two years before and Yount's goods lay unsold. Now he joined a trapping expedition to the Colorado River and began his career as a mountain man.

Although George Yount could neither read nor write (which is why, perhaps, he lost most of what he made as a farmer), he was as well-equipped as any mountain man could be. Self-reliant, inventive and ingenious, he was an expert with rifle and pistol, tomahawk, axe and plow. He made his own ammunition and was also a carpenter and shingle-splitter. He could build a cabin, and build and run a mill and a forge.

It is outside the scope of this book to recount Yount's years as a trapper in the Southwest, except to record that he reached the borders of Southern California in the same year he arrived at Santa Fe, in 1826, and was thus in the vanguard of the first pathfinders in the West, of American transcontinental trappers. But fortune continued to elude him. In Santa Fe again in 1830, Yount learned that his wife, tired of waiting for his return, was granted a divorce. Perhaps because of this, or because he did not wish to return to St. Louis still a poor man, he made up his mind to go further west, to California. He and his small band of trappers joined up with William Wolfskill and his band. They were the third party to forge their way from New Mexico to California, making their way along what became known as the Old Spanish Trail which formed almost a semicircle across the desert country of the Southwest, its length about twelve-hundred miles. They reached the pueblo of Los Angeles in 1831. (The Old Spanish Trail was the trail the trading caravans followed, and for several years it was the most important land route to California and was still used at the time of the gold rush.)

Beaver pelts were the basis of the Western-American fur trade and, according to Robert Glass Cleland, they flourished from the Artic Circle to the gulfs of Mexico and California. Alta California once had a large beaver population. Although Southern California has too little water to maintain beaver colonies, the big golden beaver abounded on the San Joaquin and Sacramento Rivers and their tributaries, and in the low, marshy regions tributary to San Francisco Bay.

First, Yount hunted the sea otter along the southern coastline, then continued to trap beaver on the inland rivers as he moved north, staying at one mission or another, or camping out as was the custom of most other travelers. He stayed at the Mission Dolores in San Francisco and helped to repair some of the dilapidated buildings at the mission of San Rafael.

Somewhere along the line, Yount met young Guy Freeman Fling who had come to Monterey on a whaleship from Boston. Fling, by report, was the first American to set foot in Napa Valley in 1827. Four years later, he led Yount there on the way to Sonoma. There are various accounts, based on reminiscence, of Yount's first sight of the valley, how he journeyed over the Indian trail to the top of Mount St. Helena and exclaimed "In such a place I should love to clear the land and make my home; in such a place I should love to live and die."

It may seem trivial to point out that it is doubtful whether Yount climbed the mountain that day with Fling. It would have meant making a long detour on the way to Sonoma. It seems more likely that from a point several miles south of the mountain he followed an Indian trail up and over the mountain ridge which divides Napa and Sonoma Counties. From the crest of the range, or even from halfway up, he would have a superb view of the heart of the Napa Valley below. I do not doubt he made up his mind then and there, that if he could secure a land grant this was where he would choose it. I have no doubt that Yount did, in due course, climb Mount St. Helena, and the claim may well be made that he was the first white man to do so.

152

At Sonoma, Yount endeared himself to Vallejo, rendering him all sorts of service and, above all, roofing Vallejo's ranch house in Petaluma Valley with shingles, thereby introducing the craft of splitting shingles into California. Perhaps Vallejo hinted that Yount would have his reward. However that may be, in the spring of 1835, he was baptized as a Roman Catholic at the Mission de San Rafael and became a citizen of Mexico. The following year Vallejo gave him a land grant of two square leagues in the heart of Napa Valley. Yount, as already noted, named it Caymus Rancho after the Kaymus group of Wappo Indians whose territory was by law now his.

The Caymus and the grizzly bears were everywhere. Straightway, with the help of the Sonoma Mission Indians, Yount built a two-story Kentucky blockhouse with loopholes to see and shoot through, and stocked it with food so that he and his friendly Indians could defend themselves and, if need be, withstand a siege. The following year he built a two-story adobe fort and later added a commodious loghouse to it in which he lived for many years. He built a sawmill and a gristmill (the first in California) and when it was worn he built a larger one.

At first, Yount's nearest neighbor was Vallejo at Sonoma, eighteen miles to the west. Vallejo, intent on subjugating the Indians and protecting the northern frontier, sensed or learned when trouble was brewing. On such occasions he launched a surprise attack and enlisted Yount's help. Likewise, when Yount had to battle against Indian raiders, Vallejo sent the Sonoma Mission braves to his aid.

Yount did, however, befriend the Caymus, as he had need of their help on the land. But there was no befriending the grizzly bear. They were so numerous that he determined to destroy every one he met, and made it a practice to go out on horseback with rifle in hand. Bear meat was appreciated at the Sonoma garrison and by the Kaymus.

His rancho became famous for its variety of fruits, among them fig trees which yielded two crops a year, and British Queen strawberries. He had honey from his fifty hives of bees, two-hundred gallons of wine a year from his Mission grapes and his livestock count, at its peak, was two-hundred sheep, five-hundred horses and two-thousand head of horned cattle.

There was a change in land use as the pastoral period of the Spanish and Mexican regimes drew to a close. Grazing land was ploughed and planted with oats, barley and wheat, and agriculture replaced the hide and tallow trade. With the increase of population due to the gold rush and the influx of settlers, flour was in increasing demand. Yount had four to eight-hundred acres of wheat, and his mill was the most productive one in the state. He had also received another land grant (in 1843), Rancho La Jota, comprising over forty-thousand acres on what is now Howell Mountain. In the summer of that same year, two of his daughters came from Missouri to join him.

Rancho Caymus became the rendezvous of the old trappers and the refuge of many an overland settler, including the destitute survivors of the ill-fated Donner Party. Yount's hospitality was boundless and he was a marvelous host. He had an extraordinary memory and, being a great raconteur, loved to tell about his hunting and trapping days and of his encounters with the Indians and the grizzly bears.

There was, however, one totally unforeseen turn of events that deeply troubled Yount. Following the onrush of gold seekers in '49, hordes of those who failed to accumulate precious metals and return home rich, turned desperados and swarmed over the land. They were, as one narrator put it, "the off-scouring of all lands," including some who came of reputable English and American families. Armed with rifles and revolvers, they became the terror of the countryside. They killed Indians for the sport of it, stole in open daylight and rounded up horses and cattle and drove them to market.

Some desperados became squatters, erected dwellings and fenced in farmland. Yount, like almost every other ranchero, was more troubled by squatters than he had ever been by Indians or grizzly bears. His squatter eviction suits filled the courts, as many as seventeen at a time, and for years the suits dragged through the courts.

However, 1855 was a big year for him and the tide turned in his favor. His first wife had died in Missouri five years before, and he married a widow, Mrs. Eliza Gashwiler. She proved to be a thorough business manager, "with a shrewdness which few can equal" and, from then on, Yount ceased to be plagued either by squatters or the slow verdict of the courts. And with small communities developing into small country towns (Napa was founded in 1848 and St. Helena in 1854) Yount commissioned a surveyor to lay out the town named Sebastopol, also the name of another community in Sonoma County. Yount's Sebastopol was renamed Yountville two years after his death.

Also in 1855, when Yount was sixty-one years old, he dictated the story of his life to the Reverend Orange Clark, and Clark rewrote the account. Both may have elaborated some of the tales, but the basic substance of the Clark "Narrative" is uncontested.

Most of what I have learned about Yount is contained in his *Chronicle of the West,* comprising extracts from his "Memoir's" and from the Orange Clark "Narrative" edited by Charles L. Camp and published in 1966.

Orange Clark said that, when he first cast his eye on Yount's career, he thought he had found "a new specimen of life." Richard Henry Dana was also impressed by Yount. In the journal he kept on his return visit to California in 1859, he gives us a completely unvarnished profile of the "old" man. By this time, Yount was often spoken of as old, and he looked older than his years — the earlier hardships, exposure and privation were clearly written on his weatherbeaten face.

Here is an extract from Dana's journal:

Tues. Dec. 20.   Took steamer for Mare Island. On board found...General Vallejo and his son-in-law Frisbie, and above all old Mr. Yount, the famous pioneer and woodsman, the first white settler in Napa Valley. All invited and insisted on my going to Napa. Glad to do it — as Napa Valley is the pride of California . . . and *old Yount is alone worth a journey there* . . . (the italics are mine).

Wed. Dec. 21 . . . Reached Yount's towards night. He has a principality here of some 12,000 acres, from Mountain to Mountain, and running lengthwise of the valley, the Napa Creek running through its centre. He owns a large mill, and has some 100 or so Indians encamped near his house, whom he employs . . . Lately married an intelligent middle aged woman, well educated etc. from New York, who takes care of his affairs, keeps his accounts, sees he is not cheated, and pays off his debts, for the old hunter has no business habits or knowledge . . . Old log house, modernized, one story huge chimney and large logs . . . burning on the fire. Hearty welcome.

In November 1861, William Brewer of the Whitney Survey camped on Yount's rancho by invitation. Brewer did not meet "the old man," however, as Yount was away at the time. Brewer knew him, though, by repute:

His story seemes like a romance . . . In his youth in a western state, a fortune teller had predicted to him his future home, settled in a lovely valley, etc. Here seemed to be the place — a fertile valley, enclosed by high mountain ridges, a rich bottom with grand trees, a stream rich in fish. (A prediction that Yount remembered when he first saw the Napa Valley with Fling.)

By this force of character and kindness he overcame the Indians and made them such warm friends that to this day many live on his ranch . . . His exploits and adventures smack of the marvelous, but he held his place, fully determined that Fate had destined this spot to be his home.

Mrs. Mollie Patten, daughter of John Lawley, who built the toll road over Mount St. Helena, who became mistress of the Toll House when she succeeded her brother Charley in operating the toll gate and the inn, had her own definition of the word "pioneer." "You weren't a pioneer at Napa unless you came *before* the gold rush as Old Man Yount had done."

These appraisals by men such as Richard Henry Dana and William H. Brewer testify that George C. Yount (given the middle name Concepción when he was baptized a Roman Catholic) became a legend in his lifetime, and was recognized by his contemporaries as a peer among pioneers. His mind clear to the end, he died on October 5, 1865.

32

Knight's Valley

Knight's Valley went unclaimed, except by the Indian, until 1843. That fall, Jose de los Santos Berryessa received a grant of 17,742 acres which covered almost all of Mallacomes (Knight's) Valley and adjoining land at the head of Napa Valley including Agua Caliente (Calistoga). Berryessa was a lieutenant of the Sonoma garrison and the grant was his reward from the Mexican Governor for years of good service.

Mallacomes Valley was much smaller than Napa Valley and secluded from it by a low divide now known as Murray Hill. A game-rich tract, it became Berryessa's private hunting preserve. Portions of the thick-walled hunting lodge he built still stand only a mile down the road from our own small ranch house. From his lodge he had the same dramatic view of Mount St. Helena's rocky north peak, and he could look out over what he must have called his paradise — a hunter's paradise at least.

However, the rate of change was as swift for Berryessa and California, as it is for us and the world today; violent, abrupt, wholesale. Certainly, as a lieutenant in Sonoma (and later in 1846, alcalde, i.e., mayor), Berryessa was well-informed of what was going on in his immediate countryside. Certainly, he would remember 1841, just two years before he received his land grant, as a year of extraordinary happenings.

In June of that year, Voznesensky and Chernykh had climbed Mount St. Helena. It is fair to assume they followed one of the Indian trails from the coast to a crossroad point, Mayacoma (which will be identified later), and from there made their way by another Indian trail to the north peak. Less credible was the story that the first party of American settlers — men and their families instead of trappers — were on their way to this new promised land.

The first overland train — a caravan of horses, oxen and mules drawing the white-topped covered wagons loaded with household goods — reached the Napa Valley that October.

Did Berryessa ponder on these events so close to home, being tired and content with a day's hunting and a dinner of venison or quail, stretched out before the fire with a bottle of Sonoma wine? My guess is that he was too pleased with his world to foresee the long shadows the events of that year would cast.

The Russian withdrawal and the arrival of the American trail-blazers marked the end of an era. The sea was no longer the main highway. The Indians, already decimated by the white man's disease and guns, were doomed to near extinction. For Berryessa and most other *Californios* of Spanish blood, the lotus days of the land grant period were almost over. Soon *los Americanos* would take over. Even the face of the land was about to change.

Here our concern must be limited to what happened to the Rancho Mallacomes. In 1846, it and all of California became a territory of the United States. At that sweep of change, many of the Spanish-speaking rancheros quit their lands, some to follow their own lowered flag back to Mexico, others merely to vanish.

The gold rush of '49 brought a flood of humanity that rapidly spread over much of Northern California, including Mount St. Helena. However, not all of the newcomers came as gold-seekers. Some preferred land, and among them was Thomas P. Knight.

Thomas Knight was a young, unmarried storekeeper in Arkansas who closed his business in 1844. He built a large wagon for himself with his own hands and loaded some leftover store goods into it, including a barrel of gunpowder. And, as common practice, he concealed two little bags of gold and silver money somewhere in his wagon. Thus, he set out, a member of the Grigsby-Ide train, bound for California in 1845.

On reaching the Sierra without event, Knight rode ahead of the party, leaving his wagon in the care of two young fellow travelers. Probably they guessed money was hidden in some secret hollowed-out pocket, discovered it, and then used a match. Whatever, the wagon caught fire, and the barrel of gunpowder exploded. Hurrying back, Knight searched the debris for hours but could recover no more than $18.50. He was convinced the two young men had found the money, covering the theft by firing the wagon.

In California, Knight took part in the Bear Flag Revolt at Sonoma in 1846, which was one of the first steps toward California becoming an American state. Thereafter, still penniless, he had no choice except to try gold hunting. Seemingly he was successful, for he came back to the Sonoma countryside. Mallacomes Valley, in all its primeval beauty, offered as fair a prospect as he could wish.

Unlike scores of other settlers who occupied abandoned ranches as trespassers or "squatters," Knight paid Berryessa ten-thousand dollars for a large portion of Rancho Mallacomes and received title to the land in 1853. He called his rancho, Muristool, added a second story to the hunting lodge, and began growing fruit and wheat and raising sheep. And, in 1856, he built a sawmill.

Oddly enough it was a habit of the chroniclers of the Old West to use the terms "white" and "civilized" to describe only those early settlers who were primarily of American or English stock. However, civilized Jose de los Santos Berryessa ranks as the first settler in Mallacomes Valley, and William and Ellen McDonnell, who came to the valley shortly ahead of Knight were the first "white" settlers. They homesteaded on U.S. government land at the north end of the valley and, for a while, were Thomas Knight's nearest white neighbors. William, who had crossed the plains as a team-driver for the Kellogg emigrant train, became, we remember, the first guide to the Geysers from the Knight's Valley approach. Ellen's parents were among the ill-fated members of the Donner Party. Their granddaughter, Florence McDonnell McCord, raised the same breed of sheep on the original holding as her grandfather William.

Calvin Holmes was another team-driver who, in 1859, purchased part of Berryessa's land. He called his ranch Mallacomes and in the 1860s, as the *History of Sonoma County* records, Mr. Holmes "erected a superb mansion and magnificent farmhouses, arranged with every design to insure the care and comfort of this stock." Both Knight's adobe house and Holmes' mansion still stand.

One of the McDonnell children, reminiscing in later years, made this often-quoted remark: "there were no white settlers between them (William and Ellen McDonnell) and the settlements on the Willamette river in Oregon." William Brewer of the Whitney Survey confirmed this, in part, saying that McDonnell told him he was "the remotest settler in this region between San Francisco and the settlers in Oregon" at the time he and his twenty-year-old wife came to Knight's Valley. This is not true.

Cyrus Alexander settled in the valley immediately north of Knight's in 1841, several years before Knight and the McDonnells arrived. Surely the only explanation for McDonnell knowing nothing about Alexander when he first came to Knight's Valley is that no one had then traversed the two-mile-long, narrow and winding canyon which separated one valley from the other. In 1859, when Bayard Taylor drove his buggy through the pass, a road of sorts following the stream bed had been made and the chasms "spanned by the rudest kind of corduroy bridges," but even so it was still an extremely hazardous road.

So began the history of what was our valley, as far as the "white" man is concerned; only some one-hundred-and-thirty years ago; all in the lifetime of my grandparents.

Knight's Valley provides another instance of the continuity in grape growing in the wine country. The *Russian River Flag* of October 8, 1874, in an article on Knight's Valley, reported that, some five years previously:

> . . . after cultivating and enjoying the ranch . . . plucking the tender grapes, the luscious peaches and juicy apples that his own hand had planted and tended, and having disposed of about half the ranch from time to time, Mr. Knight sold the rest . . .

"The rest," according to the same article, included a seventeen-acre vineyard, and the new owners expected the vineyard to produce twenty-five tons of grapes that season to be shipped to Napa County.

By 1912, grapes were the leading crop in Knight's Valley and, once again, grapes are the leading crop today. It is now recognized that, because of its soil and climate, with its backdrop of the entire length of Mount St. Helena, Knight's Valley is unique among the valleys of the Coastal Range and is also a unique grape-growing area. Beringer's has close to five-hundred acres in vines and their Knight's Valley Cabernet Sauvignons and Sauvignon Blancs are renowned nationwide. Who would ever guess, seeing the labels on these two wines, with "Knight's Valley Estate" written across them, just where Knight's Valley is, and what it looks like?

33

"The Life and Times of Cyrus Alexander"

Cyrus Alexander (1805-1872) ranks second only to George Yount as a peer of pioneers. In many respects he was different from Yount although he shared Yount's integrity and endurance. He was frail in boyhood, well-lettered as any farmer's son, and became a shrewd appraiser of men and the goods they offered. Yount was strong, unlettered, and utterly unbusinesslike, with an almost childlike trust in all men's honesty. Yet their lives followed much the same pattern.

Alexander was born in Pennsylvania, the youngest but one of eight children. He was five years old when the family moved to Illinois and settled some sixteen miles from St. Louis. Too frail to work on his father's farm, Cyrus read countless books, mostly about the lives of hunters and explorers, and these stirred his imagination as the stories of the mountain men in and around St. Louis had stirred Yount. Cyrus resolved to adventure and to become rich.

In order to earn enough to equip himself as a rover, he went to work first for one of his brothers engaged in the tanning trade, then for another who was a miller. He then purchased four yokes of oxen and a sturdy wagon to carry his tools and provisions. In 1827, when he was twenty-two years old, he set out on the four-hundred mile trek to the lead mines in northern Illinois. This first venture brought no worthwhile success, although it hardened him physically, and he returned home to await a more lucrative prospect.

Next, the fur trade between St. Louis and the Far West attracted him. He sold his oxen and wagon and purchased a good horse, a mule to carry his traps, and the essential gun. His friend, known as Uncle Sam, was a hunter and owned what was generally judged to be the best rifle in the country. Alexander was determined to have that gun, and determination was a dominant trait in his character. Once he made up his mind to do something, he did it.

"Wall, Cyrus," said Uncle Sam, "I have refused to sell my gun time and again, because it is a good un, and I can't hardly git along without it. But see-in its you and you musn't go off there without a gun, I rather guess I'll have to let you have it." A price was agreed on, and Cyrus bought a brace of percussion cap-style pistols also, and ordered traps to be made for him.

Thus equipped, Alexander joined a fur company, not as one of "the boys" (employees), but as an independent under the company's protection. He set out from St. Louis in the spring of 1831 for the Rocky Mountains and was soon known as Aleck by "the boys." He was now twenty-six years old. Yount was thirty-two when he set out from St. Louis in the caravan to Santa Fe.

Fortune eluded Aleck as it had eluded Yount. Three times he was on the verge of getting the furs he had accumulated to market, and three times his hopes of returning home to Illinois, rich enough to become a prominent land-holder, faded. The third time was touch-and-go. He and his companions were attempting to cross the upper part of the Gulf of California in a large canoe, overloaded with their guns, furs and traps. A storm arose and in turning the canoe toward the shore they had left, the boat capsized into the bitter cold water. Three of the crew struck out for shore and were never seen again. Aleck and the others clung to the bottom of the upturned boat for one long day and, just as the sun was setting, the drifting canoe struck bottom near the place they had started. Friendly Indians came to their rescue. Aleck, unable to stand, was carried ashore.

Aleck now had nothing in the world but the suit on his back and the moccasins on his feet. The great loss was Uncle Sam's gun. Having heard of the trade in hides and tallow between Lower California and Boston, he decided to head for the nearest point on the Pacific Coast and reached San Diego in 1832 or 1833. He immediately found work and soon earned enough to buy some clothes and equip himself for more adventuring.

Like Yount, Aleck hunted sea otter along the coast, and then the sea otter and the sea lion around Guadelupe Island, two-hundred miles south of San Diego. He and his companions "slew them by the wholesale" until the creatures became scarce and shy. It was a short-lived but highly profitable adventure.

Back in San Diego, Aleck found that Spanish was universally spoken and that business could hardly be conducted without it, and learned to speak Spanish fluently. He also worked briefly for Henry Delane Fitch, a prosperous merchant, in the hide and tallow trade.

Captain Fitch had come from Boston to California in 1826, and settled in San Diego. He became a Mexican citizen, married a sister-in-law of Mariano Vallejo, and his cattle grazed on the land grant he received from the Mexican Governor and his own ships carried the hides and tallow to Boston. Historian Bancroft described him as being "straightforward in his dealings, generous in disposition, frank and cheerful in manner." So Aleck found him.

Fitch took a liking for Aleck who, by this time, concluded that cattle-raising was a very profitable business. Yet he had small hope of obtaining a land grant; he was unmarried, he was not a Roman Catholic and he had no intention of giving up his American citizenship to become a citizen of Mexico. Fitch advised him to go north of San Francisco Bay to look for some good, unclaimed grazing land. If found, Fitch said he would ask the government for a land grant, would stock it, and Aleck could "run it on shares."

Aleck headed north, riding the best of his four horses. In 1841 he found good, unclaimed land in a cove of the Russian River close to what is now Healdsburg. On receiving Aleck's report, Fitch came up to judge the prospects for himself and, that same year, received a grant of eleven leagues known as the Sotoyome Rancho. This included the present site of Healdsburg and much of the surrounding territory. Fitch then drew up his contract; he would stock the ranch with horses and cattle, Aleck was to care for them, and at the end of each year would rodeo the cattle — round them up and brand and divide them. He was to have half of the increase and, at the end of four years, receive two leagues of land.

In short order, Aleck built a small redwood cabin. He improvised a primitive wagon with wooden wheels and a center shaft to be drawn by a yoke of Spanish oxen, so that he could move tools and equipment from Sonoma, some thirty-five miles to the southeast. Soon, with the help of the Digger Indians, he built a roomier house of adobe and a tannery on what is still called Fitch Mountain.

Aleck had a poor opinion of the Diggers but they were his only labor force and he befriended them, paying for their work by giving them the game he hunted on their behalf. Thus he obtained the Diggers' goodwill and as they spoke a Spanish lingo, they and Aleck understood one another well enough.

In 1843, Frank Bedwell, a former Rocky Mountain trapper, came to Aleck in search of work. Aleck made him an offer, as much for company's sake as for any work he might do. If Frank would stay for two years Aleck would give him five-hundred acres. Frank accepted. Having heard of an orchard at Fort Ross, the former Russian settlement on the coast and thirty-five miles west of the ranch, one of the first things Aleck asked Frank to do was to ride to Fort Ross, with a Digger as guide, and bring back whatever seeds and "sprouts" he could procure. The seeds and cuttings which Frank brought back were planted that fall in what became Aleck's first orchard. In due course, Bedwell received his reward, purchased about eight-hundred acres more and went in for raising sheep and growing fruit — and became very prosperous.

Seventy years later, when Mr. G.S. Call purchased the Fort Ross property, the orchard planted by the Russians was still in existence just outside the palisade. A.A. Thompson, who wrote the first history of Sonoma County in 1877, said that the Russians had an excellent and quite extensive orchard at Ross, where they grew especially fine apples and other fruits. It may well have contained three apples which are still in cultivation today. These are the Red Astrakan, a Russian apple introduced via Sweden into England where it fruited for the first time in 1816, and was brought to America in 1835; the White

Astrakan which originated in Russia or Sweden in 1748; and the Gravenstein, said to have originated in Germany about 1790. Whether the Russians at Fort Ross obtained their "sprouts" or seeds direct from Russia is hard to tell, but in all probability the White Astrakan apple tree still growing in the Alexander house garden came from one of the "sprouts" Frank Bedwell brought back from Fort Ross. Of these three apples, the Gravenstein is the most widely grown in Sonoma County and is the principal variety used for making applesauce at Sebastopol, the center of Sonoma County's applesauce industry.

Before long, Aleck knew some of his neighbors, though they were few and far between, and among them were George Yount, John Cooper of Bodega, Captain Sutter of Sutter's Fort (Sacramento) and William Gordon, a Rocky Mountain trapper who had married a Spanish-Mexican woman. Gordon, his wife, and her teenage sister, Rufina Lucerne, had come to Sonoma in 1842. Gordon had received a land grant in Yolo County the following year.

The Fitch and Gordon grants were some one-hundred miles apart. The upshot of Aleck's visits to Gordon was his brief courtship of Rufina Lucerne. What had to be said was said in Spanish. They were married by Captain Sutter at Sutter's Fort in December 1844. Rufina was fourteen-years old, Aleck was thirty-nine — a difference of twenty-five years between them. After a brief stay at the Gordon ranch, Aleck and Rufina set out on their three-day ride home to the Fitch Rancho. Rufina proved "cut-out" to be a pioneer's wife.

The following year, according to his contract, Aleck was entitled to receive two leagues of land. Now that he could be independent again, he gave up his stewardship of the Fitch ranch, and Fitch regretfully found another man to take his place. And that October (1845) Aleck took possession of his portion of the Sotoyome Rancho, although he did not receive his title and deed until September 22, 1847.

The land he chose for his portion of the Sotoyome Grant lay on the east side of the Russian River and included the land from the river's channel to a line along the foothills. The site he chose for his home was "on a small eminence over which a large stream of spring water flowed from a large hill above, and still further up, a little to the east, was a number of springs forming quite a brook, which flowed down to the valley below like a silver thread."

Here Aleck soon established Rufina and their first child in a small redwood house that would serve until he built a larger one. He made a plow, harnessed his oxen to it, and plowed some land. After sowing the wheat seed, which came from Chile, he used a brush instead of a harrow to work it into the soil. He moved his tannery over from Fitch Mountain, enlarged it and sent his Diggers out to the coast again for seashells. Lime from the shells was essential to tanning, to remove the hair from the hides. His tanned leather had a ready market at Sutter's Fort, as did the cigars he and Rufina made. Through Sutter's influence they had obtained the necessary brown paper and plug tobacco, and since *cigaratas* were in great demand, cigar-making was a profitable sideline. He planted grapevines and set out another orchard, perhaps transplanting some of the young trees growing from the slips he had obtained from Fort Ross. In the dry months of 1847 he began work on what was to be his permanent home.

Of necessity, Aleck became as inventive and ingenious as Yount, and could manufacture almost everything Rufina and he needed. He is credited with being the first in Sonoma County to build a tannery and a lime-kiln, the first to build a brick-kiln and make bricks (for Rufina's brick oven), and the first to build and run a mill, although he had a Spaniard cut the millstones. He was also extraordinarily adaptable, ever-ready to grow and raise what he could profitably market. He raised sheep, had a fine drove of hogs, gave up tanning and drove his cattle to the mines instead of killing them, "receiving almost fabulous prices for them there." His fruit and vegetables also had a ready market, and one year he raised a crop of extra large onions, sent two tons of them to the mines in an ox team and cleared about twelve-hundred dollars in gold dust.

Aleck was, of course, plagued by the predators. He had killed off most of the bears, but the coyotes, the mountain lions, the jack rabbits and the ground squirrels raided his cattle, his sheep and his crops. Now and then he raided these animals in turn, shooting and trapping. He also soaked chunks of meat in a decoction of *nux vomica*, a rank poison he obtained from San Francisco and dragged the bait across the animals' trails. He was also plagued by squatters as was every other land holder. One night a squatter set fire to his great barn. It and its contents, the fresh threshed grain and farming equipment, was a total loss.

Again like Yount, Aleck had his chronicler. In July 1850, his nephew, Charles Alexander, who knew his uncle before he left Illinois, came to California and made his way from the Russian River Valley to Alexander's ranch. He stayed with Aleck and Rufina for two years and then bought land from his uncle and lived as his near neighbor for eleven years.

Obviously, the two men had a great affection for one another. Aleck, as Charles usually referred to his uncle, was his hero; and Aleck who was usually reticent in talking about his affairs, talked freely with Charles. Sitting around the fireside on long winter evenings they talked of things past and gone, of the family and friends in Illinois, and of Aleck's adventures as a trapper and pioneer. Three years after Aleck's death, Charles felt obligated to write *The Life and Times of Cyrus Alexander.* The original manuscript came into the safekeeping of the Bancroft Library of the University of California, and in the 1960s, was made available for publication. It was edited by George Shochat and published under the title Charles gave his work by Dawson's Bookshop, Los Angeles, in 1967.

Charles used the notes he had made of certain items, but wrote his slim biography almost entirely from memory. He was, after all, familiar with the Alexander Valley scene. He wrote completely factually without any embellishments, and his narrative is, perhaps, unique in portraying Aleck' and Rufina's domestic life, and the life of a farmer in Northern California in the mid-

1800s. Some of Charles' descriptive passages evoke the Dutch and Flemish paintings of country and household life in seventeenth-century Holland.

When the wheat was ready for harvest, it was harvested with a sickle which Aleck had brought from San Diego. In threshing the wheat, Aleck followed the only method known in California at the time:

> The corral into which they drove the horses and cattle to lasso them, after a while became quite hard; into this they would pile up the grain and then the *manatha* (*Manada*) or band of mares were turned upon it to tramp out the grain . . . After threshing, the wheat would be a mass of grain and chaff . . . The most difficult part of the operation was separating the grain from the chaff. As the dry season in California lasts from the middle of May until the middle of October, they had plenty of time to work at the wheat. So when the wind was high enough, the Diggers would toss the mass up into the air with large wooden forks, and the wind would separate it for them.

Rufina's method of spinning was new to Charles. It may have been primitive and it may have been an invention of her own, he said. With the rolls of wool she procured from San Diego, Rufina busied herself spinning the rolls into yarn.

> She had a large earthen bowl, very smooth on the inside; this bowl she would place in her lap while sitting on a low chair. In this bowl she twisted a spindle with her thumb and finger; said spindle was a stick whittled in such a shape as to whirl readily on one end, similar to a boy's top; while keeping this in motion with one hand, she would *pay* out the wool with the other. In this manner she could spin enough yarn in one day for a pair of socks.

Cyrus Alexander achieved almost all he wanted. He had made a fortune; his house, begun in 1847, was the largest, the most elegantly and expensively furnished house in Alexander Valley. The walls of the lower story were two feet thick of solid adobe, the upper was frame. It was porched on two sides, painted white and roofed with redwood shingles. Close by, at the rear, was a much smaller adobe house which presumably was built on the site of the earlier redwood cabin. The fruit trees that Alexander had planted in 1846 flourished. He had spent time and money in adding the best variety of fruit trees he could procure and so achieved his ambition of having the finest "pioneer orchard" anywhere around. Near the house, he planted a fig tree and an Astrakan apple tree, both of which are believed to have come from Fort Ross. His olive trees from Spain were aboard a trading vessel berthed in San Francisco.

On the reverse side of the golden coin, he lost five of his several children, including his two eldest sons, and he suffered two strokes. He had to be driven around his land in a buggy, could no longer read and could speak only in monosyllables. But people read aloud to him and his mind was clear to the last. He died when he was sixty-seven years old, on December 27, 1872, and was buried in the little family graveyard on the top of a knoll near the house.

Charles Alexander, writing his book in 1875, often went to see Rufina. "The place is nicely fitted up; the house is surrounded with a nice yard containing shade trees, and many varieties of flowers . . . All necessary barns, stables, smoke-house, granaries, etc., are built of the best material."

Rufina talked constantly about Aleck. Three of the younger children lived with her, and a married son and married daughter lived nearby. "She is still young looking to be the mother of so many children," wrote Charles. "She is under medium height, heavy set, dark complexion, quick of movement and very industrious; she is forty-five years of age, but looks much younger." Rufina had never learned to speak English fluently, and it was difficult for anyone who did not speak Spanish to talk with her. Usually she managed to have one of her children with her to interpret. The children were obviously bilingual and Cyrus had seen to it that they were taught good penmanship. Later he had built a schoolhouse for them and the children of the other settlers.

One of the questions asked most often at the Edwin Langhart Museum in Healdsburg is "What does the word 'Sotoyome' mean?" Apparently this has been a matter of controversy since at least 1906. The museum's curator, Hannah Clayborn, has done a great deal of research to try to find the answer. The result of her work is contained in a four-page report published in the Healdsburg Historical Society's "Russian River Recorder" of July/August 1981.

Included in her report is the opinion of Mrs. Anita Fitch Grant, a daughter of Captain Henry D. Fitch, and reputedly a linguist and a student of the native tribes or groups in the area. Her interpretation of the latter part of the name was "y-o-me" meaning the place where one stays, and "Soto" was derived from the name of a Spaniard, De Soto, who was sent by the Spanish padres at San Rafael to round up some Indians to help in building the mission there. De Soto stayed at a settlement on Macama Creek and the Indians thereafter called their territory "Sotoyome" — the place where De Soto stayed. However questionable this version is, it suggests that the Spaniards went far afield in search of Indian labor, but in 1817, when the San Rafael Mission was founded, it is hard to believe there was not a sufficient supply of Indian labor close at hand.

Hannah Claybourne concludes that "At least we can now answer to those who question the meaning of the word Sotoyome: It has *definitely* been established that no one really knows!" In *The Handbook of North American Indians*, Volume 12, California, edited by Robert F. Heizer, it is said that the name "Sotoyome" is from the Pomo "Place of Sota," a chief of the Sotoyome.

34

Alexander Valley's Inheritance

The Alexander house and a good deal of the surrounding land remained in the family's ownership until Mrs. Annie Alexander died. Mr. and Mrs. Harry H. Wetzel purchased the property from the heirs of Cyrus Alexander's granddaughter in 1963. The house was not the one Cyrus Alexander built. In the 1906 earthquake, his first story adobe walls cracked beyond repair. The adobe was carted away and the redwood timbers of the upper story were used to rebuild a second house on the same site. The walls of the small adobe house at the rear also cracked and the house was left just as it was.

At the time of the purchase, the second house was in disrepair and the garden was a wilderness. But the fig tree and the Astrakan apple tree, which Cyrus Alexander had surely obtained from Fort Ross and planted close to the house, were still standing and so were the olive trees from Spain. These are now trees of great size.

When I first saw the superbly restored house and the remarkable garden, planted almost entirely with vegetables and herbs, I was mystified. I had assumed that Mrs. Wetzel was a Californian. Yet the feel and furnishings of the house reminded me of those Virginia plantation houses which have been continually lived in, and speak of the present as well as the past. In particular, Brandon on the James River in the Virginia Tidewater came to mind.

The garden, one of the most ornamental kitchen gardens I have seen, also seemed to echo faintly and on a much larger scale, the small, formal kitchen gardens in Williamsburg, Virginia's eighteenth-century colonial capital, which were intended from the beginning to be decorative as well as useful.

The riddle was solved when Mrs. Wetzel told me later that she came from an old Virginia family and had been born and raised in the Tidewater, a few miles from Williamsburg. She has, quite unconsciously, imparted the atmosphere of the plantation house on the 1906 Alexander house. And, oddly enough, Cyrus Alexander, just as unconsciously, imparted another aspect of the plantation house when he built, as Charles told us, his stables, smokehouse, granaries, etc., in the yard between the house and garden and the rear. Between the plantation and the Williamsburg house and garden, there was a service yard with a smokehouse, a granary (for corn instead of wheat) and other "dependencies," as these essential outbuildings were called. Perhaps the farmers in Illinois had similar service yards.

Unless one has a sense of place or is familiar with Tidewater, Virginia, I do not think most people would detect the influence of a Virginia hand. The touch is a light one and does not superimpose itself on the present or on the Wetzel family's tastes and interests. Mr. and Mrs. Wetzel are, however, proud of the fact that only two families have owned the property. They have established a certain continuity in ownership by respecting, in countless detailed ways, what they have indirectly inherited from Cyrus Alexander and they treasure every item of Alexander memorabilia. The photographs of Cyrus and Rufina have pride of place over the fireplace in the high-ceilinged living room and there is also a portrait of Captain Fitch on the wall quite close beside them.

The small adobe house in the service yard in which Cyrus and Rufina lived until the much larger family home was built, has been restored and is now used as a game room. The schoolhouse, built in 1868, has been moved nearer the main house and now serves as a guest house. It is reached by a broad stone path which leads from the end of the garden, across a little creek bed, to a hillside above. Cyrus Alexander had a Spaniard cut his millstones. The schoolhouse path was laid by a Mexican.

As for the garden, Mrs. Wetzel deliberately set out to create what she calls a westernized Williamsburg kitchen garden, and she had an English landscape gardener from Santa Rosa to help her carry out the design. It is a large garden and has a spaciousness about it that goes far beyond the confines of a small-town garden. The vegetables are grown in regimented rows, and the pole beans form a wide hedge six to eight feet tall. The massed plantings of globe artichokes and herbs such as lavender, sweet basil and various sages, border the flowing contours of the broad paths which are covered with the brown shredded redwood bark. These bold plantings, often overspreading their boundaries, soften the forefront of the vegetable growing area and almost mask the underlying formal design.

Mrs. Wetzel is a hard-working, highly knowledgeable gardener, and is well-aware that she has the soil, the climate and, above all, an abundance of pure spring water to aid her. But she follows the golden rule of all good gardeners — she puts back into the soil more than she takes out of it.

She is a great lover of trees. One side of the road leading up from the highway to the house is lined with sweet gum (Liquidambar) trees which are native to Virginia and other eastern states. Cyrus Alexander sent Frank Bedwell and a Digger Indian to Fort Ross to get the slips of fruit trees he planted in 1843. Mrs. Wetzel drove her pickup some two-hundred miles to a nursery south of San

Francisco to pick out and bring back her sweet gum trees. In the orchard, slips from the old white Astrakan apple tree have been grafted on new apple trees, so that a new generation of Astrakans may grow along with the old. The orchard also contains Gravenstein apple trees. And as all cordonned fruit trees should be trained by only one pair of hands, it is Mrs. Wetzel who trains the line of cordonned pear trees which separate the service yard from the garden.

Cyrus Alexander was ever ready to buy the latest and the best equipment with which to work his land. A threshing machine of sorts became available in 1853; he bought one for his grain harvest, along with a winnower and a fan-mill which was used with the thresher, and he bought grain-cradles and cradled his grain instead of cutting it with sickles.

The Wetzels, in accordance with the trend of the day, put 240 acres of their land into grapes. Harry Wetzel Jr., the winemaster, makes his Cabernet Sauvignon, Chardonnay, Johannisberg Riesling and Gewurztraminer in the family winery just below the Alexander graveyard knoll. The Wetzel vinyardist and the vintner have the best and latest equipment. The grapes are harvested by a mechanical harvester. This was invented by the late Mr. Wallace Johnson, whose family winery, Field Stone, is just a little way down the road from the Wetzels and whose land was once part of the Alexander grant.

Sheep still run on the hills above and the coyotes still make their raids until the county trapper slows them up for a season. So much has changed and so much remains unchanged. Cyrus Alexander would be pleased and intrigued by the up-to-date equipment. Rufina would marvel at the cold-storage structure in the service yard which preserves the surplus fruit and vegetables, and she would be in her element when the Wetzel children, and their children come in and out of the house.

Cyrus would, however, probably ponder over the interest people in the Napa, Knight's and Alexander Valleys have today in the Digger Indians. Cyrus, we remember, had a poor opinion of them. Richard Dana, William Brewer and that intrepid Englishwoman, Isabella L. Bird who traveled alone in America, Canada and the Orient, and who was in Northern California in 1873, found the Diggers utterly unprepossessing in appearance — the ugliest Indians in North America. But photographs of the Diggers belie their ugliness and Grace Carpenter Hudson (1865-1937), "the painter lady" of the Pomos of Mendocino County, saw attractiveness if not beauty in some of their faces. Her picture, "Little Mendocino" (1893), brought her into the limelight. It portrayed a papoose wrapped in a blanket and securely tied with strong cord in its basket resting against the foliage of a redwood tree. From then on she painted innumerable portraits of the Pomo, mostly of children and young men and women, and a comparatively few adults. They were undoubtedly flat-nosed and sturdy, but not ugly in the eyes of today. Grace Hudson's Pomo portraits, like the Wappo and Pomo basketry, and their obsidian arrowheads and spear points, are now collectors' items and museum pieces.

35

The Wappo Indian

Surely nothing could be less ghostly than a tax bill. So we thought until we received the notice sent by the tax collector of Sonoma County. The bill informed us that our acre was a part of the Rancho Mallacomes, of which we had never heard.

Naturally, when we paid the bill in Santa Rosa, we inquired about the "rancho." The clerk we questioned hauled up a huge record book to show that "the title deed of the old Mexican land grant makes your property a part of Rancho Mallacomes or Moristul y Plan de Agua Caliente."

I copied the long, romantic-sounding title, which conjured up a vanished world that survived only in the official records. *Agua Caliente,* Hot Springs in Spanish, we already knew applied to Calistoga. No one locally could enlighten us about the origin and meaning of the other names and it was a good two years before we rounded up the story of Rancho Mallacomes or Moristul.

We learned from the University of California's Anthropological Records that Moristul was from the Indian dialect Mutistul: *muti,* meaning "north," and *tul* meaning "valley," the valley north of *Agua Caliente* (today, Knight's Valley, north of Calistoga). Mallacomes, pronounced May-yah-*ko* - mace, was the Spanish phonetic rendering of the Indian name *Mayacoma,* from *mayoc* and *noma,* meaning "standing" and "place." (Incidentally, the language of the Indians and the Californios were not unlike phonetically and the Indians readily picked up Spanish words and phrases that baffled them in English.)

There was an intriguing explanation for the name "standing place." Several Indian trails, from north, south, east and west, crossed at some point in the valley north of *Agua Caliente.* It was Indian practice for one traveling band to leave a stick "standing" at the crossroads to tell those following behind which direction to take from there. The name Mayacamas is still applied to the mountains extending northwest of Mount St. Helena.

In pursuing the origin of the names on our tax bill we read the late

Alfred L. Kroeber's classic, *Handbook of California Indians,* first published by the Smithsonian Institution. We learned almost all we know about the California Indians in general from this book, and in particular, about those whose territory included Knight's Valley.

The California Indians differed from all others in North America. They were divided into some five-hundred groups, each speaking its own dialect, each more like a big family than a tribe. The size of each group was determined by those natural resources of its area that would provide food, water and shelter. The birth rate was instinctively balanced with Nature's supply, so the group rarely suffered want.

In turn, each village of the group had its own commonly recognized preserve. Its people fished, hunted game and gathered roots, seeds and berries only within the village's common grounds. Such wars as happened were seldom more than quarrels over trespassing and ended when the first man was wounded or killed. His side lost the dispute. But there were some exceptions.

Professor Kroeber records that Alexander Valley (along the Russian River above Healdsburg) is one of the few tracts which changed ownership from one Indian group to another. The Russian River was essentially a Pomo river and the western Wappo had but one village of any importance on it. This was Pipoholma, inhabited by the Mishewal (Wappo) — the "mishe-warriors" — under a chief, Michahel.

About 1830, and a few years before the first Spanish settlements in the Russian River Valley, on a day in the fall, the Mishewal gathered some acorns and stacked them in piles on their side of the creek which was the boundary line between their territory and that of the Pomo. Then the Mishewal returned home to Pipoholma. The Pomo stole the acorns during the night.

It was easy for the Mishewal to trace the thieves. The next night, Michahel and some ten of his men crept into the nearby Pomo village and killed two Pomos. The next morning, the Mishewal attacked again in force, slew some of the Pomo and burned the village. The survivors, along with the inhabitants of six other neighboring Pomo villages, fled downstream from Healdsburg. While the Mishewal were cremating the fallen, the Pomo sent word that they wanted to end the feud. A meeting ensued, gifts were exchanged, and Michahel told the Pomo they could return in peace to their abandoned villages. But the Pomo were fearful, and they chose to re-establish themselves elsewhere and allow the Mishewal to occupy the settlements in question.

Broadly speaking, the Wappo territory embraced Napa, Knight's and Alexander Valleys, Mount St. Helena, and Cobb Mountain further north, and adjoined that of the Pomo to the west and north. Although their territory was mostly in the mountains, their settlements were in the valleys.

The Spanish soldiers, impressed by the indians resistance when they were rounded up for life and work at the mission, called them *guapo* — "courageous," "valiant" and "bold." Wappo, the Americanized spelling of *guapo,* became firmly established and has not been replaced by the aboriginal name. The mountain men, the trappers and the hunters who were the first pathfinders to California in the 1820s, gave them another name. Seeing the women digging for roots for food, they called them "Digger" Indians. Today, the name "Digger" applies mostly to those Indians north of San Francisco Bay.

Wappo and Pomo were similar in their habits, but Professor Kroeber made a distinction between them — that the Wappo were the mountaineers and the Pomo the wealthier lowlanders. Professor Kroeber also spoke of the Wappo as being more nearly "autochothone" than almost any other family group; autochothone meaning one sprung from the land he dwells on.

One of the earliest recorded descriptions of the Pomo along the Sonoma coastline was given by Kostronitonov, manager of the colony at Fort Ross for seven years. And it may well apply to the Wappo also:

> They are gentle and peaceable and very clever, especially in comprehending material objects. Only as a consequence of their excessive indolence and unconcern do they appear to be quite stupid; they need to watch an easy or complex activity but once in order to be able to imitate it immediately.

Clever as they were in comprehending material objects, the Pomo and the Wappo excelled in basketmaking. Their baskets were not only utilitarian but a form of art. The Pomo created the original models, but the baskets of the Wappo are "practically indistinguishable for Pomo wares," and these reputedly are the finest in California; some say among the best in the world. Their baskets were made for every conceivable use, including water carriers and pots for boiling which, of course, were watertight.

The men of the village made the basket traps for trapping birds, fish and small animals, and also made the granaries for holding the acorns and other harvested foods. The granary was not strictly a basket, but a strong, upright, container woven around three or four stakes and capped with a thatch roof. The women made all the household baskets with their intricate finishing and ornamenting which involved weaving designs colored by vegetable dyes. The gift basket, often adorned with feathers was, in its most elaborate form, a marvel of meticulous detail. Decorated with black wavy quail plumes, the tiny scarlet caps of the acorn woodpecker, bits of flicker yellow and blue-green from the mallard duck, it was also sometimes ornamented with clam-shell beads and iridescent abalone pendants.

Stonework was another speciality in which the Wappos excelled. They used the raw materials so plentifully strewn around them; obsidian, a black volcanic glass; cryptocrystalline churt, jasper, chalcedony and flint. Working only with stone tools which would leave the modern craftsman helpless, they turned out mortars and pestles, other utilitarian objects, and ornaments of a symmetry probably unsurpassed by any other aboriginal workers in stone. They made prime arrow and spear heads from obsidian by handchipping and flaking and, from photographs, these appear to be identical to those obsidian "lance" heads made c.7000 B.C. which were found at Chatal Huyak, Antolia, one of the earliest of Neolithic cities.

I like to think of the Wappo as being akin to England's Stone Age man, the flint-worker who was as fearful of the hairy mammoth as the Wappo of the grizzly bear. Those ancient Britons were the forerunners of the stone masons who centuries later worked the gargoyles, the flowers and leaves and all the elaborate tracery in stone found in Europe's medieval cathedrals. If the Stone Age man failed to raise his artisanship to an art, at least he attained a perfection of simplicity limited only by his tools; the Wappos achieved likewise.

The Wappo and the Pomo were described by the white man as indolent. Yet before the Spanish padres made them labor in ways they were entirely unused to, they worked as hard as any free-lance artisan today. They had to, to provide themselves with enough food to live. The marvel is that they used what spare time they had in producing stonework and basketry of such high order.

36

Paradise Lost

The Wappo's world was a primeval paradise and they had no reason to believe that it would not last forever. Until the white man's coming, the Indian and the grizzly bear of the north bay area, each in his own sphere, were monarchs over plenty. No ax had touched the trees that marched in regiments and brigades over the northerly slope of every hill. The redwoods, tallest of trees, often three-hundred feet high and twenty feet thick at the base, had been youthful contemporaries of Julius Caesar. No plow had broken the soil. Wild oats grew shoulder high across the valley floor. Wildlife abounded. Like the Indian, the coyote, the big mountain cats and the grizzlies, killed only to eat or to defend themselves. There was living room for all.

Early settlers in the Napa Valley noted that the Indians lived in contentment beside the many springs and streams, while the grizzlies, as George Yount recounted, "were everywhere — upon the plains, in the valleys and on the mountains . . . and it is not unusual to see fifty or sixty within the twenty-four hours." At the Sonoma Mission, Padre Altimira observed "the benignity of the climate," the lofty shade trees, the luxuriance of the wild grapes. To hunter and priest alike, the theme was tranquility and plenty.

Yet, with their coming that tranquility was to end. Priest and hunter, trailing gunpowder, rum and disease behind them, foredoomed the Indians and the bears. The rising flow of settlers brought a change of world almost overnight: in a gun flash, a triumphant laugh, in a thin wreath of smoke that lingered for a moment in the sunlit air. Never again would life be as it had always been.

The slaughter of the bears began at once, gunpowder being a more potent killer than a bow-string, white men less willing to keep peace with wild neighbors who raided sheep and cattle. In fairness to the pioneers, we must concede that a grizzly in the backyard was not compatible with quiet living. The grizzly was so formidable that he had few natural enemies, and was the

174

undisputed monarch of the wild, possibly for a million years, until gunpowder annihilated him. At his peak, he weighed a good twelve-hundred pounds and stood ten feet tall when reared up on his hind legs. Inevitably, he went with the white man's occupancy of the land.

On one day in June 1823, the soldiers of the Sonoma Mission finished off ten grizzlies as a starter of a new Hundred Years War. George Yount, who probably accounted for more grizzlies than any other single hunter, said he often killed as many as five or six in one day. By 1923, the grizzly was declared extinct in California — except for its memorial emblem on the state's Bear Flag.

The Indian vanished even more quickly than the bears. Altimira found them either friendly, timid, or only slightly hostile at worst, easily dispersed by the blast of a small brass cannon. In 1831, George Yount made a guess that from three-thousand to five-thousand Indians were living in and near the Napa Valley. In 1838, he reported that hardly a handful remained. Smallpox brought in by the white man had disposed of the others.

A historian of the time wrote that the pestilence "paved the way for peaceable occupation of this territory by immigrants," adding: "There were not enough Indians left to offer any serious resistance to the free occupancy of their former hunting grounds by civilized man."

Civilized? Benjamin Franklin's comment on that question was: "Savages we call them, because their manners differ from ours, which we think the perfection of civility. They think the same of their's."

Professor Kroeber, writing as an American researcher, reported facts however unpleasant. His comment on the efforts of the Spanish mission padres to save souls was that Indian souls were saved only at the inevitable cost of lives. "The brute upshot of missionization, in spite of its kindly flavor and humanitarian root, was only one thing: death. What the Franciscan began with his concentrations the Americans finished by mere settlement."

A lot of things went down with the crumbling of the Indian world. The Wappos and the Pomos were the last of the master basketmakers, the last of the great aboriginal stoneworkers. Many of their animal brothers went with them: the wolf, the wapiti, and other predators, and the grizzly bear. Suddenly, in the land where there had been room for all, there was room only for an exclusive few. How incredible it seemed to us that all this happened in my own grandmother's day, just over a hundred years ago.

One dominant character who survived the holocaust was the valley oak, though these are far fewer than they used to be, for they once studded the floor of almost every valley. The Spaniards called it "El Roble," or *the* oak, to mark it as the largest of all of California's oaks. The fact that it is useless for lumber and makes indifferent firewood perhaps explains the great wide-spreading tree's survival. We had three of them on our acre, the largest estimated to be more than three-hundred years old. We called this tree "the patriarch" because it was a family tree that provided home and board to a varied company.

It had once helped feed the Indian and the grizzly bear and now, in springtime, the golden oriole comes to this patriarch to build its hanging-basket nest in a streamer of hanging Spanish moss. The plain titmouse, the big tree's true friend, feeds year-round on the insects which destroy both leaves and acorns. Another year-round resident, the red-headed California woodpecker, stores acorns in the oak tree's bark, a practice that caused his colloquial name, acorn woodpecker. Come winter, "the patriarch's" trunk and limbs are studded from tip to toe with acorns like a coat of mail.

The so-called Spanish moss which occurs in Knight's and Alexander Valleys and many other valleys of the Coast Range is *Ramalina reticulata,* a conspicuous lichen, its netted structure hanging from the branches of trees, in particular of oak trees. True Spanish moss is a flowering plant found mainly in the southern states and is a member of the pineapple family.

In Indian days the acorns were harvested by man and beast as well as by the birds. For the Indian, as for the woodpecker, the acorn was a staple food. When leached, it had an excellent flavor and was ground into sweet meal, which was baked into bread or boiled in a gruel.

The acorn was a staple of diet for the grizzly also. The bear would feed on the acorns lying upon the ground and, if there were not sufficient fallen nuts, it would jump on to an oak limb and swing and jerk until it broke, branches and acorns, and probably bear all coming down together.

Surely the grizzlies came to our patriarch as they guzzled their way from oak grove to oak grove throughout the valley, until fat and so heavy their bellies dragged along the ground. And just as surely, the Indians came too, for festival as well as harvest. The Indians would wait their turn though, for they always gave the grizzly the right of way. They felt a closer kinship with the big bear than with any other creature and knew that if he was left alone, he would leave them alone.

When the bears moved on, their own harvest completed, the Indians held their Acorn Festival. Decking themselves with feather-head-nets filled with eagle down, or a forehead band of red-shafted flicker's quills, they danced the night away beneath the trees. A campfire lighted the scene for, by then, it was late fall, growing cold, and the life of the village soon became more inviting than life in the wild all around.

37

Moristul

One of the maps in the *Archaeology of the Napa Region,* is of Wappo territory and shows their campsites and permanent valley villages. One campsite and one village in our valley are both marked Mutistul and we tried to pinpoint the village.

To begin with, no one we asked knew anything about Mutistul or Moristul, nor had they ever heard of any Indian village in our valley. The only answer we got was "old Mr. So-and-so, he's eighty now, has lived here all his life; he may know."

We learned little tapping the memories of old-timers. But we were amazed to discover an undercurrent interest in Indians and, in many cases, a deep respect and how many said that they had a few Indian things, if we'd care to step inside to see them. Stored away in many country household cupboards were fine examples of baskets, arrowheads and mortars — the heavy stone bowls, from eight to twelve inches wide, and the grinding stones, rounded to fit the hand, which served to grind seeds, especially acorns.

The widow of a man of pioneer family had an array of mortars in her garden. Her husband, she told us, had been a long-time friend of Professor Kroeber. The two had gone searching for Indian relics together, often along the streams after heavy rains which dislodged fast-held curios — or to use the ugly professional word, artifacts.

We visited her again and were given an Indian bowl and grinding stone of our choice. We put the bowl to use as a bird bath, setting it by one of our spiggots on the lawn near the big oak tree, much to the birds' delight, especially the woodpeckers, the bluebirds and goldfinches who thronged to it all summer long. One spring we counted seventeen robins drinking from the bowl at one time.

I suspect that over the months our question, "Have you ever heard of an Indian village hereabouts," earned us the reputation of having "gone over the hill." Always the answer was a shake of the head and an amused look. It seemed that Moristul was lost indeed except to the long memory of the county tax collector.

Knowing that all villages of the first Californians had been on or near year-round streams out of elemental necessity, we began exploring stream banks in our vicinity. Once we thought we had a clue. Meeting an odd character who looked like a trapper of the early days, he told us that the Indians came to his particular creek for the runs of steelhead in the spring.

"Was there a village nearby?" At that, the interest left his eyes. For some reason or other the question was unwelcome. He shrugged his shoulders, mumbled something about a mound across on the other bank of the stream, and that was all.

Months had gone by. We had just about given up our search as hopeless, when our neighbor from whom we had bought our acre, solved the mystery. I had never mentioned Moristul in talking to her, why I now can't imagine, because her large holdings were billed for taxes under the same grant as our own.

During a visit, my eye caught an Indian basket perched on a balustrade in her high-ceilinged hallway. At once, I asked the question I had asked so fruitlessly over and over again.

"Oh, yes," she said as casually as if I had asked if she had a good colt for sale. "Moristul, Mutistul or however you spell it, I'll show you where it was." She explained that ten years or so earlier, upon acquiring their land in Knight's Valley, she and her sister, afire with curiosity also, had set out to find Moristul. A former owner of the land, then an old man, had granted at last, and most unwillingly, that there had been an Indian village nearby.

"Up aways on the hill," he had said vaguely. "Try as we would to pin him down, he was evasive about the exact spot. But he knew."

His wife, then dead, had never wished their children or anybody to know just where the village had been. She had wanted the Wappos' sanctuary to be left undisturbed, so the old man kept faith.

He did say he had found numerous Indian relics, all witness to the site of the village, and had presented them to a museum in San Francisco for safekeeping. Ironically, the museum had been destroyed and the relics lost in the earthquake of 1906, but not before they had been adjudged of great antiquity.

In the intervening years, the land had been in the possession of a sawmill operator. Logging roads had been cut over the old trails, an area cleared for the mill and the best of the huge trees lumbered off. With a helpless shrug, our friend swept a vague half-circle with her arm: "Here's all that's left of Moristul."

Not all. Later we were shown a field, then planted in young walnut trees, where, after a rain, it was still easy to find arrowheads and chips of obsidian brought to the surface. The source of supply was relatively close at hand, on what is known as Glass Mountain on the Silverado Trail in Napa County, and obsidian arrowheads, being the best of all, were important items of trade.

We paused to make a mental survey of the site, knowing that we were as near as we would ever come to Mayacoma — Mallacomes, the crossroads and the Standing Place. Hereabouts the Wappo stood or squatted, ready to barter with all who passed their way.

From the north came iris cord used for deer snares and sinew-backed yew bows that were superior to local bows of mountain mahogany. From the northeast, from what is now Lake County, came magnasite beads that had been baked and polished. Mussels, seaweed, clamshell disc beads, and the shell of haliotis or abalone as the Spaniards called it and which yields mother-of-pearl, were brought in from the west along the coast. Pieces of abalone shell were often attached to the body of a basket as danglers to catch and reflect the light. Clamshell beads were sometimes woven into a basket's rim, or strung on a milkweed string and worn around the neck. Clamshell discs were also used as money.

Money is what you make it. The Wappos were rich by such standards of natural resources at hand. They could offer skins of the black and brown bears, acorns, roots of wild plants, brodiaea and other lily bulbs, the leaves of *nicotiana,* their mild wild tobacco, woodpecker-scalps, talcum powder from silky-hued steatite, and fine vermillion make-up paint from powdered cinnabar for festive occasions. The abundance of obsidian blanks and chips and the proximity of Glass Mountain suggest that the making of arrowheads was a flourishing industry.

Undoubtedly, the Standing Place, like all trading posts, would have been a news center as well, and the Wappo would have been posted on all events of consequence near and far. The coast Miwoks whom Chaplain Fletcher recorded as running "very swiftly and long" and who reported the presence of Drake and his crew "as it seemed a great way up into the countrie," would surely have carried the strangest news that had ever reached the Wappo — some two-hundred years before the coming of the Spaniards and the Russians.

Far away from the highway where tall woodwardia fern grew along one of the streams and the clear sweet spring-fed waters swirled among the moss-covered boulders, we knew that somewhere nearby, but two or three miles by crowflight from our small ranch house, was where Moristul had been.

We went back there many times. The woods, despoiled as they were of big timber, were still beautiful. Here and there a giant fir survived, considered by loggers too irregular to be worth felling, in a day when lumber was more plentiful than it is today. There were tall young trees everywhere sifting sunlight and in spring, wildflowers colored the open glades and wine-dark trilium were abloom thickset along the stream.

About the place was that silence of long deserted places. We had been told we might regard the land as our own to explore as we wished. "If you want to, dig. I'm sure the ghosts won't mind, if you dig with respect, as I'm sure you will."

But dig I did not. I was content to pick up an arrowhead that the rains or a harrow had brought to the surface, and it gave me a curious deep satisfaction to hold it in my hand, knowing that only a skilled Indian's hand had held it before me.

And for another reason I stayed my spade. I felt that I owed the men of Moristul a debt and had no right to disturb their sanctuary. With their ghosts all round about us, the wide open spaces of the West were no longer so wide, so empty, or so lonely as I once thought them to be.

For the record, I should add that there are still approximately two-hundred Wappo Indians living in the Russian River Valley region. And I am now doubly glad I did not dig into the soil round about Moristul.

In the intervening years since we lived in Knight's Valley, I have learned that digging for Indian relics is illegal. Archaeology is far more sophisticated than it used to be. The layers of soil provide the prehistoric record of a site. Even pollen can be recovered by a meticulous sifting of the soil, and the plants which yielded it identified. This, in turn, leads to a wider knowledge of plants which were used medicinally. To dig haphazardly and raise some relic is to remove that relic from its context, and may be likened to tearing pictures out of a book and throwing away the text.

Epilogue

This stir of change and these perpetual echoes
of the moving footfall, haunt the land.

In listening for those phantom footfalls we did discover, what Stevenson had no time to do, that many of those footfalls left their mark. I also discovered that since Stevenson's day and on up to the present there has been a continuity in the stir of change and the perpetual echoes of the footfall of a highly cosmopolitan company of travelers and settlers who have been drawn to what is now commonly called The Wine Country. Many of these have also left their mark.

The region is richer in its literary associations. In the last thirty years, the Arthur Haileys, M.F.K. Fisher, Idwal Jones have come here; so have Hildegarde Flanner, and her husband, the artist and architect Frederick Monhoff. There is a lack of landscape painters — the age of the great landscape paintings has long since gone. But photographers have been drawn here, in particular Philip Hyde, well known for his photographs of the Sonoma coastline. These have followed in a tradition that had already been marked out.

Today a different breed of men have come here too. There are the film writers, and famous chefs who have made the region a gourmet's paradise. There is also a change in attitude of both long-time residents and the newcomers. Unlike the pioneers who had little time or thought to record a present, they are keenly interested in making a record of their own history, and in preserving and restoring what are now the old homes, the old wineries and the memorabilia concerning them.

A line may, perhaps, be drawn between the traveler and the tourist. Either way they come here — from all over the world. Some come to tour the wineries and taste the fine wines; others, the students, the scholars and the specialists come from Samoa, from Pakistan, from everywhere, to the Silverado Museum which houses one of the world's largest collections of Stevensoniana. And there are those interested in the region's history who visit the Sharpsteen Museum in Calistoga, and the Edwin Langhart Museum in Healdsburg.

One is no longer permitted to drive up the tortuous road to the summit of the north peak on Mount St. Helena, but the hikers can follow it to the top. There are now other ways to see the vast panorama unfold. Glider planes soar noiselessly along the wind-currents in the sky above, and there are rides to be had in multicolored balloons that float above the landscape.

Much has changed, much remains unchanged. The face of the land has changed only according to man's use of it; the grape vine now possesses the territory that formerly belonged to prune and walnut orchards and pasture land. Inevitably, Mount St. Helena is still the presiding genius of what Gene Dekovic, himself a writer and photographer, in his latest book calls *This Blessed Land*.

Bibliography

Aldington, Richard. *Portrait of a Rebel.* London: Evans Brothers, 1957.

Alexander, Charles. *The Life and Times of Cyrus Alexander.* Ed. George Shochat. Los Angeles: Dawson's Bookshop, 1967.

Archuleta, Kay. *The Brannan Saga.* Calistoga: Archuleta, 1977.

Atherton, Gertrude. *My San Francisco — A Wayward Biography.* Indianapolis, New York: Bobbs-Merrill, 1946.

Atherton, Gerturde. *Adventures of a Novelist.* New York: Liveright, 1932.

Bancroft, Hubert Howe. *History of California.* 7 vols. San Francisco: 1884-1890.

Beard, Yolande S. *The Wappo — A Report.* Banning, California: Malki Museum Press, 1979.

Belloc, Hilaire. *The Contrast.* London: J.W. Arrowsmith, 1923.

Bird, Isabella L. *A Lady's Life In The Rocky Mountains — Letters On Her 1873 Tour.* Ed. Daniel J. Boorstin. Norman, Oklahoma: Oklahoma Press, 1979.

Brewer, William H. *Up and Down California, Letters.* Ed. Francis P. Farquhar. Berkeley: University of California Press, 1977.

British Library. *Sir Francis Drake.* London: British Museum Publications, 1977.

Brough, James. *The Prince & The Lily.* New York: Coward, McCann & Geoghegan, 1975.

Boynton, Searles R. *The Painter Lady — Grace Carpenter Hudson.* Eureka, California: Interface, 1978.

Camp, Charles L. (ed.). *George C. Yount — His Chronicle Of The West.* Denver, Colorado: Old West Publishing Co., 1966.

Caughey, John Walton. *California.* New York: Prentice Hall, 1971.

Cleland, Robert Glass. *This Reckless Breed of Men.* Ed. Harvey C. Carter. Albuquerque: University of New Mexico Press, 1976.

Dana, Richard Henry. *Two Years Before The Mast — And Letters And Journals.* Ed. John Haskell Kemble. Los Angeles: Ward Ritchie Press, 1964.

Duflot de Mofras, Eugene. *Duflot de Mofras' Travels on the Pacific Coast.* trans. by Marguerite Eyer Wilbur. Santa Ana, California: 1937.

Duhaut-Cilly, Augusta Bernard. *A Visit To The Russians in 1828*, An episode translated from the French by Charles Franklin Carter. San Francisco: The Grabhorn Press, 1946.

Federal Writers' Project. *California.* New York: Hastings House, 1945.

Field, Isobel. *This Life I've Loved.* London: Longmans Green, 1936.

Furness, J.C. *Voyage To Windward.* New York: Sloane, 1951.

Gerson, Noel B. *Because I Loved Him. Life & Loves of Lillie Langtry.* New York: William Morrow, 1971.

Gibson, James R. *Imperial Russia In Frontier America.* New York: Oxford University Press, 1976.

Gilliam, Harold. *Island In Time.* San Francisco: Sierra Club, 1962.

Goss, Hellen Rocca. *The Life and Death of a Quicksilver Mine.* Los Angeles: The Historical Society of Southern California, 1958.

Gregory, Tom. *History of Solano and Napa Counties, California.* Los Angeles: Historic Record Company, 1912.

Green, Floride. *Some Personal Recollections of Lillie Hitchcock Coit.* San Francisco: The Grabhorn Press, 1935.

Gudde, Erwin G. *California Place Names.* Berkeley: University of California Press, 1960.

Hanson, Harvery J. and Miller, Jeanne Thurlow. *Wild Oats in Eden — Sonoma County in the Nineteenth Century.* Santa Rosa, California: Hanson & Thurlow, 1962.

Haas, Robert Bartlett. *Muybridge: Man In Motion.* Berkeley: University of California Press, 1976.

Hart, James D. (ed.). *From Scotland to Silverado.* Cambridge: The Belknap Press of Harvard University Press, 1966.

Heizer, Robert F. (ed.). *The Archaeology of the Napa Region.* University of California Anthropological Records. Vol 12. No. 6. Berkeley: University of California Press, 1953.

Hendricks, Gordon. *Eadweard Muybridge: the father of the motion picture.* London: Secker & Warburg, 1975.

Hennessy, James Pope. *Robert Louis Stevenson.* London: Jonathan Cape, 1969.

Holdredge, Helen. *Firebelle Lillie.* New York: Meredith Press, 1967.

Hoover, Mildred Brooke. *Historic Spots in California.* Stanford: Stanford University Press, 1966.

Hutchinson, W.H. *California.* Palo Alto: American West Publishing, 1969.

Issler, Ann Roller. *Happier For His Presence — San Francisco and Robert Louis Stevenson.* Stanford: Stanford University Press, 1949.

Issler, Ann Roller. *Our Mountain Hermitage — Silverado and Robert Louis Stevenson.* Stanford: Stanford University Press, 1950.

Jenkins, Olaf P. (ed.). *Geologic Guidebook of the San Francisco Bay Counties.* (State of California, Dept. of Natural Resources, Division of Mines. Bulletin 154.) San Francisco: 1951.

Jones, Idwal. *Vines In The Sun.* New York: William Morrow, 1949.

Kingman, Russ. *A Pictorial Life of Jack London.* New York: Crown Publishers, Inc., 1979.

Kroeber, Alfred L. *Handbook of the Indians of California.* (Bureau of American Ethnology Bulletin, Vol. 78.) Smithsonian Institution, Washington, D.C. Reprinted Berkeley: California Book Co., 1953.

Langtry, Lillie, (Lady de Bathe.) *The Days I Knew.* London: Hutchinson, 1925.

Lockwood, Charles. *Suddenly San Francisco. The Early Years of an Instant City.* San Francisco: The San Francisco Examiner, 1978.

Lewis, Oscar and Hall, Carroll. *Bonanza Inn.* New York: Alfred A. Knopf, 1939.

London, Charmian. *The Book of Jack London.* New York: The Century Co., 1921.

Mackay, Margaret. *The Violent Friend.* Garden City, New York: Doubleday, 1968.

Maugham, W. Somerset. *A Writer's Notebook.* Garden City, New York: Doubleday, 1949.

McGlaschan, C.M. *History of the Donner Party, A Tragedy of the Sierra.* Truckee, CA: 1979. 11th Edition reprint. San Francisco: 1918.

Magoon, Genevieve S. *The Story of Guenoc Ranch.* Honolulu: Tong Publishing Co., 1976.

Muscatine, Doris. *Old San Francisco.* New York: G.P. Putnam's Sons, 1975.

Myrick, David F. *San Francisco's Telegraph Hill.* Berkeley: Howell-North Books, 1972.

Menefee, Campbell A. *Historical and Descriptive Sketch Book of Napa, Sonoma, Lake and Mendocino Counties.* Napa: Reporter Publishing House, 1873.

Morton, J.B. *Hilaire Belloc: A Memoir.* London: Hollis & Carter, 1955.

O'Brien, Bickford (ed.). *Fort Ross — Indians — Russians — Americans.* Jenner, CA: Fort Ross Interpretive Association, Inc., 1980.

Powell, Laurence Clark. *California Classics. Los Angeles: The Ward Ritchie Press, 1971.*

Robertson, William Graham. Life Was Worth Living: The Reminiscences of William Graham Robertson. New York: Harper & Bros, 1931.

Scott, Reva. *San Brannan and the Golden Fleece.* New York: Macmillan, 1944.

Sichel, Pierre. *The Jersey Lily.* Englewood Cliffs, NJ: Prentice-Hall, 1958.

Smith and Elliot, . *Napa Valley Historical Sketch.* Oakland: Smith & Elliot, 1878.

Speaight, Robert. *The Life of Hilaire Belloc.* New York: Farrar, Strauss & Cudahy, 1957.

State of California. *California Landmarks.* Sacramento: Department of Parks & Recreation, 1971.

Stellman, Louis J. *San Brannan, Builder of San Francisco.* New York: Exposition Press, 1953.

Stevenson, Robert Louis. *Treasure Island.* London: Cassell, 1883.

Stevenson, Robert Louis. *The Silverado Squatters.* London: Chatto & Windus, 1883.

Stevenson, Robert Louis. *A Child's Garden of Verses.* London: Longmans, Green, 1885.

Stevenson, *The Silverado Journal.* San Francisco: The Grabhorn Press, 1954.

Storer, Tracey I. and Tevis, Lloyd P. *California Grizzly.* Berkeley: University of California Press, 1955.

Sudworth, George B. *Forest Trees of the Pacific Coast.* Washington D.C.: U.S. Department of Agriculture Forest Service, 1908.

Swearingen, Roger. *Prose Writings of Robert Louis Stevenson.* Hamden, CT: The Shoe String Press, 1908.

Taylor, Bayard. *Home and Abroad.* (2nd Series). New York: G.P. Putnam, 1862.

Thompson, Robert A. *A History of Sonoma County.* Oakland: Thos. H. Thompson & Co., 1877.

Thompson, R.A. *The Russian Settlement in California.* Oakland: Biobooks, 1951.

Thompson, Thos. H. *Historical Atlas Map of Sonoma County.* Oakland: Thos. H. Thompson & Co., 1877.

Topolos, Michael and Dopson, Betty. *California Wineries, Napa Valley.* St. Helena: Vintage Image, 1974.

Magazines and Journals

Eastwood, Alice. "Early Botanical Explorers on the Pacific Coast," *California Historical Society Quarterly,* Vol. XVIII No. 4 (December 1939).

Goss, Helen Rocca. "Lillie Langtry and Her California Ranch," *Historical Society of Southern California Quarterly,* (June 1955).

Herr, Pamela. "Lillie on the Frontier," *The American West.* Vol. XVIII. No. 2. (March/April 1981).

Howe,, John Thomas. "A Collection of Russian Plants," *Leaflets of Western Botany.* Vol. 11. No. 2. San Francisco: Academy of Sciences, 1937.

Palmquist, Peter E. "Carleton Watkins," *The American West.* Vol. XVII. No. 4. (July/August 1980).

Scully, Toni. "Guenoc Winery," *Wine Country.* July, 1982.

Truman, Maj. Ben C. "Knights of the Lash," *The Overland Monthly,* 1898.

Newspapers

Napa County Recorder. April 10, 1885.
Napa Daily Register. February 5,6,8, 1875. April 10, 1885. May 28, 1885.
Russian River Flat. October 8, 1874.
San Francisco Chronicle. February 5,6,7,8, 1875.
St. Helena Star. June 1,8, 1885. August 28, 1885.

Unpublished Manuscripts

Lyman, W.W., Jr. "Memoirs." 3 vols. St. Helena, 1978.

Martin, Noel B. Jr. *The Drake Navigators Guild and the Quest for Portus Novae Albionis.* Project for Dr. Lawrence Kinnaird History 281B Seminar in North American History. Univ. of California, Berkeley, May 1959.

Napa Valley Wine Library. "History of Napa Valley: Interviews & Reminiscences of Long-Time Residents." 3 vols. St. Helena, 1981.

Stewart, George R. "Stevenson in California. A Critical Study." Unpublished Master's thesis, University California, Berkeley, 1921.

Swearingen, Roger. "Robert Louis Stevenson and the Napa Valley — Chronology." Unpublished manuscript. Silverado Museum, St. Helena, 1980.

Turner, Maggie. "The Oak Knoll Ranch." Research study compiled for Napa County Historical Society, Napa, 1948.

Index

Joan Parry Dutton

Joan Parry Dutton was born in England and educated there
and in France and Germany. Gardening and gardens, both
cultivated and wild, have been a life-long interest; she is also
a plant historian. After traveling widely in Europe, and a visit
to South America, she came to this country in 1949 to see
America by way of its gardens. On her journey, which took
her three years, she traveled some 15,000 miles through
almost every state, looking at gardens, both famous and
unsung, and wild areas as remote as Goat Rocks in the Far
Northwest. She has been associated with the Colonial
Williamsburg Foundation since 1950, and lived in
Williamsburg for ten years. Most of her American life has
been spent in northern California, and she now lives
in St. Helena.

A Note About The Book

The typeface use in this book is ITC Garamond, a contemporary version of the design by Claude Garamond, the French type founder, in 1540. The composition was done by Casey Hobbs Design in Napa, California and the printing and binding was done by the Kingsport Press in Kingsport, Tennessee. The design is by Gene Dekovic.